improvise
FOR REAL

Understand the music you hear.
Play the music you imagine.

By David Reed

Improvise for Real

By David Reed

ISBN: 978-0-9846863-6-0

Illustrations and cover design by Mireia Clua Geli

Book design and layout by Jessé Rodrigues

Edited by Amy Nicholson

Jam tracks and other support resources at ImproviseForReal.com.

Table of contents

What I hope to give you

I wrote this book for everyone who dreams of understanding music and being able to enjoy creating it for themselves. I want you to know that there is nothing "wrong" with you if you haven't yet found your path in music. All human beings are capable of imagining and creating beautiful music, and there is nothing stopping you from enjoying the thrill of creating your own music almost immediately. All you need is a little help visualizing the materials of your art so that you can begin to enjoy working with them.

You do not need to know anything at all about music theory to get started. All you need is an open mind and any instrument that produces musical notes (guitar, bass, piano, trumpet, saxophone, violin, etc.). You will begin improvising on the very first day, and you will use improvisation itself as your own personal vehicle to move around and explore our musical system. You will learn how to connect with and play from your musical imagination, where you will discover that you have an endless supply of beautiful, creative ideas. And you will learn to use a simple but powerful *musical map* to gradually build your own personal understanding of harmony.

This method is completely open-ended. How far you go is up to you. Even if you never go beyond the first two exercises, this alone will enable you to improvise with confidence in any musical situation for the rest of your life. But if you go further you will see things with more clarity. You will begin to recognize and understand the sounds in the music all around you. You will be able to play any song you hear, in any key. And you will compose your own pieces just as easily as you might draw a picture.

But none of that is really very important. What I really hope to give you is a chance to discover and connect with a part of yourself that you didn't know existed. And I hope to show you a vision of harmony not as a set of rules about "right notes" and "wrong notes" but rather as an infinite beautiful landscape that you can discover at your own pace. Most of all I hope you enjoy the journey. Life is too short to waste time imitating others. Be yourself and discover *your own music*!

Why we play

Do you remember the first time a piece of music really thrilled you? Maybe that was the moment you knew you wanted to be a musician. Or maybe you just felt the music's power without thinking about its consequences. But in that moment you tasted something that you would later spend a good part of your life searching for again and again.

Your experience then was uncomplicated by music theory. The magic was not in the scales, the chords or a clever use of syncopation. You felt the music in your body and you didn't need anybody to tell you that the music was great.

This book is about honoring that experience. We play because we want to live in that moment. We do not play to impress others with how much we know. We play with humility and gratitude, thankful for each moment and for every beautiful sound.

Our dysfunctional relationship with music

Most of us lead something of a double-life with respect to music. On the one hand we have our real, natural experience of music in our daily lives. We have our favorite songs and maybe even a favorite band. We listen to music at home, in our cars, on headphones and almost everywhere we go. We sing melodies quietly to ourselves and tap rhythms with our hands and fingers. We even go to concerts just to sit quietly and concentrate all our attention on listening to music. And when the music is really good it can give us goose bumps, bring tears to our eyes or make us laugh out loud. In all of these innocent and unselfconscious ways we demonstrate both our love and our comprehension of music.

But then we have something called "music classes". This bizarre ritual, normally led by a sympathetic guide called a "music teacher", consists of staring at hundreds of little black dots on a piece of paper and trying to extract an elaborate sequence of notes from a musical instrument without violating any of the sacred laws of posture and hand position. Many of us patiently complied with this routine for *years* because we innocently assumed that there must be some kind of a connection between music classes and actually understanding music.

But amazingly, there doesn't seem to be any connection at all. On the contrary, it seems that no matter how much formal music training we endure, we never get around to actually understanding all that music that surrounds us and permeates every aspect of our daily lives. This little oversight gives rise to a whole host of strange contradictions:

- Children who love music but hate music lessons

- Music theory "professors" who have never actually created any music

- Brilliant classical musicians who are intimidated by a friendly jam session

- Jazz improvisers who can't play simple pop songs by ear

- Concert pianists who can't play "Happy Birthday" without sheet music

What's going on here? How does a person "study music" for 10 years or more and still not understand *children's songs*? How come most music teachers couldn't write a song to save their lives when there are so many successful songwriters with no formal education whatsoever?

And most importantly, why do so many musicians feel ashamed of their current level of knowledge and ability? In Africa you can spot the musicians by their warm smiles and tremendous positive energy. In New York you can spot the musicians by their worried faces and their chain smoking. What is it about our education system that turns so many beautiful and sensitive little children into frustrated, self-abusing adults?

What I am going to try to show you in this book is that our situation not only has a perfectly logical explanation, but more importantly it has a *solution*. The explanation is simple enough: we have not been studying music at all. Most of us have never had any idea how to study music so instead we studied something else called "music theory".

The solution is equally simple: study music.

The origins of music education

Our traditional approach to teaching music has some wonderful things that we should take great care to preserve. But it also contains some pretty spectacular failures, and I think it's important to recognize them before moving on. I think that if you can understand why we teach music the way we do, you'll have a much easier time finding your own path, both in music and in life.

Let's start by recognizing some things that we do very well. We do a great job of teaching students to play their instruments. Our teaching methods have been refined and perfected over many generations, and we are making these methods even better with new research into early childhood learning, motivational psychology, body mechanics, repetitive motion injury and other issues. We are even beginning to incorporate learning traditions and innovations from other parts of the world (e.g. Suzuki) with interesting results. We also do a great job of teaching general music literacy skills like reading and writing sheet music, basic music theory, and so on.

But despite all our advances, we seem to have overlooked entirely the whole question of how to actually create music. In every other art form, students begin to practice their own creative expression right from the very first day. Painting, drawing, sculpture, poetry and creative writing classes all give students the opportunity to experience the creative process as a normal part of their learning.

It's only in music that the creative process remains shrouded in mystery, the exclusive domain of ancient "composers" and the occasional child prodigy. You would think that our music teachers were a bunch of ogres who refuse to let their students express themselves creatively. But quite the contrary, most music teachers would LOVE to incorporate these creative activities in the classroom! And many are bravely venturing into this territory on their own. But it's not at all obvious how to do it. Most music teachers simply don't have any methodology for empowering students to create their *own* music.

But how can such a glaring oversight exist? Almost every musician fantasizes about creating his or her own music someday. How can we have an entire industry dedicated to "teaching music" and never get around to actually showing anybody how to create music?

I believe that the answer to this question lies in the European origins of our most basic ideas about what it means to teach music. Remember, for centuries the primary goal of classical music education was to produce orchestra performers capable of reading a piece of sheet music and correctly playing the composer's ideas. And this is no small task. It requires both a formidable control over one's instrument and also a very high level of skill at reading complicated musical phrases on a written page. It also requires great sensitivity and expressive power, since without these the music would sound dull and lifeless.

This curious breed of musician unites several personality traits that are highly contradictory. He must have the precision control of a world-class athlete in order to execute the very fine motor skills involved in playing his instrument. But he must also have the extreme mental agility required to read and instantly decipher impossibly complex rhythms coded into symbols on a page. He must be sensitive enough to feel and express the beauty in every line that he plays, but he must be detached enough to play whatever music is handed to him without complaining.

This is the context in which our music education system evolved. The goal was to produce a kind of super-performing robot-person that could play any piece of music on demand and make it sound heavenly. There was, however, one ability that was not required of these super-performers, and that was the ability to create music for themselves. In the European classical tradition, the performer's role is not to understand music but to execute it.

It's easy to imagine how this set of circumstances led to the development of two fundamental attitudes in the teaching of music:

Knowledge comes from outside. Musicians start out empty initially. They must be taught what to play and how to play it. The musician's role is to practice each new technique until he can execute it convincingly.

Musicians play for others. A musician's purpose is to delight audiences and impress other musicians. His success can be measured by the number of gigs he gets, the salary he earns and also the respect and fame he enjoys among other musicians.

Both of these attitudes have to do with preparing the musician to be a professional performer capable of earning a salary by working for others. This is very different from our modern idea of a musician as a thinking, feeling human being who wants to grow, to create and to experience life for himself. What I'm trying to suggest is that at its very roots our music education system is actually a kind of vocational school. It was designed to produce qualified employees who could serve a useful function. And this attitude is so thoroughly ingrained in our culture that we continue to teach music this way today even though it no longer makes any sense whatsoever.

Our entire world has changed. For most people, there are no more orchestra gigs and no more royal families commissioning great works of art. There aren't even any more traveling jazz groups that call you at the last minute for a substitution. From a professional point of view, the golden era of the musician as performer is basically over.

But the best part is only just beginning. We are standing at the edge of the most amazing moment in our history, in which every single person in the world can have access to the same knowledge of harmony that was possessed by Bach or Mozart. Imagine an entire world of people discovering music for themselves and creating all sorts of wild and fantastic compositions.

What if everyone you knew could pick up an instrument and improvise freely together? You might be at home with your family on a lazy Sunday morning and suddenly Grandma would turn to you and say, "Wanna jam?" Or imagine if you had the ability to recreate the most powerful moments from the most beautiful concerts you have ever heard, those moments that gave you goose bumps or brought tears to your eyes. Imagine if you could enter that world whenever you wanted to.

This fascinating world of sounds is open to everyone 24 hours per day, and there is no charge for admission. All we have to do is forgive ourselves for whatever mistakes we might have made in the past, and learn to think about music in two fundamentally new ways:

All knowledge is self-knowledge. Inside the imagination of every person there exists a whole universe of sounds, thoughts, feelings and desires. This universe expands with every new sound we hear and every emotion we feel. The musician's path is to discover these elements within himself and learn how to express them.

We play for ourselves. Studying music is a way for us to contemplate the beauty of nature, and it's also a daily practice that enables us to connect privately with ourselves. This practice is available to everyone as a means of enjoyment and personal growth, regardless of their level of knowledge or skill. A musician's success can be measured only by his own satisfaction with the relationship he has with music.

If you are open to these two new ideas, then you are ready to begin the liberating journey to your own musical creativity. The path may be surprising to you, so I want to start by explaining how improvisation is normally taught and why we will take such a different route.

The rules and formulas paradigm

Most modern improvisation courses are a poor environment for a sensitive young music lover. Students come to discover the beautiful world of harmony but instead find themselves drowning in a sea of rules, formulas and definitions. Students are taught to rely on music theory to determine the "correct notes" for improvising in any given musical situation. And they are required to memorize a seemingly endless inventory of scale patterns, licks and phrases that they are supposed to spit out during their solos to demonstrate their "mastery" of the material. The whole paradigm of these courses is not to help you discover harmony but simply to tell you *what to play*.

Ironically your two greatest gifts as a musician, your ear and your imagination, play almost no role in all this musical training. Students learn how to read sheet music and play appropriate scales, but they never learn to *hear* the most basic elements from which all of this musical material is made. This is why so many jazz musicians can't even play their favorite song in a different key. They can only play it in the key in which they memorized it because they don't really understand it at all. And needless to say, improvising along with other styles like flamenco, classical music, free improvisation or Middle Eastern music is out of the question entirely. Theory and formulas don't work when there are no written chord symbols to work with.

But the biggest problem with this formula-based approach to making music is that it doesn't give us the artistic satisfaction we long for. If you had hoped that musical improvisation would be a way to get in touch with your creative side, and express your *own* musical ideas directly from your imagination, then this mechanical paint-by-numbers approach is a big disappointment.

What seems to be missing from every improvisation course I have ever seen is the idea of the improviser as a thoughtful, sensitive person with his *own* ideas and values. If your teachers just gave you the basic information that you really need in order to begin expressing yourself creatively through music, you would be amazed at how simple harmony really is. The only reason why improvisation seems complicated is that students are being asked to memorize an endless list of gimmicks and formulas just so they can sound exactly like everybody else. In other words, we have become so preoccupied with sounding "good" that we have forgotten about playing *our* music, even though that was what drew us to musical improvisation in the first place.

The ironic thing is that none of the great improvisers in history ever studied music this way. They all tell the same story of discovering harmony for themselves. They talk of spending countless hours playing simple melodies and contemplating the sound of each note. From working class jazz musicians all the way up to the most celebrated artists of the 20th century, one image is absolutely constant. It's the image of a solitary human being, lost in thought and completely absorbed in the world of sounds. Not one of these great musicians talks of learning tricks and formulas. You never heard Miles Davis say, "Things really took off for me when I found that book of jazz scales."

In other words, the musical studies of these great improvisers were not directed outward in search of techniques and formulas. Their search was inward, a kind of personal meditative *practice* that gave them a powerful mastery over the sounds of our musical system. Today there is nothing stopping any of us from cultivating this same daily practice in our own lives. The key is to stop looking for answers in the rules and formulas paradigm. The answers are all to be found in the world of sounds, and you need to discover that world for yourself.

Improvise for Real is about returning to our original dream, to what drew us to musical improvisation in the first place. We didn't get into this looking for tricks and formulas to impress other people with our knowledge. We wanted to improvise because we imagined how great it must feel to express ourselves creatively through music. We dreamed of performing beautiful spontaneous concerts with other people, expressing the unique music that lies inside of us. Why would anybody trade this dream for a bunch of formulas? If we can't even be ourselves when we are playing music, then why play at all?

True musical improvisation is just as beautiful and exciting as you imagined it would be. And the thrilling experience of improvising for real is available to absolutely everyone, regardless of experience or skill level. So if you're one of those people who have always thought that harmony and improvisation must be very difficult, then you are in for a wonderful surprise. Musical improvisation is the easiest thing in the world. You just relax, listen to that inner voice we all have, and play what you hear.

If you're like most people, you probably have no idea what I'm talking about, or how you could ever actually do this. But don't worry. That's the subject of this book. You are about to discover an exciting alternative to the rules and formulas paradigm. Studying music for real does not mean accumulating more techniques to use in your solos. It means learning to use those two awesome resources that are the very essence of a musical artist: your ear and your imagination.

Creating a new musical practice

Let's start our journey together with a moment of brutal honesty. When you look at your instrument, what do you *feel*?

Do you feel love?

Do you feel excitement and wonder?

Do you see your instrument as the doorway to your own personal paradise?

Unfortunately, not everybody can answer "yes" to all of these questions. Some feel a vague sense of boredom or indifference toward their instrument, as if they were not finding their true purpose in music. And some people actually feel frustration, guilt or even fear.

It's worth remembering that music was the world's first physiotherapy. The only reason human beings began to sing, to dance and to play musical instruments was the intense physical pleasure that they felt from doing so. If we no longer feel this ecstasy when we play our instruments today, then maybe we have forgotten something important. I wonder what a primitive musician living 30,000 years ago would think about the idea that music could be a source of guilt or fear.

For the next few months I want to propose an experiment. I want you to make a small space in your life for a new musical activity that has nothing to do with anything else in your musical life. Don't worry about trying to understand how this new practice fits in with other things you may have studied. Just think of it as a musical hobby that you are going to try for a while.

You don't need to stop your other musical activities or change them in any way. If you already have a practice routine going and you feel it's important to continue it, then by all means do so. You can still keep all your goals and objectives, your areas for improvement and all that material you would like to master someday. The only thing I ask is that you leave all that other stuff far out of your mind whenever you practice the activities described in this book. Work on the other stuff as much as you want, but then set aside a few minutes each day to just enjoy relating to music in a different way.

Our work here is about creating something very special just for you. You don't have to share it with anybody if you don't want to. It's entirely yours to explore and enjoy for the rest of your life. It will lead you on fascinating adventures when you are up to the challenge. And it will be your comfort and protection when things aren't going your way. In the beginning it will feel kind of like a game, and little by little it will gradually evolve into something else. But at no point will I ever ask you to play well or to impress anybody with your skills. This new musical practice is exclusively for your own enjoyment.

The Five Exercises

If you've glanced at the table of contents of this book, you may have noticed that in the entire Improvise for Real method there are only five exercises. It probably goes without saying that these five exercises are not like homework assignments to be completed and checked off your list. What they actually represent are five different levels of musical abstraction which together form a complete method for lifelong musical growth. Each exercise is in fact a whole area of musical study, but I have included in this book the most essential ways to work on each of these five areas.

The Five Exercises are presented in a specific order because each exercise builds upon the previous ones. But they are cumulative in the sense that you don't "move on" from one exercise to the next. The goal is to learn all five so that you can take control of your own musical development. Each time you sit down to practice, you are the one who will decide where to focus your energies.

Each of the Five Exercises described in this book contains enough ideas and activities to keep you busy for a lifetime. So don't make the mistake of thinking that you need to master each exercise completely before starting the next one. It doesn't work that way! You will continue to learn and grow in all five of these areas for the rest of your life. So just learn the exercises at whatever pace feels right to you. Remember that you always have complete freedom to decide how much work you do at each level.

You also have complete freedom to decide how far you go in IFR. Many students never go beyond Exercise 2 because they do not feel the personal need to know all the details of the harmony that surrounds them. They can already improvise beautifully over any tune in any key, and for them this is the right level of understanding to give them an enjoyable musical experience. If your goal is be able to participate in jam sessions or improvise solos in a musical group, you will achieve this with Exercise 2. You will learn how to orient yourself in any piece of music using nothing more than your ear, and you will learn how to express your own ideas in any musical context.

If, on the other hand, your goal is to develop yourself completely as a creative musical artist, then Exercise 2 is just the beginning. To reach your full potential as a musician, improviser, composer and teacher of music, you will need to become a master of harmony. This is the work we do in Exercises 3 and 4. These exercises are especially important for the musicians who actually create the harmonic environment in any musical group (bass players, guitarists and piano players). But they are really for anyone who wants to discover and understand the beautiful world of tonal harmony.

Students who go as far as Exercise 5 will discover the fascinating world of free improvisation. You will learn to apply your knowledge of tonal harmony in a more abstract way that enables you to instantly respond to whatever is going on around you musically and to participate in this conversation without needing written chord changes. You will learn to depend on your ear and your imagination as the only orientation you need.

These are the exercises that have helped me and my students to understand music and enjoy creating it. But ultimately every artist is self-taught. I can accompany you for a part of your journey, but your life is your own. It's up to you to decide what is important, what is beautiful, and what you need to do in order to grow. Your freedom as an artist begins with the freedom to study what *you* want to study, in the manner that is most enjoyable to you. But I hope that I can help you by showing you a way that you can discover our musical system for yourself and connect with your own musical imagination.

At our website you'll find other components of the IFR method which work together with the concepts in this book to accelerate your musical learning. These resources will make your practicing more fun, more creative and more effective.

Here are some of the most important tools to add to your music practice:

- **IFR Jam Tracks** - The IFR Jam Tracks line is a complete course in modern harmony. It leads you step-by-step through the complete harmonic journey described in this book, with creative insights and illustrations every step of the way. Every harmonic situation described in this book is a complete lesson in the IFR Jam Tracks series, giving you the opportunity to experience these beautiful sounds for yourself and practice improvising your own music in that situation.

- **Sing the Numbers** - This is IFR's ear training course designed specifically for improvisers. In IFR we believe that your sensitivity and your love of music are your greatest gifts as an improviser. And so your ear training program should also be artistic and beautiful. Sing the Numbers uses beautiful songs and melodies to teach you about music. Through this process you'll learn to recognize the sounds in the music all around you, and you'll learn to express the sounds you imagine on your instrument.

- **Video courses and workshops** - Video is such a powerful medium for learning music because you can hear the sounds and see the exercises being performed. We're working hard to create IFR video courses for every instrument family and I invite you to check out what's already available. We also offer workshops on improvisation, harmony and ear training, all based on the IFR method.

- **IFR Blues Mastery Course and the IFR Standards Workouts** - These courses will teach you how to apply the skills you're learning in IFR to the musical styles of blues and jazz. The IFR Blues Mastery Course gives you everything you need to truly master blues harmony and enjoy improvising over the blues. And the IFR Standards Workouts will teach you how to improvise over the most popular jazz standards played in jam sessions.

You'll find all of this at ImproviseForReal.com.

Special note to guitar and bass players: Please skip the following chapter and go directly to the version of Exercise 1 written specifically for your instrument. We do Exercise 1 differently on these instruments.

Exercise 1: Landscape

Objective: To continuously improve in your ability to...

Clearly visualize your entire musical range and move effortlessly across it.

Since truly improvised music is created in the imagination, the most important technical skill to the improviser is the ability to instantly play any sound that he imagines. It's important to understand that this capacity is entirely mental. It has nothing to do with playing fast. Flying through scales with the metronome clacking away at 200 beats per minute might impress the neighbors but it doesn't necessarily make you a better improviser.

The improviser's objective is not speed of execution but clarity of vision. Imagine being able to see in your mind the entire map of a large city at once. That's how we would ideally like to feel about our entire musical range. The goal is to achieve a deep sense of *orientation* that accompanies us no matter where we might be on our instrument. If you're on the note Ab for example and your melodic idea requires you to go up a minor third, or go down a perfect fourth, you don't want your creative flow to be interrupted by having to puzzle over these intervals. The idea is to be able to see the entire musical landscape at once so that you can easily imagine any type of movement across it. That way you can stay focused on the joy and fun of creating music.

The key to Exercise 1 is to just relax and enjoy yourself. The only thing you might find difficult about the exercise is overcoming the feelings of guilt that make you want to move on to something more "serious". Most beginning improvisers are in such a hurry to make music that they never take the time to just enjoy moving around their instrument. But there is nothing more important for you to master than the actual musical terrain which underlies everything you will play in the future.

In Exercise 1, the notes on your instrument have no musical significance whatsoever. Just forget about music for now. Don't be distracted by any thoughts about melody, harmony, tonality, scales, etc. Try to just unwind and have fun moving around your instrument as if you were a child playing in a field. The only goal is to gain confidence moving around within your musical range.

I recommend that you focus exclusively on Exercise 1 for a few days, and then just use it as a quick daily warm-up. If you are a beginner, you might spend the initial period just doing the first two activities (Discovery and Staircase). If you are already a very experienced musician you might go directly to Exercise 1 - Mastery Level. But whatever your situation, investigate Exercise 1 thoroughly for a few days and then just keep it in mind as a daily warm-up. You can also think of Exercise 1 as a place that you can always come back to whenever you want to improve your clarity of thinking and mental quickness.

One of the most important goals of Exercise 1 is to learn to see the notes on your instrument as one long unbroken chain of half steps. This is an important part of liberating yourself from the constraints of key signatures and theory. The idea is to see all of the notes as equals. Your entire range should feel like one long connected staircase that you can move up or down as you please. So let's start by simply playing all of these notes in their natural consecutive order. I call this simple exercise "Discovery".

Discovery

1. Close your eyes.

2. Play the lowest note that you can comfortably play on your instrument. Try to produce the most beautiful sound you can. Enjoy this note and give it your full attention.

3. Now move up exactly one half step and play the new note. Again you should make a special effort to produce the most beautiful sound you can.

4. Now very slowly continue to move up in half steps, pausing at each note to just relax and enjoy the sound.

5. Keep moving up in half steps until you reach the highest note that you can comfortably play without straining.

6. Now begin to come down very slowly, one half step at a time until you reach the very bottom of your range. Try not to rush through the exercise.

Do this exercise for as long as you find it interesting and enjoyable. When you start to feel very confident doing it slowly, try moving through your range more quickly and see what happens. There is no upper limit to the amount of speed, fluidity and confidence with which you can move across your musical range. So you are never really "done" with the above exercise. But after doing it a few times you will probably want to move on to something more interesting. So in the next activity we will incorporate some freedom of movement into our practicing.

Staircase

1. Close your eyes.

2. Choose any random note on your instrument and play it.

3. Move down exactly one half step and play the new note.

4. Keep moving down in half steps until you decide you have gone low enough.

5. Whenever you decide, start coming back up in half steps and keep moving up for as long as you want to.

6. Continue to wander around your musical landscape in half steps, changing direction freely wherever you feel like it.

This is the version that reminds me of a child playing around on a staircase. Especially as you begin to gain confidence and a little bit of speed, you can start to play freely with rhythm and syncopation as part of the exercise. By changing direction often you can create wild be-bop sounding phrases.

If there is any region that you find especially confusing or difficult, just stay there. Keep moving back and forth across the problem zone until it becomes your favorite stretch of musical terrain. In my own playing, the regions that used to give me the most trouble are now the parts that I enjoy most. When you struggle through an awkward fingering or some other technical issue that complicates your movement in a particular part of your range, you end up feeling a great deal of affection for that little piece of land. It comes to have a personal meaning for you that no other musician can entirely relate to. So take your time and enjoy having these experiences for yourself.

Exercise 1 Daily Meditation

Once you have gained a basic level of comfort with moving around your musical landscape, you can begin practicing IFR Exercise 2: Melody. From that point on you won't need the exercises above any more. Instead, we will replace them with a simple daily meditation. It only takes a few minutes and it's fun to do. Depending on your mood it can be playful, serious, calm or violent. So be creative and use this meditation to express whatever you are feeling in the moment:

1. Close your eyes.

2. Pick a note, any note. From now on we will start every exercise this way. You shouldn't always pick the same note. But don't think too much about it either. Just pick a note completely at random. This is a great way to practice one of the most essential skills of the improviser, which is the ability to orient oneself instantly with a single note. You never know where you are going to be when you will want to paint a certain musical shape on your instrument. So it's important that each exercise begin with a moment of complete disorientation. Don't shy away from the areas where you are less comfortable. These are the *best* places to start because the whole point is to become equally comfortable with *all* of the notes on your instrument. If this is your first time then jump right in with a weird note like G flat.

$$G\flat$$

3. Enjoy this note for as long as you want to. Try to produce the most beautiful sound possible, the purest example of how you really want the note to sound. Play the note several times and really listen to the sound. Sing along with the note if your instrument allows you to do so. *Use* this note to help you relax and prepare your mind for the rest of the exercise.

4. Move to the note exactly one half step below. For example if you started on G flat then the new note would be F natural. Play this note just like you played the first one, and try to notice all the same things. Don't rush ahead. Take a minute to just stay here and enjoy this note.

$$F$$

5. Alternate between the two notes. As you alternate, notice what you are actually doing physically with your hands and body to change between the two notes. Improvise for a minute with just these two notes. Be playful. Even with just two notes you can express a whole world of music just by playing with rhythm, tone and dynamics. Think about conga

players who can make music for hours with just two drums in front of them.

F Gb

6. Now your focus expands to include a third note a half step above these two. (In our example the new note would be G natural.) Improvise freely with all three notes. You don't need to always pass chromatically through all three notes. You can also jump directly between the lowest and highest notes without passing through the middle note. But as you play, try to visualize all three notes at once.

F Gb G

7. Now expand the range downward again, adding a half step below these three. (In our example the new note would be E natural). First practice moving up and down through the entire series of four notes. Then practice connecting every possible combination of notes within this region. Improvise freely with all four notes, jumping around however you like within this little region. As you do this, remember to continue to visualize all four notes at once. It is the simultaneous visualization of all of the notes that makes the exercise beneficial.

E F Gb G

8. Add a final note a half step above these four. (In our example the new note would be A flat.) This brings us to a total of five consecutive notes separated by half steps. Work on connecting every single one of these notes to every other. Become an expert in moving all around this little region as if you were doing drills on a basketball court. Then improvise freely with all 5 notes for as long as you like. Take time to enjoy the special sound effects created by using some of the notes while omitting others. For example try improvising with just the notes E, F and Ab while omitting Gb and G. What does that sound like? What about using only the notes F, Gb and Ab? Imagine other combinations and see how long you can play with just these 5 sounds. While you are doing this, try to maintain all five notes in your consciousness as if you were looking down on this musical terrain from above.

E F Gb G Ab

Essentially all you are doing in this exercise is just directing your attention to a single note and then slowly expanding your focus outward to encompass a small region of the musical landscape. Since you are the one who decides how you will play with the notes, even beginners should find it easy and relaxing. But over time this simple daily meditation will give you more confidence and clarity of thought than you could ever achieve by practicing scales.

Beware of the temptation to advance through the steps too quickly. The secret to the exercise is in taking lots of time with each step before you move on to the next. Deep learning only takes place *after* something has already become familiar. For beginners this can be a difficult concept to understand. We are accustomed to moving ahead just as quickly as we are able to. But that's precisely what blocks the really deep learning that we are after. If your mind is always working, thinking about the next note or making some other sort of calculation, then your attention is always on your own thoughts instead of on the *experience* of playing the notes. So try to get out of your own head. Focus on a couple of notes and really jam with them. Listen to them, express yourself with them and forget about what comes next. Then when you are thoroughly exhausted, that's when you can move on to the next step.

(NOTE to piano players: You are probably thinking to yourself that this exercise is ridiculously easy for you, even with your eyes closed. And you are right. In fact a big part of Exercise 1 is just to help other musicians see their musical range as clearly as you already see yours. But keep reading because you'll find the exercise a bit more challenging when we get into larger intervals. And remember that you can move on to Exercise 2 whenever you want. Do what makes sense for you!)

(NOTE to violin, viola and cello players: For the above exercise you don't necessarily need to use the specific fingering that you would normally use to play the "chromatic scale". You only need this uncomfortable fingering when you want to play various half steps consecutively. But whenever you want to move up or down a whole step then by all means use the fingering that is most comfortable for you. For example in Step 6 above (with the notes F, Gb and G), anytime you move from F directly to G (without passing through Gb) you can just use the finger you would normally use for this whole step movement. There is no reason to use the chromatic scale fingering except when you literally want to play F, then Gb and finally G.)

If you like to practice in a way that offers more speed and stimulation, you may want to invent more challenging ways to move across your musical landscape with half steps. But remember that the goal is not merely to execute the chromatic scale with speed and fluidity. What we are after is something much deeper than that. Our goal is to feel oriented and completely at home no matter where we might be on our instrument. This feeling takes time to cultivate but is available to everyone and it seems to me that there are two keys to achieving it:

- Take the time to experience every corner of your musical landscape.

- Be playful and enjoy fully whatever notes you are using at the moment.

If you are a beginner or if you only want to play music as a hobby, the above exercises will give you everything you need to enjoy a lifetime of musical improvisation. But if your desire is to become the very best improviser you can possibly be, then you should take Exercise 1 to a much deeper level. You still don't necessarily need to spend a lot of time on it. Even just a few minutes per day will take you very far over time. But whereas the casual player will outgrow the need for Exercise 1 relatively soon, you will want to keep growing in this area for the rest of your life. We do that with Exercise 1 - Mastery Level.

Exercise 1 - Mastery Level

In Exercise 1 - Mastery Level, we practice the same daily meditation you learned earlier but we extend it to include every interval in the musical octave. The first interval you should study after the half step is the whole step. To illustrate, here are the notes you would use to perform the exercise with whole steps, starting on the same note Gb as we did earlier:

1. The first note would be Gb.

$$Gb$$

2. The second note is E, since it's one whole step below Gb.

$$E \qquad Gb$$

3. The third note is Ab, since it's one whole step above Gb.

$$E \qquad Gb \qquad Ab$$

4. The fourth note is D, since it's one whole step below E.

$$D \qquad E \qquad Gb \qquad Ab$$

5. The fifth and final note is Bb, since it's one whole step above Ab.

$$D \qquad E \qquad Gb \qquad Ab \qquad Bb$$

Just as you did with half steps, you should practice this meditation with whole steps in every part of your musical range until you can move effortlessly all over your instrument in whole steps. Then you can try increasing the interval to a minor third, then a major third, then a perfect fourth, etc. Maybe one day you practice with a very big interval and the next day you go back to half steps. Later when we get into specific harmonic shapes like major and minor chords you can incorporate these shapes into the game as well. The possibilities are endless.

But don't be in any rush to move on to higher intervals. Just relax and allow yourself to spend about five minutes a day exploring some small corner of your musical landscape in whatever way appeals to you in the moment. The goal of the exercise is not to "advance" to higher levels. The goal is almost exactly the opposite: to lovingly contemplate your musical range from every possible point of view, without a care in the world.

Note: The following supplement is for guitarists only.

Exercise 1: Landscape (for guitar)

Objective: To continuously improve in your ability to...

Clearly visualize your entire musical range and move effortlessly across it.

Since truly improvised music is created in the imagination, the most important technical skill to the improviser is the ability to instantly play any sound that he imagines. It's important to understand that this capacity is entirely mental. It has nothing to do with playing fast. Flying through scales with the metronome clacking away at 200 beats per minute might impress the neighbors but it doesn't necessarily make you a better improviser.

The improviser's objective is not speed of execution but clarity of vision. Imagine being able to see in your mind the entire map of a large city at once. That's how we would ideally like to feel about our entire musical range. The goal is a deep sense of *orientation* that accompanies us no matter where we might be on our instrument. If you're on the note Ab for example and your melodic idea requires you to go up a major third, or go down a major sixth, you don't want your creative flow to be interrupted by having to puzzle over these intervals. The idea is to be able to see the entire musical landscape at once so that you can easily imagine any type of movement across it. That way you can stay focused on the joy and fun of creating music.

The key to Exercise 1 is to just relax and enjoy yourself. The only thing you might find difficult about the exercise is overcoming the feelings of guilt that make you want to move on to something more "serious". Most beginning improvisers are in such a hurry to make music that they never take the time to just enjoy moving around their instrument. But there is nothing more important for you to master than the actual musical terrain which underlies everything you will play in the future.

In Exercise 1, the notes on your instrument have no musical significance whatsoever. Just forget about music for now. Don't be distracted by any thoughts about melody, harmony, tonality, scales, etc. Try to just unwind and have fun moving around your instrument as if you were a child playing in a field. The only goal is to gain confidence moving around within your musical range.

Guitar players practice Exercise 1 in a special way to take advantage of a wonderful property that the guitar has. The guitar is in some ways even more visual than the piano. By "visual" I mean that all musical intervals, melodies, chords, etc. correspond to exact physical shapes on the neck of the instrument. This gives the guitarist a tremendous advantage in learning to understand and truly internalize harmony. Your instrument literally has a double life. In addition to being your means of self-expression and musical creation, it also serves as your own personal workspace where you can visually arrange musical shapes and contemplate their sounds.

You are going to learn Exercise 1 in two phases. The first goal is to learn to visualize the notes on your instrument as one long unbroken chain of half steps. This is an important part of liberating yourself from scale drawings and memorized key signatures. The idea is to see all of the notes as equals. Your entire range should feel like one long connected staircase that you can move up or down as you please.

We achieve this on the guitar by practicing a technique that I call "Cloud", which is simply a way to visualize all of the notes that surround you at any given time. You will only practice this preliminary technique for a little while before moving on to "Mobility", which is the real technique that we will use as a complete approach to movement on the guitar. But this initial period of practicing Cloud is a tremendous exercise in visualization and an important mental preparation for Mobility, so please don't skip this critical step!

Cloud

To begin with, please take a minute to look at the following drawing of the guitar neck. Make sure you understand its orientation. It represents approximately what you would see if you were to look down at your left hand while playing the guitar.

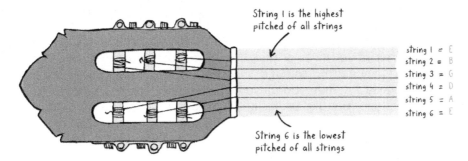

The traditional tuning of the guitar (E, A, D, G, B, E) is irregular in the sense that not all strings are separated by the same interval. Some guitarists (like myself) avoid this inconvenience by adopting a perfectly regular tuning. But I am going to assume that you use the standard guitar tuning and I will show you how to visualize notes across all of the strings on your guitar.

The open strings are tuned such that the interval between adjacent strings is always a perfect fourth, except in one location. The exception is the interval between the 2nd and 3rd strings, which is only a major third:

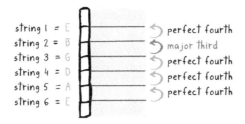

This observation will have a lot more significance to you in the coming weeks. But for now the only thing you really need to get out of this discussion is the fact that the guitar tuning is irregular, and that the exact location of this irregularity is the border between strings 2 and 3. For this reason, the unbroken chain of half steps (which can also simply be called the "chromatic scale") is also irregular at exactly this point. The entire set of notes available to you at any time (or what I call the "cloud") takes the following form on the guitar:

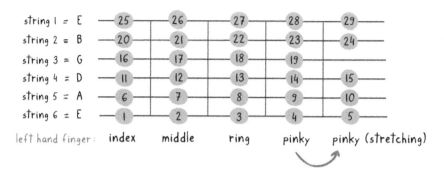

string 1 = E	25	26	27	28	29
string 2 = B	20	21	22	23	24
string 3 = G	16	17	18	19	
string 4 = D	11	12	13	14	15
string 5 = A	6	7	8	9	10
string 6 = E	1	2	3	4	5
left hand finger:	index	middle	ring	pinky	pinky (stretching)

Don't be overwhelmed by all the numbers inside the circles. I just put them there to show you the order of the notes in pitch from lowest to highest. Imagine yourself playing these notes one at a time, starting with circle 1 and ending with circle 29. This is how we visualize the unbroken chain of half steps on the guitar. The finger indication is very important. No matter where you are on the guitar neck, for now you MUST always use the exact fingering indicated above. Notice that your little finger or pinky has the "double duty" of covering all the notes on two different frets. Follow this rule meticulously for the entire time that you practice the Cloud version of Exercise 1. When you move on to Mobility you can go back to playing notes with whatever fingers you feel like using. But for Cloud you need to use this exact fingering even when it seems uncomfortable or illogical. We use this rather strange fingering because it helps us to mentally visualize and remember where the notes are. Remember, in the future you are not even going to use this fingering so don't stress out about the fact that you feel slow or clumsy doing it this way. Just do it anyway. It's only a trick to help your memory, and you'll find that it really does help you to see more clearly what you're doing.

The important thing about the above drawing is that this cloud of notes always looks the exact same no matter where your hand is on the guitar. If you are playing way down low on the guitar then your index finger might correspond to the 1st fret. If you are playing way up high then your index finger might be at the 9th fret. But in both cases the notes available to you take on the exact same form, the one represented in the above drawing.

As you can see, there is no great mystery regarding half step movement within a particular string. If you want to move up a half step you just move up one fret. The story only becomes interesting at the borders between one string and the next. Pay special attention to these borders as you move around in the cloud. Here is a beginning version of Exercise 1 for guitar players that we can call "Cloud Practice 1":

Cloud Practice 1

Step 1: Pick a note, any note.

> We start every exercise this way. You shouldn't always pick the same note. But don't think too much about it either. Just pick a note completely at random. This is a great way to practice one of the most essential skills of the improviser, which is the ability to orient oneself instantly with a single note. You never know where you are going to be when you will want to visualize a certain musical shape. So it's important that each exercise begin with a moment of complete disorientation. Just place your left hand anywhere on the guitar neck and align your fingers properly so that each finger

corresponds to a specific fret. Choose any string at random and play any note on that string, using the appropriate finger.

Step 2: Enjoy this note for as long as you want to.

As you play the note make sure that each of the other fingers stays aligned with its corresponding fret. Close your eyes. You should still be able to visualize your hand with each finger aligned to a specific fret. Keeping your eyes closed, can you also visualize all of the rest of the notes in the cloud drawing above?

Step 3: Move to the note exactly one half step below.

For example if you started on circle number 22 (played with your ring finger) then the new note would be circle number 21 (played with your middle finger). Make sure your hand is still perfectly aligned with one finger per fret. Keep your eyes closed for this and all remaining steps.

Step 4: Continue moving down in half steps as far as you want to.

Step 5: Whenever you decide, change direction and begin to move upward.

Step 6: Continue playing, changing direction whenever you feel like it.

Move around freely within the cloud with your eyes closed, visualizing exactly where you are in the cloud drawing the entire time. If you are careful to maintain your left hand properly aligned with one finger per fret (except the pinky finger which stretches to perform its double duty), then you should be able to move wherever you want without becoming disoriented. The key is to do the exercise slowly and visualize the cloud drawing in your mind every step of the way.

This is just one of many ways to practice Cloud but it's the most important, and it is the foundation of everything to come. So don't rush on to the next thing. Stay with this simple exercise until you can do it in your sleep. Even after you understand the exercise, keep practicing it at least once every day for the first few weeks. You might "get" the idea intellectually right from the very beginning. But your subconscious mind needs time to reprogram itself to imagine this cloud of notes as your musical universe. So take a few minutes each day to perform this simple relaxing exercise.

To make it more enjoyable you can play freely with rhythm, phrasing and syncopation. In other words, don't trudge through the notes as if you were performing a military drill. Be playful and change direction a lot. Instead of playing all the notes in a boring sequence like this:

...try to dance through the entire cloud like this:

One thing you should understand is that the numbers inside the circles don't have any purpose beyond just trying to show you how this exercise works. In fact with my own private students I don't even use these numbers because I can just show them the exercise directly on the guitar. So while you're practicing Exercise 1, please don't put any effort into remembering the little numbers inside the circles. Your only objective is to visualize the cloud and practice moving around within it. We will never actually talk about these circle numbers again in this book.

Work on Cloud Practice 1 until you get to the point where moving from one note to the next becomes essentially effortless. You should be able to literally pick up the guitar, place your left hand anywhere on the neck and start moving through the cloud in either direction.

Once you have gained this level of confidence moving around anywhere in the cloud, then you can take your practicing to the next level. The next step is to separate each of the notes by whole steps instead of half steps. For example if you randomly pick circle 22 as a starting point, then the next note below would be circle 20, then circle 18, then 16, etc. As with half steps, the goal is not simply to trudge through the notes in a systematic, boring way. Take time to enjoy yourself. Be rhythmic and playful, dancing around in the cloud using little whole step jumps. You will find that some places are more difficult than others to visualize this whole step jump. When you run into difficulties, don't stress out. Just stay there and enjoy practicing your jump as if you were a martial artist training in the dojo.

Once you have mastered half steps and whole steps, you have reached an important plateau. These are the only two intervals you need in order to play all of the material that you are going to see in IFR Exercise 2: Melody. So this is also the moment when your practicing needs to break into two parallel paths. You should go ahead and begin working on Exercise 2 just as soon as you are ready, but you should also continue to grow your abilities in Exercise 1.

I'll explain Exercise 2 when we get there. But right now I want to keep going in Exercise 1, to show you how you can continue to grow in your mastery of the basic musical landscape of your guitar. This new exercise that I am going to show you will become the primary way that we will visualize any kind of movement on the guitar.

Mobility

The Mobility exercise is a simple concept but explaining it in a book takes a lot of words. Once you understand the movements in the exercise, you'll find it both fun to practice and incredibly liberating. It's only the initial explanation that takes some effort. But each movement is explained and illustrated in this chapter, and you'll find video demonstrations of the exercise at ImproviseForReal.com.

Mobility: half steps

The idea behind Mobility comes from making a couple of important observations about the relationships between the notes in Cloud. By reducing our Cloud experience to a couple of key observations, we can carry these principles with us wherever we go, and thus move freely around the entire guitar without even bothering to visualize the entire cloud at once. Let's look again at the Cloud drawing with numbers representing each note:

string 1 = E	25	26	27	28	29
string 2 = B	20	21	22	23	24
string 3 = G	16	17	18	19	
string 4 = D	11	12	13	14	15
string 5 = A	6	7	8	9	10
string 6 = E	1	2	3	4	5
left hand finger:	index	middle	ring	pinky	pinky (stretching)

The first observation we need to make about the above drawing is what the interval of a half step *looks like* between one string and the next. Consider what the half step interval looks like between the lowest string (string 6) and the next string up (string 5):

The two circles shown are actually circles numbered 5 and 6 in the cloud drawing above. But they no longer have numbers because I don't want you visualize the entire cloud anymore. I just want you to notice the relationship between these two notes. Notice that they are separated by that uncomfortable distance that corresponds to the pinky finger stretching in the Cloud exercise. In Mobility, we don't actually maintain this uncomfortable stretch. Instead we simply shift our hand exactly one fret and *relax in the new position*. If you don't get the idea exactly, just grab your guitar and keep reading. When you do it for yourself you'll see what I mean.

Got your guitar? Great. Now play any note on the low E string with your pinky finger. (Choose a note that is high enough on the neck so that you can execute the movement shown in the drawing above.) Align your left hand properly using one finger per fret. There should be no stretching involved at this point. You should simply have all four fingers resting on the low E string while you play the note under your pinky finger.

Now, if you wanted to move *down* a half step in pitch, that would be obvious. You would just play the note under your ring finger on the same low E string. But if you wanted to move *up* a half step, you would have two choices. Both choices involve a change of "position". On the guitar, a position simply means the fret with which your first finger is aligned. If you move your entire hand one fret closer to the body of the guitar, we say that you have moved up one position. One way to move up a half step would be to do just that, to move your entire hand up one position closer to the body of the guitar, and play the new note that falls under your pinky.

But the other way to do it would be to make a "Mobility jump" to the next string. You would actually move *down* one position and play the note that falls under your index finger on the next string. In all the movement feels like opening your hand for a big stretch, playing the new note and then relaxing in the new position.

If you don't follow me, there is a simple way for you to discover this same movement for yourself. Just go back to the drawing of the entire cloud, the one that has the little numbers in the circles. Play circle number 5 with your pinky and then circle number 6 with your index finger. Go back and forth between these two notes about a hundred times telling yourself, "This is what the half step looks like between the two lowest strings on my guitar." That's all I'm trying to show you.

Now let's take a look at the next two strings:

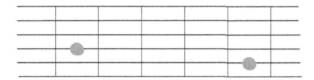

Here we have the exact same situation. So again we can conclude that this is what the half step looks like between strings 5 and 4. Practice this movement several times to start getting this idea into your muscle memory. As you alternate between the notes, remember to pause after each note to relax in the new position. This means that just after playing the new note, take a moment to relax and align your hand again in the new position so that you have exactly one finger per fret. Don't let your hand hover above the guitar neck in a stretched posture trying to cover all five frets at once.

The half step movement is also the same for the next two strings:

Again, practice this a few times while saying to yourself, "This is what the half step looks like between these two strings as well." But now take a look at what happens in the critical region between the second and third strings on your guitar:

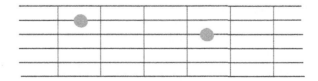

Notice that the half step movement between these two strings is different. Here the half step is what your hand naturally gives you, without any need for changing position. (If you don't see this clearly, just go back to the cloud drawing with the numbers in the circles. What we are talking about right now is the movement between circles numbered 19 and 20 in the cloud drawing.) Practice this movement by alternating several times between these two notes while thinking to yourself, "This is what the half step looks like in this funny special zone on my guitar between the second and third strings. Everywhere else I need to stretch and change position, but here the half step is what my hand naturally gives me."

Finally let's take a look at the last pair of strings:

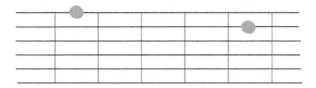

Here we return to the normal situation. Practice this movement several times saying to yourself, "The two highest strings are normal strings again. The half step here requires me to stretch and change position." Once you are clear about this, go back and practice half step movement between all of the other strings again. Remember to practice moving down just as much as moving up. In other words, pick a note at random to play with your *index* finger, and think through how you would jump to the next lower string moving *down* a half step. Make sure you have no doubt whatsoever in your mind about how to move in either direction from one string to the next by the interval of a half step.

I know this probably seems like the most trivial observation in the history of the world, but it is precisely what is going to allow you to master your entire guitar in no time. So just be patient and learn this concept deeply! Following is a simple game that you can play to practice Mobility in half steps.

Mobility Practice 1 (half steps)

Step 1: Pick a note, any note. (This means any finger, any string, any fret.)

Step 2: Move down a half step using *one* of the two possible movements:

Same String - Just move down one fret on the same string. If you already have a finger at that fret you can use it. But you can also take advantage of this moment to change the position of your left hand if you want to.

Different String - If instead you want to play the new note on the next string down, just make a Mobility jump to connect the two strings. But remember that the only Mobility jumps we know are based on connecting our index finger and our pinky finger. So regardless of what finger you used to play the prior note, now you must physically move your hand and change position to put your index finger on the last note you played. (You don't need to actually play the prior note again with your index finger. Just place your index finger there as a momentary visualization trick.) Now that your index finger is on the last note you played, you can use the Mobility jumps you learned earlier to visualize where to put your pinky finger on the next lower string in order to move down exactly one half step.

Step 3: Keep moving down in half steps as long as you want to.

Remember that you are free to move down a single string as long as you want to (until you run out of string!) or make a Mobility jump to the next lower string at any time.

Step 4: Whenever you decide, change direction and start moving up using *either* method:

Same String - Just move up one fret on the same string. You can use a finger that is already there or change position if you want.

Different String - Regardless of what finger you used to play the prior note, now you must physically move your hand and change position to put your pinky finger on that note. (Again, this is our momentary visualization trick because our Mobility jumps only work between index and pinky fingers.) Now with your pinky finger on the last note you played, you can use the Mobility jumps you learned earlier to visualize where to put your index finger on the next higher string in order to move up exactly one half step.

Step 5: Keep moving up in half steps as long as you want to.

Step 6: Continue playing, changing direction whenever you feel like it.

I'm sorry it takes so many words to explain the exercise. In the beginning, just trying to get through my explanation to form your own idea of the exercise can be pretty tiring. But all I'm really trying to encourage you to do is to move around your guitar neck freely in *both* dimensions:

- Moving up and down the frets on a single string

- Mobility jumping from one string to the next

You'll have to practice a bit in order develop confidence and fluidity. But soon your hand should be able to float all around the neck of your guitar with continuous half step motion. Be free and playful! This is not the time to be conservative. Be a show-off, like the little kid who rides his bike all around the neighborhood with no hands. If your hand is way down low on the guitar neck (in the first position, for example), don't feel that you need to stay there. You can fly all the way up that string by changing positions until you reach the very highest frets on your guitar, and only then make a Mobility jump to the next string. We are not looking for the most efficient and "logical" way to move up or down in half steps. What we want is complete freedom of movement. Our idea is to effortlessly float all over the guitar neck, freely mixing the two dimensions of motion.

Mobility: whole steps

Before moving on to whole steps, I suggest you take at least a few days to practice moving around purely in half steps. It's important that you keep your focus on half steps until this movement becomes fluid and effortless all over your guitar. That's when you are ready to move on to the whole step, which is the other essential movement that we need to master. Once we get whole steps down we can relax for a moment because these are the only two intervals we need for IFR Exercise 2: Melody.

To understand whole step movement, take a minute to go back to the cloud drawing with the numbered circles. You can visualize whole step movement between the low E string and the next string up by looking at the circles numbered 4 and 6 in the cloud drawing. Notice that there is no stretching involved. The movement looks like this:

To try it for yourself, play any note you want on the low E string with your pinky finger. Align your left hand properly so that you have exactly one finger per fret, and then alternate between this note and the one that falls directly under your index finger on the next string up. While you do this, say to yourself, "This is what the whole step looks like between the two lowest strings on my guitar." It's a simpler movement than the half step because you don't need to change position. Both notes fall directly under your fingers.

We have the same situation with the next two strings...

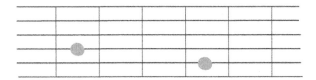

And the next two strings...

And just like before, the situation changes at the border between strings 2 and 3:

Here the interval of a whole step does not even require the entire length of your hand. Don't get hung up on the question of which fingers to use for these two notes. You can play the lower note (on string 3) with your pinky finger and the higher note (on string 2) with your middle finger. Or you can play the lower note with your ring finger and the higher note with your index finger. The point is simply to visualize the actual displacement on your guitar neck from one note to the next. Practice by alternating between these two notes while thinking to yourself, "This is what the whole step looks like in this funny zone between the second and third string."

Finally between the highest two strings of the guitar, the situation goes back to normal:

Take a minute to practice these whole step movements across all the strings on your guitar. Once you've got it clear in your mind, take a look at the following exercise which we will use to practice whole step movement over the entire guitar. (It's exactly the same as the exercise for half steps, but here's the detailed explanation anyway.)

Mobility Practice 2 (whole steps)

Step 1: Pick a note, any note.

Step 2: Move down a whole step using one of the two possible movements:

Same String - Simply play the note two frets lower on the same string. If you already have a finger at that fret you can use it. But if you prefer you can actually move your hand and change position.

Different String - Regardless of what finger you used to play the prior note, now physically move your hand and change position to put your index finger on that note. (This is our momentary visualization trick.) Now you can use the Mobility jumps you learned earlier to visualize where to play on the next lower string in order to move down exactly one whole step.

Step 3: Keep moving down in whole steps as long as you want to.

Again, you can move down a single string as long as you want or make a Mobility jump at any time to the next lower string.

Step 4: Whenever you decide, change direction and move upward using either method:

Same String - Just move up two frets on the same string. You can use a finger that is already there or change position if you want.

Different String - Regardless of what finger you used to play your last note, now physically move your hand to put your pinky finger there. Now you can use the Mobility jumps you learned earlier to visualize where to play on the next higher string in order to move up exactly one whole step.

Step 5: Keep moving up in whole steps as long as you want to.

Step 6: Continue playing, changing direction whenever you feel like it.

In Mobility, just as in Cloud, we will also eventually practice larger intervals like minor thirds, major thirds, fourths, etc. And later in the book when we get into specific harmonic shapes like major and minor chords we will incorporate those shapes into the game as well. But already with half steps and whole steps you have everything you need to improvise all over your guitar in any key. So don't be in any hurry to move on. Take your time to really understand the Mobility jumps and convince yourself that they are true. Go back and practice Cloud, and notice how the Mobility jumps are contained right there in Cloud. Do both exercises every day with whatever interval you feel like practicing. For now don't even worry about how you will eventually use these skills that you are developing. Just think of Landscape as short daily meditation that you can use to begin your practice routine. For a few minutes each day, just try to relax and give your full attention to the simple act of moving around the musical landscape on your guitar.

Note: The following supplement is for electric and upright bass players only.

Exercise 1: Landscape (for electric and upright bass)

Objective: To continuously improve in your ability to...

Clearly visualize your entire musical range and move effortlessly across it.

Since truly improvised music is created in the imagination, the most important technical skill to the improviser is the ability to instantly play any sound that he imagines. It's important to understand that this capacity is entirely mental. It has nothing to do with playing fast. Flying through scales with the metronome clacking away at 200 beats per minute might impress the neighbors but it doesn't necessarily make you a better improviser.

The improviser's objective is not speed of execution but clarity of vision. Imagine being able to see in your mind the entire map of a large city at once. That's how we would ideally like to feel about our entire musical range. The goal is a deep sense of *orientation* that accompanies us no matter where we might be on our instrument. If you're on the note Ab for example and your melodic idea requires you to go up a major third, or go down a major sixth, you don't want your creative flow to be interrupted by having to puzzle over these intervals. The idea is to be able to see the entire musical landscape at once so that you can easily imagine any type of movement across it. That way you can stay focused on the joy and fun of creating music.

The key to Exercise 1 is to just relax and enjoy yourself. The only thing you might find difficult about the exercise is overcoming the feelings of guilt that make you want to move on to something more "serious". Most beginning improvisers are in such a hurry to make music that they never take the time to just enjoy moving around their instrument. But there is nothing more important for you to master than the actual musical terrain which underlies everything you will play in the future.

In Exercise 1, the notes on your instrument have no musical significance whatsoever. Just forget about music for now. Don't be distracted by any thoughts about melody, harmony, tonality, scales, etc. Try to just unwind and have fun moving around your instrument as if you were a child playing in a field. The only goal is to gain confidence moving around within your musical range.

Bass players practice Exercise 1 in a special way to take advantage of a wonderful property that the bass has. The bass is in some ways even more visual than the piano. By "visual" I mean that all musical intervals, melodies, chords, etc. correspond to exact physical shapes on the neck of the instrument. This gives the bassist a tremendous advantage in learning to understand and truly internalize harmony. Your instrument literally has a double life. In addition to being your means of self-expression and musical creation, it also serves as your own personal workspace where you can visually arrange musical shapes and contemplate their sounds.

You are going to learn Exercise 1 in two phases. The first goal is to learn to visualize the notes on your instrument as one long unbroken chain of half steps. This is an important part of liberating yourself from scale drawings and memorized key signatures. The idea is to see all of the notes as equals. Your entire range should feel like one long connected staircase that you can move up or down as you please. We achieve this on the bass by practicing a technique that I call "Cloud", which is simply a way to visualize all of the notes that surround you at any given time. You will only practice this preliminary technique for a little while before moving on to "Mobility", which is the real technique that we will use as a permanent approach to movement on the bass. But this initial period of practicing Cloud is a tremendous exercise in visualization and an important mental preparation for Mobility, so please don't skip this critical step!

Cloud

To begin with, please take a minute to look at the following drawing of the bass neck. Make sure you understand its orientation. It represents approximately what you would see if you were to look down at your left hand while playing the electric bass. (Upright bass players please follow along as if you played the electric bass. The following drawings are for the fretted electric bass but all of the concepts are applied in the same way to the upright bass.)

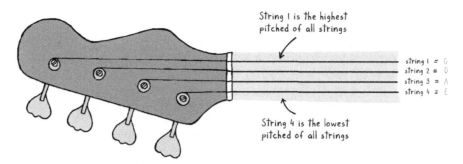

The open strings are tuned such that the interval between adjacent strings is always a perfect fourth. This observation will have a lot more significance to you in the coming weeks. But for now the only thing we are interested in is the entire set of notes available to you at any time. This set of notes (or what I call the "cloud") takes the following form on the bass:

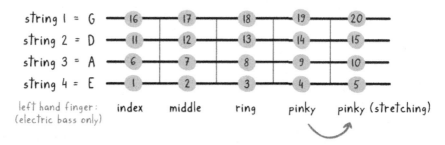

Don't be overwhelmed by all the numbers inside the circles. I just put them there to show you the order of the notes in pitch from lowest to highest. Imagine yourself playing these notes one at a time, starting with circle 1 and ending with circle 20. This is how we visualize the unbroken chain of half steps on both the upright and the electric bass.

The finger indication is for electric players only. No matter where you are on the bass neck, if you are an electric player for now you MUST always use the exact fingering indicated above. Notice that your little finger or pinky has the "double duty" of covering all the notes on two different frets. Follow this rule meticulously for the entire time that you practice the Cloud version of Exercise 1. When you move on to Mobility you can go back to playing notes with whatever fingers you feel like using. But for Cloud you need to use this exact fingering even when it seems uncomfortable or illogical. We use this rather strange fingering because it helps us to mentally visualize and remember where the notes are. Remember, in the future you are not even going to use this fingering so don't stress out about the fact that you feel slow or clumsy doing it this way. Just do it anyway. It's only a trick to help your memory, and you'll find that it really does help you to see more clearly what you're doing.

Upright players will have to make their own decisions about fingering using the (1, 2, 4) concept or any other technique. But you should still mentally visualize the above cloud drawing just as electric players do. The exercise is the same for both electric and upright players. It's just that upright players need to use their imagination a bit more to visualize the cloud, because their left hand will be moving around a lot more than the electric player's hand.

The important thing about the above drawing is that this cloud of notes always looks the exact same no matter where your hand is on the bass. If you are playing way down low on the bass then your index finger might be at the first fret. If you are playing way up high then your index finger might be at the ninth fret. But in both cases the notes available to you take on the exact same form, the one represented in the above drawing.

As you can see, there is no great mystery regarding half step movement within a particular string. If you want to move up a half step you just move up one fret. The story only becomes interesting at the borders between one string and the next. Pay special attention to these borders as you move around in the cloud. Let's look at a beginning version of Exercise 1 for bass players.

Cloud Practice 1

Step 1: Pick a note, any note.

> We start every exercise this way. You shouldn't always pick the same note. But don't think too much about it either. Just pick a note completely at random. This is a great way to practice one of the most essential skills of the improviser, which is the ability to orient oneself instantly with a single note. You never know where you are going to be when you will want to visualize a certain musical shape. So it's important that each exercise begin with a moment of complete disorientation. Just place your left hand anywhere on the bass neck and play any note you wish with the appropriate finger.

Step 2: Enjoy this note for as long as you want to.

> As you play the note make sure that each of the other fingers stays aligned with its corresponding fret. Close your eyes. You should still be able to visualize your hand with each finger aligned to a specific fret. Keeping your eyes closed, can you also visualize all of the rest of the notes in the cloud drawing above?

Step 3: Move to the note exactly one half step below.

> For example if you started on circle number 11 (played with the index finger on electric bass) then the new note would be circle number 10 (played with the pinky finger on electric bass). Electric players should make sure their hand is still perfectly aligned with one finger per fret, except for the pinky finger which sometimes stretches to perform its "double duty". Keep your eyes closed for this and all remaining steps.

Step 4: Continue moving down in half steps as far as you want to.

Step 5: Whenever you decide, change direction and begin to move upward.

Step 6: Continue playing, changing direction whenever you feel like it.

Using nothing but half steps, you should be able to move around freely within the cloud with your eyes closed, visualizing exactly where you are in the cloud drawing the entire time. For electric players, if you are careful to maintain your left hand properly aligned with one finger per fret (except the pinky finger which sometimes needs to stretch), then you should be able to move wherever you want without ever becoming disoriented. Upright players will have to work harder to imagine the cloud map at all times. But in both cases the key is to do the exercise slowly and to visualize the cloud drawing in your mind every step of the way.

This is just one of many ways to practice Cloud but it's the most important, and it is the foundation of everything to come. So don't rush on to the next thing. Stay with this simple exercise until you can do it in your sleep. Even after you understand the exercise, keep practicing it at least once every day for the first week. You might "get" the idea intellectually right from the very beginning. But your subconscious mind needs time to reprogram itself to imagine this cloud of notes as your musical universe. So take a few minutes each day to perform this simple relaxing exercise.

To make it more enjoyable you can play freely with rhythm, phrasing and syncopation. In other words, don't trudge through the notes as if you were performing a military drill. Be playful and change direction a lot. Instead of playing all the notes in a boring sequence like this:

...try to dance through the entire cloud like this:

One thing you should understand is that the numbers inside the circles don't have any purpose beyond just trying to show you how this exercise works. In fact with my own private students I don't even use these numbers because I can just show them the exercise directly on the bass. So while you're practicing Exercise 1, please don't put any effort into remembering the little numbers inside the circles. Your only objective is to visualize the cloud and practice moving around within it. We will never actually talk about these circle numbers again in this book.

Work on Cloud Practice 1 until you get to the point where moving from one note to the next becomes essentially effortless. You should be able to literally pick up your bass, place your left hand anywhere on the neck, play any note at random and immediately begin moving by half steps in either direction through the entire cloud.

Once you have gained this level of confidence moving around anywhere in the cloud, then you can take your practicing to the next level. The next step is to separate each of the notes by whole steps instead of half steps. For example if you randomly pick circle 17 as a starting point, then the next note below would be circle 15, then circle 13, then 11, etc. As with half steps, the goal is not simply to trudge through the notes in a systematic, boring way. Take time to enjoy yourself. Be rhythmic and playful, dancing around in the cloud using little whole step jumps. You will find that some places are more difficult than others to visualize this whole step jump. When you run into difficulties, don't stress out. Just stay there and enjoy practicing your jump as if you were a martial artist training in the dojo.

Once you have mastered half steps and whole steps, you have reached an important plateau. These are the only two intervals you need in order to play all of the material that you are going to see in IFR Exercise 2: Melody. So this is also the moment where your practicing needs to break into two parallel paths. You should go ahead and begin enjoying Exercise 2 just as soon as you are ready, but you should also continue to grow your abilities in Exercise 1.

I'll explain Exercise 2 when we get there. But right now I want to keep going in Exercise 1, to show you how you can continue to grow in your mastery of the basic musical landscape of your bass. This new exercise that I am going to show you will become the primary way that we will visualize any kind of movement on the bass.

Mobility

The Mobility exercise is a simple concept but explaining it in a book takes a lot of words. Once you understand the movements in the exercise, you'll find it both fun to practice and incredibly liberating. It's only the initial explanation that takes some effort. But each movement is explained and illustrated in this chapter, and you'll find video demonstrations of the exercise at ImproviseForReal.com.

Mobility: half steps

* A special note to upright players:

> The following description of the Mobility exercise includes many comments about finger position that are for electric bass players only. This is because on the electric bass the Mobility jumps correspond to exact finger movements, and I want to make these movements clear. You will obviously not use the same fingerings, but please follow along with this explanation anyway and try to imagine how you would do the Mobility exercise on an electric bass. This will help you visualize the Mobility jumps on your upright bass as well because the actual movements are identical. The only thing that changes is the fingering, since you will make your own decisions about which finger to use for each note. Because of the freedom of left hand movement that the upright bass requires, you will have to concentrate a bit harder in the beginning in order to visualize the Mobility jumps. But with a little practice you can do the exercise just as easily as electric players. The first step is simply to get clear about the movements themselves, and to do that I would ask you to imagine for a moment that you are an electric player, and follow along with the examples below.

The idea behind Mobility comes from making a couple of important observations about the relationships between the notes in Cloud. By reducing our Cloud experience to a couple of key observations, we can carry these principles with us wherever we go, and thus move freely around the entire bass without even bothering to visualize the entire cloud at once. Whenever we want to change strings we will simply make a "Mobility jump" to the new location and continue playing. Let's look again at the Cloud drawing with numbers representing each note:

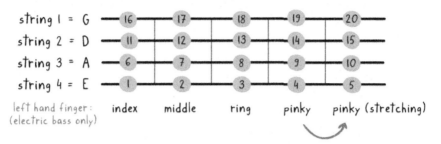

The first observation we need to make about the above drawing is what the interval of a half step *looks like* between one string and the next. Consider what the half step interval looks like between the lowest string (string 4) and the next string up (string 3):

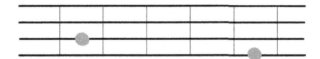

The two circles shown are actually circles numbered 5 and 6 in the cloud drawing above. But they no longer have numbers because I don't want you visualize the entire cloud anymore. I just want you to notice the relationship between these two notes. Notice that they are separated by that uncomfortable distance that corresponds to the pinky finger stretching in the Cloud exercise. In Mobility, we don't actually maintain this uncomfortable stretch. Instead we simply shift our hand exactly one fret and *relax in the new position*. If you don't get the idea exactly, just grab your bass and keep reading. When you do it for yourself you'll see what I mean.

Got your bass? Great. Now play any note on the low E string with your pinky finger. (Choose a note that is high enough on the neck so that you can execute the movement shown in the drawing above.) Align your left hand properly using one finger per fret. There should be no stretching involved at this point. You should simply have all four fingers resting on the low E string while you play the note under your pinky finger.

Now, if you wanted to move *down* a half step in pitch, that would be obvious. You would just play the note under your ring finger on the same low E string. But if you wanted to move *up* a half step, you would have two choices. Both choices involve a change of "position". On the bass, a position simply means the fret with which your first finger is aligned. If you move your entire hand one fret closer to the body of the bass, we say that you have moved up one position. One way to move up a half step would be to do just that, to move your entire hand up one position closer to the body of the bass, and play the new note that falls under your pinky.

But the other way to do it is to make a Mobility jump to the next string. You will actually move *down* one position and play the note that falls under your index finger on the next string. In all the movement feels like opening your hand for a big stretch, playing the new note and then relaxing in the new position.

If you don't follow me, there is a simple way for you to discover this same movement for yourself. Just go back to the drawing of the entire cloud, the one that has the little numbers in the circles. Play circle number 5 with your pinky and then circle number 6 with your index finger. Go back and forth between these two notes about a hundred times telling yourself, "This is what the half step looks like between any two strings on my bass." That's all I'm trying to show you.

Now let's take a look at the next two strings:

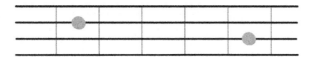

Here we have the exact same situation. But practice this movement several times anyway just to get it into your muscle memory. Think to yourself that this is what the half step looks like between these two strings as well. As you alternate between the notes, remember to pause after each note to relax in the new position. This means that just after playing the new note, take a moment to relax and align your hand again in the new position so that you have exactly one finger per fret. Don't let your hand hover above the bass neck in a stretched posture trying to cover all five frets at once.

The half step movement is of course also the same for the highest two strings:

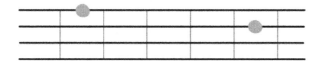

Again, practice this a few times while saying to yourself, "This is what the half step looks like between these two strings as well."

I know this probably seems like the most trivial and useless observation in the history of the world, but it is precisely what is going to allow you to master your entire bass in no time. So just be patient and learn this concept deeply! Following is a simple game that you can play to practice Mobility in half steps.

Mobility Practice 1 (half steps)

Step 1: Pick a note, any note. (This means any finger, any string, any fret.)

Step 2: Move down a half step using *one* of the two possible movements:

> Same String - Just move down one fret on the same string. If you already have a finger at that fret you can use it. But you can also take advantage of this moment to change the position of your left hand if you want to.

Different String - If instead you want to play the new note on the next string down, just make a Mobility jump to connect the two strings. But remember that the only Mobility jumps we know are based on connecting our index finger and our pinky finger. So regardless of what finger you used to play the prior note, now you must physically move your hand and change position to put your index finger on the last note you played. (You don't need to actually play the prior note again with your index finger. Just place your index finger there as a momentary visualization trick.) Now that your index finger is on the last note you played, you can use the Mobility jumps you learned earlier to visualize where to put your pinky finger on the next lower string in order to move down exactly one half step.

Step 3: Keep moving down in half steps as long as you want to.

Remember that you are free to move down a single string as long as you want to (until you run out of terrain!) or make a Mobility jump to the next lower string at any time.

Step 4: Whenever you decide, change direction and start moving up using *either* method:

Same String - Just move up one fret on the same string. You can use a finger that is already there or change position if you want.

Different String - Regardless of what finger you used to play the prior note, now you must physically move your hand and change position to put your pinky finger on that note. (Again, this is our momentary visualization trick because our Mobility jumps only work between index and pinky fingers.) Now with your pinky finger on the last note you played, you can use the Mobility jumps you learned earlier to visualize where to put your index finger on the next higher string in order to move up exactly one half step.

Step 5: Keep moving up in half steps as long as you want to.

Step 6: Continue playing, changing direction whenever you feel like it.

I'm sorry it takes so many words to explain the exercise. In the beginning, just trying to get through my explanation to form your own idea of the exercise can be pretty tiring. But all I'm really trying to encourage you to do is to move around your bass neck freely in *both* dimensions:

- Moving up and down the frets on a single string

- Mobility jumping from one string to the next

You'll have to practice a bit in order develop confidence and fluidity. But soon your hand should be able to float all around the neck of your bass with continuous half step motion. Be free and playful! This is not the time to be conservative. Be a show-off, like the little kid who rides his bike all around the neighborhood with no hands. If your hand is way down low on the bass neck (in the first position, for example), don't feel that you need to stay there. You can fly all the way up that string by changing positions until you reach the very highest frets on your bass, and only then make a Mobility jump to the next string. We are not looking for the most efficient and "logical" way to move up or down in half steps. What we want is complete freedom of movement. Our idea is to effortlessly float all over the bass neck, freely mixing the two dimensions of motion.

Mobility: whole steps

Once you can move effortlessly all over your bass in half steps you are ready to move on to the whole step, which is the other essential movement that we need to master. Once we get whole steps down we can relax for a moment because these are the only two intervals we need for IFR Exercise 2: Melody.

To understand whole step movement, take a minute to go back to the cloud drawing with the numbered circles. You can visualize whole step movement between the low E string and the next string up by looking at the circles numbered 4 and 6 in the cloud drawing. Notice that there is no stretching involved. The movement looks like this:

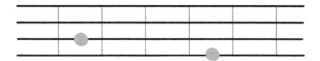

To try it for yourself, play any note you want on the low E string with your pinky finger. Align your left hand properly so that you have exactly one finger per fret, and then alternate between this note and the one that falls directly under your index finger on the next string up. While you do this, say to yourself, "This is what the whole step looks like between any two strings on my bass." It's a simpler movement than the half step because you don't need to change position. Both notes fall directly under your fingers.

It's the same situation with the next two strings...

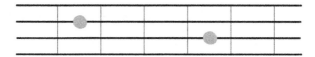

And the highest two strings...

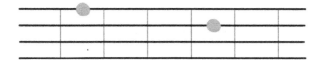

Take a minute to practice these whole step movements across all the strings on your bass. Then take a look at the following exercise which we will use to practice whole step movement over the entire bass. (It's exactly the same as the exercise for half steps, but here's the detailed explanation anyway.)

Mobility Practice 2 (whole steps)

Step 1: Pick a note, any note.

Step 2: Move down a whole step using one of the two possible movements:

Same String - Simply play the note two frets lower on the same string. If you already have a finger at that fret you can use it, or you can change position if you feel like it.

Different String - Regardless of what finger you used to play the prior note, now physically move your hand and change position to put your index finger on that note. (This is our momentary visualization trick.) Now you can use the whole step Mobility jump to play the note that falls under your pinky finger on the next lower string.

Step 3: Keep moving down in whole steps as long as you want to.

Again, you can move down a single string as long as you want or make a Mobility jump at any time to the next lower string.

Step 4: Whenever you decide, change direction and start moving up using either method:

Same String - Just move up two frets on the same string. You can use a finger that is already there or change position if you want.

Different String - Regardless of what finger you used to play your last note, now physically move your hand to put your pinky finger there. Now you can use the whole step Mobility jump and play the note that falls under your index finger on the next higher string.

Step 5: Keep moving up in whole steps as long as you want to.

Step 6: Continue playing, changing direction whenever you feel like it.

In Mobility, just as in Cloud, you should also eventually practice larger intervals like minor thirds, major thirds, fourths, etc. Can you already imagine what these larger Mobility jumps look like on the bass? Here are a few to consider:

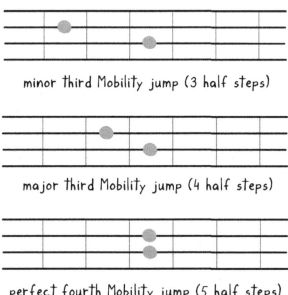

minor third Mobility jump (3 half steps)

major third Mobility jump (4 half steps)

perfect fourth Mobility jump (5 half steps)

augmented fourth Mobility jump (6 half steps)

perfect fifth Mobility jump (7 half steps)

Later in the book when we get into specific harmonic shapes like major and minor chords we will incorporate those shapes into the game as well. But already with half steps and whole steps you have everything you need to improvise all over your bass in any key. So don't be in any hurry to move on. Take your time to really understand the Mobility jumps and convince yourself that they are true. Go back and practice Cloud, and notice how the Mobility jumps are contained right there in Cloud. Do both exercises every day with whatever interval you feel like practicing. For now don't even worry about how you will eventually use these skills that you are developing. Just think of Landscape as short daily meditation that you can use to begin your practice routine. For a few minutes each day, just try to relax and give your full attention to the simple act of moving around the musical landscape on your bass.

The architect and the bricklayer

Before we start talking about harmony I want to tell you a story that will help you understand the shift we need to make in our musical thinking. The story is about an architect and a bricklayer.

Each morning the bricklayer goes to work and begins his day by reviewing the plans he is given. These plans tell him exactly what structures he has to build and where he has to build them. He never knows exactly what the final building will look like, but it doesn't matter because his job is just to implement whatever is written in the plans.

These building plans were designed by an architect. They are based on a long list of customer requirements combined with the architect's own understanding of aesthetics, functionality, safety considerations, zoning laws, the cost of different building materials, etc. The architect may work for a year or more on the design of a single building. Then a whole team of people works for many more months to turn this high level design into an actual project plan with specific tasks for construction workers like our bricklayer.

The bricklayer is very good at his job but in his heart he dreams of being an architect himself someday. He imagines himself designing entire buildings and passing orders on down to bricklayers and other contractors. Sometimes in his free time he sits and contemplates his bricklaying plans trying to comprehend their logic. But no matter how much he studies his instructions, he never really understands the architect's thinking. The architect's work seems like magic and our poor bricklayer wrongly concludes that he just doesn't have what it takes to be an architect.

The problem is that the architect works with different tools and a different language, and he follows a completely different methodology from that of the bricklayer. It's not that our bricklayer is incapable of becoming an architect. He just needs to go to architecture school and start to think about the kinds of things that architects think about. He will never understand architecture by studying his bricklaying instructions, because the information is simply not there.

This is exactly what happens to musicians who try to understand harmony by studying their "instructions" (classical sheet music, jazz lead sheets, etc). Our system of key signatures, chord symbols, notes and rests, etc. is a very efficient way to tell a performer exactly what he is supposed to play. But as a language for understanding harmony our notation system is a complete disaster. It's not that creating music is difficult. It's just that you'll never understand it if you are trapped in the language of the performer. Just like the bricklayer's instructions, the design information is simply not there.

If you want to create music yourself you need to abandon the musical language of performers and adopt a musical language adequate for composers. In other words you need to start from scratch and take a fresh look at harmony through the eyes of a child. What you will find is that if you can just set aside all those distracting "bricklayer" questions, harmony is actually quite simple. In fact it's ridiculously simple.

Seven little notes

All of the music you have ever heard in your life is based on just seven notes.

(Please take a moment to reflect on that. It's a big statement.)

We have literally spent centuries applying our musical creativity to a simple constellation of seven notes. They make up the music of every classical composer you can think of, as well as all of contemporary pop music, rock, funk, blues, jazz, soul, bossa nova and everything else. From the most raucous heavy metal to the sublime meditations of Miles Davis, you are hearing the same seven notes over and over again.

The seven notes are called very simply the "major scale", and from this scale comes every musical sound you have ever heard. It may seem very surprising that so much music can be made from such a simple little set of materials. But what's even more amazing is that you *already* recognize these seven notes in the music all around you. You had them memorized before you could even speak. You are not accustomed to naming them because nobody ever pointed them out to you. But your subconscious mind is already highly trained in their use.

This is why, for example, you are able to recognize the melody to "Happy Birthday" no matter what key it's in. What you are really recognizing is just a particular sequence of notes from the major scale. In other words, the very fact that you are able to recognize the melody at all means that on a subconscious level you *already know what the notes are*. And "Happy Birthday" isn't the only melody that we recognize in this way. It's just one example among thousands. Literally every time you whistle a tune, sing a song or recognize a familiar melody you are demonstrating your knowledge and command of the seven notes that make up our musical system. They are like a second language to you, and you know them so well that you use them masterfully without even realizing that you're doing it.

I'll show you an example. Take a moment to recall a familiar melody from your childhood. It could be a Christmas carol or a pop song or a TV jingle or whatever. Sing the first couple of lines out loud and make sure that you are singing well enough for the melody to be recognizable.

--- Really, please actually *do* this exercise instead of just thinking about it. It only takes a second. Sing each note clearly and really *feel* each note as you sing it. When you have finished you can move on with the reading. Sing the melody now. ---

Great, now here is the point. Most likely you sang the melody in a totally different key from the original key in which you heard it. But starting from any random pitch you are able to perfectly place all those half steps and whole steps in just the right places so that the melody is correctly reproduced in the *new key* that you are imagining now. This transposition from one key to another would probably take you ten minutes to figure out with pencil, paper and music theory. But for your subconscious musical mind (which we can also simply call "the ear"), the transposition is absolutely effortless. This simple exercise demonstrates that you are already an absolute master of tonal harmony. It also gives you perhaps your first glimpse at *where* your musical genius resides.

Most people don't consider singing a simple tune to be a particularly impressive feat. But it is a very small step indeed to be able to *play* these notes on any instrument as well. In fact one of the very first skills you will acquire as a result of practicing IFR is the ability to effortlessly play on your instrument any melody you can imagine, in any key that you wish. In one fell swoop you will inherit an instant repertoire that consists of every song you have ever heard.

Reflecting on this revelation that all our music is based on just seven notes, you might think to ask why none of your music teachers ever told you this. The answer is that they probably *didn't know*. If you have ever been exposed to anything at all of "music theory", you have seen a wonderful example of how well-intentioned people can invent an explanation that is vastly more confusing than the material they were trying to explain in the first place.

The power of direct experience

But *why* is music theory so dense and complicated? Why is there this contradiction between the elegant beauty of music and the clumsy drudgery of music theory?

I believe that the problem is not with music theory itself, but with our attempts to use it as a substitute for direct, personal experience.

Imagine for a moment that I wanted to know everything there is to know about your home town where you grew up. You may not realize what an expert you are on the subject of your home town. But we would both be in for a long night if you had to explain it *all* to me. For starters there's your family's house (don't forget all the different rooms), your friends' houses, your school with all its classrooms, your favorite places to play outside, all the streets and street corners, all the restaurants, the grocery store, the bank, the post office and lots more places that only you would know about. I'll bet there are literally hundreds of places that you can clearly remember if you think about it long enough.

And that's just the beginning. Even if you narrow it down to just one of these locations, you find that there are still countless details to explain: floor, ceiling, walls, doors and windows, light fixtures, furniture and perhaps dozens of small objects.

And it doesn't even stop there. Even if you focus on just one of the objects in the room, you still find that words are not even adequate to describe completely this one single thing!

So much for the power of words.

But now imagine if you could just *take me there*. You could show me around and take me to all those places that you wanted to share with me. In just the first few minutes alone the sudden rush of sights, sounds and smells would already fill my mind with more details than you could ever possibly give me in words.

Your home town is a good metaphor for harmony. There is nothing particularly difficult about harmony, but it's just not the kind of thing that can be easily reduced to words and theories. This beautiful world of sounds must be experienced first-hand. If you just go there and experience this world for yourself, you will find that you really don't need a whole lot of theory to keep track of where things are. But if you remain outside this world and try to learn about it through second-hand explanations, if you try to reduce this rich world of sounds and sensations to a bunch of formulas and definitions, that's when you find yourself before an impossible task.

This is why music theory seems so difficult and confusing. It's just not possible to get any real understanding of music unless you experience it for yourself. You need to create the sounds yourself and hear them over and over again. You need to play with them freely, combining them in all different ways. In other words, you need to *improvise*. Most people falsely believe that you need to understand harmony before you can improvise. But actually it's the other way around. You need to improvise in order to understand harmony.

So really, learning to improvise is not the "goal" of the IFR method. Improvisation *is* the method. It's how we investigate new concepts and discover their meaning for ourselves. My job is to organize your experiences so that you gradually come to have an understanding of our

47

entire musical system. Your job is simply to play with and enjoy whatever sounds we happen to be studying at the moment. If we both do our jobs correctly, then your practicing should always be enjoyable, interesting and fun. But you will also be developing a deep personal mastery of harmony that cannot be explained in words.

A genuine understanding of music is available to anyone, but the only way to achieve it is through direct personal experience. Unfortunately, music classes are just about the worst place to go to gain this experience. Most music teachers are intensely uncomfortable letting students just experience notes and chords for themselves. They think that in order to justify the price of the class they need to "explain" something. This is the biggest mistake of our entire music education system. An artist can't get by with second-hand explanations. An artist needs to have direct personal experience with the materials of his art.

Understanding begins with listening

Every composer uses sounds for one reason only. Each sound makes the audience feel a particular sensation, and the composer wants to lead the audience through these sensations in a particular way. For example if a piece of music is written in a minor tonality with lots of dark and sad chords, the audience can feel this. The audience can *feel* the difference between major and minor.

Similarly, the audience also perceives perfectly the sensations of tension and release in the music they hear. The way Western harmony works is that at every moment during a piece of music, the listener feels a certain attraction toward a particular note. This note is called the *tonal center*. But it doesn't matter what it's called. Just think of it as a gravitational center that exerts a force of attraction on you. Essentially your subconscious mind is always wanting to relieve its tension by returning to this tonal center. Every sound you hear that is not this tonal center produces a kind of tension in your mind. Some of these sounds are more tense than others, but each one produces a very specific sensation in your mind and body.

In addition to these feelings, at any given instant during a musical performance the audience is also subconsciously aware of exactly seven notes that make up the music's *tonality* at this moment. This is perhaps the most "hidden" of your subconscious abilities because you kind of have to go digging around in your mind a bit in order to discover that you are in fact imagining exactly seven notes.

But what all this amounts to is that the very first role model you should strive to emulate in your musical career is a surprising one: *the audience*. The audience already perceives essentially everything there is to know about any particular piece of music. And if you think about it, this makes perfect sense. In fact it couldn't be any other way. Why would composers put sounds in their compositions if the audience weren't capable of perceiving them?

The mistake we make as musicians is in thinking that "understanding music" is a project that should take us off in some different direction from the experience of the audience. Our teachers convince us to abandon our role as listeners and focus our attention on theories and formulas. But the path to understanding music starts with the very same experience that the casual listeners in the audience are already enjoying. We musicians don't need to go off and join some strange cult in order to learn the secrets of music. If we want to understand music more deeply than the people sitting around us in the audience, we just need to listen more closely. Our experience is not different from theirs. It is only deeper. Our road to musical understanding begins with recognizing and using the very same sensations that everybody else in the audience is already feeling. By becoming aware of these natural processes that *already* occur in your mind and body when you listen to music, you can discover the secret of those musical geniuses who immediately know how to play any piece of music that they hear.

You can begin this process right now. Here is a simple exercise that you can do anytime you listen to music. Try it first with very simple music like Christmas carols, folk songs, country music, children's songs, etc. The exercise consists of trying to consciously feel the song's *tonality* and the *tonal center*:

1. Listen to the song with your full attention for at least one full minute. Don't think about anything else. Just relax and enjoy the song and really listen.

2. Shut off the music if you can, or move away from it physically so that you don't hear it so loudly anymore. (Do this quickly because we don't want to lose the sensation of the music in our mind.)

3. Sing a note that you can clearly remember from the song. It could be the last note you heard or it could be the sound of any particular word or phrase. But try to remember the sensation of one particular note and sing it to yourself.

4. Now try to imagine a note one step lower than this one. But don't think about it too much! If you think too hard you will be able to imagine some other scale that has nothing to do with the music you just listened to. Just relax and move downward to whatever seems to be the next lower note you hear in your mind. Then move down another note, then another, etc.

5. Keep coming down until you reach what you feel to be the most "final" note of the whole bunch. This is the note that makes you feel a sensation of permanent relaxation. For example when the song ends, this note would be a good choice for the last note.

If you can get as far as step 4, and you are able to clearly imagine a whole series of notes after listening to a song, then what you have clarified for yourself is the song's tonality. Essentially, you have abstracted from the song the seven notes from which the entire song is made. As you move down through your singing range you might actually sing a lot more than seven notes. But all you are really doing is simply repeating the seven notes of the tonality in different octaves. You may not realize that there are exactly seven notes but that doesn't matter right now. The exciting thing about this exercise is simply discovering that the notes which make up the entire harmonic environment of a song become automatically separated, organized and stored in your subconscious mind whenever you listen to music.

This means that despite the bewildering jumble of sounds and sensations flooding in through your ears, somewhere in your mind there is a set of seven neat little boxes where you will find precisely the seven notes from which the entire song is made. This is an organizational feat that you could never pull off consciously. It would be impossible to consciously recognize and sort out the notes that make up all those chords and melodies. But even absolute beginners (including little children) can perfectly sing the seven notes that make up the tonality of any song, simply by relaxing and allowing themselves to imagine whatever notes "occur to them". Take advantage of this internal process that is available to you. Look within yourself to clarify the notes that make up the tonality of every song you hear. You don't have to name the notes or understand them in any way. Just hear them in your mind and sing them to yourself.

Step 5 of the exercise challenges you to decide for yourself which of the seven notes is the tonal center. This may or may not be clear to you. If you don't feel any particular note as the tonal center, then just turn the music back on again. As you listen to the music, ask yourself the question, "Which of these notes or chords sounds like the ground floor of the song's harmony, the place where everything is relaxed and final?" If you still don't feel it, just keep listening. Almost every song ends by returning to the tonal center. So you can actually teach yourself what the tonal center feels like just by waiting until the end of every song and noticing that moment. The sensation you have in your body when you hear the last chord of a song is what the tonal center feels like.

You won't always be successful in performing this exercise with any particular song. In fact in your first few attempts you might not even get past step 3 (imagining clearly one single note from the song). But if that's as far as you get in the beginning, then just keep taking the exercise to step 3. The important thing is to be actively in search of these sensations within yourself. Remember that it is not about guessing how the music works. It's about *noticing* what the music is already doing inside your body.

If you simply can't get started with this exercise, don't panic. Just set it aside for now if you don't know exactly how to do it. When you begin to practice IFR Exercise 2: Melody, this will all be much clearer. For now just know that whenever you listen to music two things automatically happen:

1. Your subconscious mind imagines exactly seven notes that make up the song's tonality.

2. One of these notes attracts you especially as the tonal center.

Breaking the spell

The biggest difficulty that both beginners and advanced musicians alike have with understanding harmony is the ridiculous naming system that we use. Our system of naming notes is so nonsensical that most beginners simply can't believe it. They just figure that music must be very complicated since the language we use to talk about it is so complicated.

But there is a dirty trick hidden inside every music lesson, and it has to do with the names we use for the notes. These names are so misleading that it is almost impossible to see even the simplest relationships between them. This is one reason why people can study music all their lives and never even notice that they are always playing the same seven sounds. It's as if our entire society were under a spell that prevents us from seeing what is right before our eyes.

To begin with, you should understand that music is *relative*. The absolute pitches of the notes in any song *do not matter*. What makes the song sound the way it does is the relationship between the notes. You could transpose the entire song up or down a half step and nobody would even notice, even though the name of every single note would change in the process. In fact any piece of music can be perfectly reproduced in any key you want, whether it be a simple blues or the entire Requiem Mass of Mozart.

For this reason, the language we use to think and talk about music must also be relative. If you hope to make any sense at all of music, you need to look beyond the absolute note names like F# and Bb and adopt a language that corresponds to the way music really works. In every single key the seven notes of the major scale always sound exactly the same. So the first step to understanding music is to give these notes *permanent names* that do not constantly change depending on what key you're in. You could give these seven notes any names you like, but I use the numbers 1 through 7 because it's the simplest way I know to talk about seven things and easily remember their order:

$$1 \quad 2 \quad 3 \quad 4 \quad 5 \quad 6 \quad 7$$

Soon you will learn to visualize these seven notes anywhere on your instrument. But first we need to look at the entire set of notes in our musical system. This is where we come into contact with the unfortunate naming system we have inherited. But don't despair. They are only names. If you can learn to look beyond the names you will have no trouble at all.

In all there are twelve available notes in our musical system. They have the following names:

$$A \quad A\# \quad B \quad C \quad C\# \quad D \quad D\# \quad E \quad F \quad F\# \quad G \quad G\#$$

Notice that there is no sharp note between B and C, nor between E and F. This is an important detail.

Now, the sharp notes can also be called the next note flatted. For example A# is the same as Bb. So we could also list the notes in the following way:

$$A \quad B\flat \quad B \quad C \quad D\flat \quad D \quad E\flat \quad E \quad F \quad G\flat \quad G \quad A\flat$$

But the truth is that both ways of naming these notes are misleading. In reality the note A# has absolutely nothing at all to do with the note A. It is not "the note A raised up a half step" as is commonly taught to children. It is in fact a *different* note. There is no more relation between A and A# than there is between E and F. They are simply neighbors, and nothing more.

The only redeeming value of this naming system is that it does help us to see clearly the structure of the major scale, at least in one key. The notes that have "clean names" (names that do not require sharps or flats) are precisely the notes that belong to the major scale of C:

$$C \quad D \quad E \quad F \quad G \quad A \quad B$$

Because of this, our naming system makes it very easy for us to visualize the notes in the key of C. And this would be wonderful if we always played in the key of C. But there's just one small problem. We almost NEVER play in the key of C!

Do you have any idea how few classical pieces are actually written in the key of C? Hardly any jazz tunes are written in C either. The only tunes I know in the key of C are a bunch of country songs and some reggae. And most of those musicians don't even use sheet music!

The sad reality is that our entire naming system is designed to facilitate talking about notes in a key in which we almost never play. The key of C is only one of twelve possible keys, and yet we name all of our notes relative to this one key.

This is why, for example, a perfectly simple melody in the key of E will appear to have all sorts of "sharp notes". In fact there is nothing "sharp" about the notes at all. The notes themselves are just the seven notes of the E major scale, and they sound just as simple and sweet as the notes of any other major scale. The only thing complicated about them is their *names*, because we are stuck with this bonehead naming system which describes everything relative to the key of C.

Unless you have been playing and thinking about music for some time, you may not completely follow what I am trying to say. But you can still understand the important point that you need to take away from this chapter. From time to time we will need to refer to the notes by their absolute names (Bb, F#, C, etc.) but I want you to understand that they are *only names*. You need to start thinking of every single note as a completely separate entity, exactly equal to its neighbors in value and importance. Bb, F# and C are all exactly equal. They are just three different notes among the twelve that exist in all.

Your concept of the notes on your instrument needs to become as clean and pure as the following drawing:

•   •   •   •   •   •   •   •   •   •   •   •   •

The work you are doing in Exercise 1 will help you achieve exactly this. It may seem like kind of a silly game, but what it's really about is learning to relate to the notes on your instrument in a new way that is not complicated by their unfortunate names. This is the first step to breaking the spell that has prevented us from understanding music.

The magic key

In this chapter I am going to show you something that is very special to me. It is something very simple, and it has been around for a long time. I certainly didn't invent it myself. It is mentioned (at least briefly) in almost every harmony course that exists. But despite the fact that a lot of people seem to "know" what I am about to show you, nobody seems to care much about it or use it in any conscious way.

In fact, I have never met *anyone* who truly grasped all of its implications until I showed them. To me it's like an old, rusty forgotten key that has the remarkable ability to open every door in the world. I love this key. And although it doesn't offer much in the way of explanations, once you learn to use it you won't need any explanations because you will understand literally everything there is to know about harmony.

Please take a couple of minutes to really look at the following drawing:

$$1 \quad \cdot \quad 2 \quad \cdot \quad 3 \quad 4 \quad \cdot \quad 5 \quad \cdot \quad 6 \quad \cdot \quad 7 \, | \, 1$$

Doesn't look like much, does it? If you've studied music theory at all you probably already know exactly what this is. It's simply a visual representation of the major scale in any key. But take a good look, because you are looking at nothing less than the map of your musical imagination. Every musical sound you have ever heard in your life is located somewhere in the above drawing. From the screaming guitar solos of Eddie Van Halen to the string quartets of Shostakovich, it's all right there on your map. And if you become as addicted to the IFR method as I am, you will spend the rest of your life contemplating this simple little drawing from infinite points of view.

Don't be put off by the numbers. There is nothing cold or mathematical about our work. The seven notes could just as easily have more friendly names like Jimmy, Fluffy, Grandpa, etc. But I use numbers because it's the simplest way to name seven things and remember their order. Just think of them like street addresses or signposts that indicate where each sound "lives".

Each item (whether it be a number or a little dot) in the drawing above represents a single note in the unbroken chain of half steps that you are learning to visualize in Exercise 1. If you imagine this series of half steps in any particular region as the following drawing:

•   •   •   •   •   •   •   •   •   •   •   •   •

...then you can also visualize the major scale anywhere in this region:

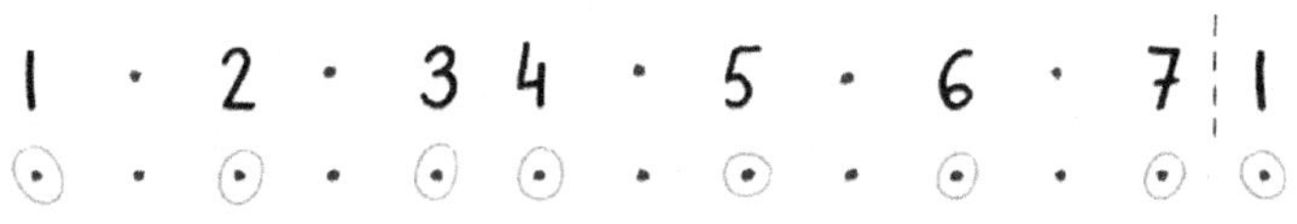

$$1 \quad \cdot \quad 2 \quad \cdot \quad 3 \quad 4 \quad \cdot \quad 5 \quad \cdot \quad 6 \quad \cdot \quad 7 \, | \, 1$$

⊙ • ⊙ • ⊙ ⊙ • ⊙ • ⊙ • ⊙ ⊙

Notice that the little "curtain" that separates note 7 from the following note 1 is not a note at all. It is merely a reminder that we are entering a new octave. It's there to remind us that the following note 1 is actually the exact same note as the original note 1 at the beginning of the scale, except that it's one octave higher. The entire major scale has only seven notes. But I often include an additional note 1 in my drawings just so that you can see clearly the interval between note 7 and the following note 1, which is a half step.

Since you have now been practicing Exercise 1 with half steps for a little while, I trust that you can pick any region on your instrument and move around comfortably within this region by half steps. So please grab your instrument and try the following activity which will allow you to hear for yourself the seven notes of our major scale.

(Playing activity)

Pick a note, any note. But don't pick an obvious note like C. Be courageous and pick an unusual note like A natural or D flat. This will be note 1.

$$1$$

Move up *two half steps*. This is note 2. Practice alternating between both notes.

$$1 \quad \cdot \quad 2$$

Move up *two more half steps* above note 2. This is note 3. Play for a moment with all three notes.

$$1 \quad \cdot \quad 2 \quad \cdot \quad 3$$

Now move up only *one half step* above note 3. This is note 4. Play with all four notes for a minute.

$$1 \quad \cdot \quad 2 \quad \cdot \quad 3 \quad 4$$

Move up *two more half steps* above note 4. This is note 5. Play with all five notes for a minute.

$$1 \quad \cdot \quad 2 \quad \cdot \quad 3 \quad 4 \quad \cdot \quad 5$$

Move up *two more half steps* above note 5. This is note 6. Play with all six notes for a minute.

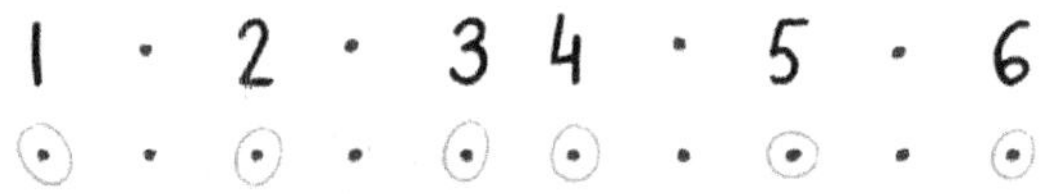

$$| \quad \cdot \quad 2 \quad \cdot \quad 3 \quad 4 \quad \cdot \quad 5 \quad \cdot \quad 6$$

Move up *two more half steps* above note 6. This is note 7. Play with all seven notes for a minute.

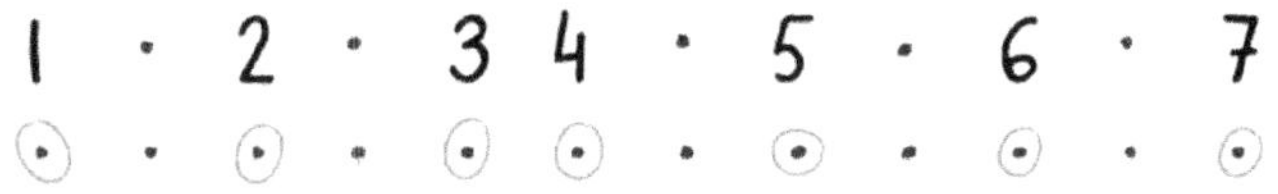

$$| \quad \cdot \quad 2 \quad \cdot \quad 3 \quad 4 \quad \cdot \quad 5 \quad \cdot \quad 6 \quad \cdot \quad 7$$

Move up *one last half step* above note 7. This is note 1 again, in the next octave. Improvise freely with all eight notes for a few minutes.

$$| \quad \cdot \quad 2 \quad \cdot \quad 3 \quad 4 \quad \cdot \quad 5 \quad \cdot \quad 6 \quad \cdot \quad 7 \quad |$$

If you want to convince yourself that the above drawing works in all keys, just go back and pick a new starting note as your note 1. As long as you respect the intervals shown in the above drawing you should be able to perfectly reproduce the major scale in any key, simply by visualizing every whole step and half step along the way.

Before we move on, I want to make some observations that are going to seem very obvious to you. But these observations are so important and so useful that you should repeat them to yourself as a personal mantra until you know them by heart:

"There is a whole step between notes 1 and 2."

"There is a whole step between notes 2 and 3."

"There is only a half step between notes 3 and 4."

"There is a whole step between notes 4 and 5."

"There is a whole step between notes 5 and 6."

"There is a whole step between notes 6 and 7."

"There is only a half step between note 7 and the following note 1."

Go back and look at the drawing above of the major scale while you repeat each of these phrases to yourself. Once you are able to visualize the entire drawing of the major scale in your mind, you will no longer need the mantra because you will literally see in your mind the distances between the notes.

I was actually given all of the clues necessary to start using the above drawing when I was about 10 years old. But it would be another 20 years before I would have any idea what to do with this information. That's because the drawing itself is not the discovery. You see, when you find an old key, the object itself is no great cause for excitement. It's not until you start *using* it, and you discover its remarkable ability to open every door in the world, that you begin to realize that you have found something very special, a *magic key*.

What's special about this key is that it contains literally everything there is to know about Western harmony. (When you get to IFR Exercises 4 and 5 you will see that this is no exaggeration. Even the "outside notes" that appear constantly in modern jazz and contemporary classical music are nothing more than displaced fragments of this very drawing.) The fact that so much music can be understood with so little theory is nothing short of astonishing. But even more astonishing is the fact that nobody ever tells you this, despite its being a rather important detail. I mean, if all of Western harmony can be understood with one little drawing, how do you teach a course on harmony and forget to mention that?

Maybe on some dry academic level they do mention briefly that all of Western music is based on the major scale, but only as a kind of historical trivia. It's like telling somebody that our spoken language is based on ancient Latin. There is nothing for a person *to do* with this information. But the major scale is not just a piece of historical trivia. It is the actual material of which all modern music is made. It is the source of every sound that we recognize as "musical", and its structure is the central architectural theme in every song you have ever heard. You can literally listen to the radio for hours without ever hearing a note that is not one of these seven. And those chords you're hearing in the background are nothing but the seven basic chords that can be built from these seven notes.

The remarkable discipline with which we stick to the major scale in our songwriting is even more amazing when you consider that we don't even do it on purpose. Take for example the melodic and beautiful reggae music of Bob Marley. With very rare exceptions, every one of his songs is perfectly contained within the seven notes and seven chords of the major scale, even though he composed songs in all different keys. Now do you think Bob Marley stayed perfectly within the major scale out of respect for his grade school music teachers? Was he consciously thinking about the key signature of each song? ("Hmm...this song is in the key of A major so I better remember to sing C#, F# and G# in my melodies.")

Of course not. He simply sang the notes he *imagined* and he used chords on his guitar that *sounded correct* to his ear. And he is not the only songwriter who does this. All over the world people are composing songs by ear, singing melodies that they imagine while fumbling for the chords that sound right. Through trial and error they eventually get everything to sound "just right" to their ear. They don't even realize that the end result simply places all the notes and all the chords in just the right places so that it all fits perfectly within one particular major scale. In other words, the ear was feeling the seven notes of the major scale all along, and would not be satisfied with the composition until all other notes were eliminated. Like a sculptor chipping away at a block of marble, the final result is always the major scale.

Isaac Newton and Michael Jordan

Sir Isaac Newton was one of the greatest theorists of all time. His mental achievements were so important that he is considered one of the most influential men in history. Newton clarified and organized many aspects of our physical world including the concepts of gravity, mass, inertia, friction, force and momentum. His work was a historic victory for the entire human race. But despite all his mental clarity, Sir Isaac Newton would have sucked at basketball.

Michael Jordan on the other hand was one of the greatest basketball players of all time. Sports writers still talk about his superhuman physical abilities. But what was special about Michael Jordan was not in his body at all. Plenty of guys were bigger, stronger, quicker, etc. What allowed Jordan to run circles around the other guys was his *mind*. Specifically, he had a superior command of the principles of gravity, mass, inertia, friction, force and momentum. But unlike Newton, he studied these principles in the purest and most intimate way possible, by living them through his physical body. And even though his work was entirely *non-verbal*, Michael Jordan was just as fascinated by nature as was Sir Isaac Newton three centuries earlier.

We all know instinctively that if you want to become a great basketball player you don't go to your physics teacher asking for help. You go to a basketball coach who probably flunked physics in high school. But that doesn't matter because he has a different kind of knowledge that is more valuable to you. He knows how to guide you through the *experiences* you need to have in order to become a great basketball player.

The difficulty most beginning musicians have with improvisation is that they have no "basketball coach" to guide them. Instead their music teachers give them theory to memorize. But this is like sending a young basketball player off to look for answers in a physics textbook.

Theory and mastery are two completely different things. In fact "theory" is not even on the road to mastery. It's a different road altogether, and it takes you to a different place. Theory is essential to intellectuals who want to understand nature and put words around it. But it is practically irrelevant to the artist.

We musicians need to follow the example of world-class athletes. Michael Jordan learned about the law of gravity not by sitting at a desk memorizing mathematical formulas but by spending countless hours in the gym all by himself practicing free throws. Each time he lifted the ball, spun it around in his hands, tested its weight and then launched it into the air he was performing a ritual meditation that deepened his already intimate relationship with the basic elements of his game. If you want to be a truly great improviser, you need to cultivate this same intimate relationship with every sound in our musical system.

Exercise 2: Melody

<u>Objective</u>: To continuously improve in your ability to...

Relate sounds to the major scale and the major scale to your instrument.

There is an important difference between the improviser and the classical musician. Whereas the classical musician primarily interprets music written by others, the improviser creates his own music in the moment. What they have in common is that both musicians study the physical aspects of playing their instruments in order to produce the most beautiful and expressive sounds possible. But the improvising musician must also take on a whole other field of study which is the art of the composer.

For this reason the practice routine of the improviser looks very different from the practice routine of the classical musician. As improvisers, our work might look like a wild jam session one minute and a Zen meditation the next. One day we might be at the piano, gently humming to ourselves while playing a couple of chords. Another day we might be at the park fooling around with a few notes under a big oak tree. Or another day we might appear to be doing absolutely nothing at all, just listening to the radio with our eyes closed.

On the surface our practicing may not look as "serious" as the technical scale studies of the classical player. But there is a method to all this madness. The improviser *needs* to have all of these different experiences with the notes of our musical system. We need to discover their beauty for ourselves before we can share that beauty with other people. We approach every sound with curiosity, humility and an open mind. Practicing for us is not just about improving our ability to execute the notes. It's about discovering the *meaning* of each note, and the melodic possibilities that it offers us.

In this chapter I am going to show you a wide variety of musical activities that will help you enter the beautiful world of harmony and discover its lessons for yourself. There is no list of things that you are required to learn, and there will be no final exam. Your only objective is to enter that world of sounds and to spend as much time as you can exploring and enjoying it. The more time you spend inside the world of harmony, discovering its beauty for yourself, the faster you grow. You don't need to worry about whether you are discovering the things that you are "supposed to" discover.

But there are two pieces of advice that I can give you which will help you to get the most out of your practicing. The first is to pay special attention to any sound that you find beautiful. These sounds are the precious gems that you will one day share with your audience, and they are the only thing that matters. When you find one of these beautiful sounds, maybe a special interval or a short little melody, stop everything. Don't move on. Stay there and enjoy the sound for as long as you possibly can. Forget about whatever other exercises you had planned for the day. They don't matter. The real lesson is right here in the present moment.

The reason why these moments are so important is because the sounds that you find especially beautiful won't be the same sounds that I find beautiful. So what is really happening in these moments is that you are discovering *your music*. These sounds have an almost hypnotic power over you because they speak directly to some part of you that you can only access through music. Don't resist their beauty. Play these sounds over and over again until you feel them so strongly that you continue to hear them in your mind even after you stop practicing.

My other piece of advice is to simply notice where each of these beautiful sounds is located on your tonal map. What I mean is to notice where you are on your tonal map whenever you find a sound or a melody that you especially like. If you notice exactly which notes make up each beautiful melody you discover, then these melodies themselves will teach you the meaning of every note in our musical system. At that point you become not merely a searcher of beautiful notes but in fact a true musical master who sees beauty and potential in *every* note.

So let's get started with IFR Exercise 2: Melody. You will find it to be a relaxed and enjoyable discovery process in which you will finally learn how to express all of those beautiful sounds in your musical imagination.

Seven Worlds

To begin with, we need to see how we can use the seven notes of the major scale to create seven different harmonic worlds that we can explore. To understand how this is possible, remember that the major scale has no beginning and no end. It is simply a pattern that extends infinitely in both directions on your instrument. So instead of this drawing of an isolated major scale which I showed you earlier...

...a better representation of the situation would be this drawing:

It's the exact same scale, but in this drawing we are showing more clearly that the scale extends infinitely in both directions. With this image in mind, here is a way that you can hear for yourself the seven harmonic worlds contained within the major scale:

1. Start by randomly choosing any note of the major scale to work on. For example, let's choose note 2. We are going to use this note as our *tonal center* and it will serve as both the floor and ceiling of the musical range that we are going to study:

2. Now pick any note on your instrument as the starting note. We are going to build the scale up from this note, so make sure you choose a note that is low enough so that you can comfortably play an entire octave above this starting note. For our example, let's say you choose the note Bb.

3. Starting on Bb and respecting the intervals in the drawing above, we arrive at the following notes:

$$2 \cdot 3 \: 4 \cdot 5 \cdot 6 \cdot 7 \: 1 \cdot | \: 2$$

$$B\flat \cdot C \: D\flat \cdot E\flat \cdot F \cdot G \: A\flat \cdot B\flat$$

4. Play this resulting scale in ascending order...

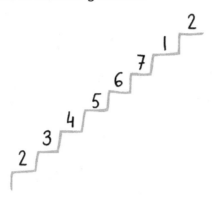

...and then in descending order:

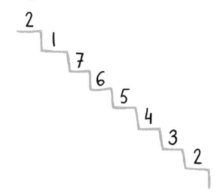

That's all there is to it. Simply by using a particular note of the major scale as both the floor and ceiling of the musical range you are going to explore, you can create the sensation that this note is the tonal center. This changes the way all of the other notes in the scale will sound to your ear. Now let's look at some of the ways that we can explore these seven worlds.

Play the Map

Now it's time to enjoy the real musical exploration of this harmonic world. Wander freely around the entire region enjoying every sound and melody that you encounter. Take your time to really connect with and feel each note. As you play each note, you may notice that the note doesn't give you the same sensation that it does when you play the scale in its original order from 1 to 7. That's because now your ear is feeling note 2 as the tonal center, which changes the meaning of every other note in the scale.

Notice that now note 1 no longer feels like the "ground floor". Now it's just one more note of the scale. Now note 2 is the one that feels like the ground floor and this also changes the way every other note will feel to you. So take your time to get to know each of the notes in this new way. As you play the notes, it may help to look at the following drawing just to visualize the part of the map that is relevant to your current adventure.

$$2 \cdot 3 \ 4 \cdot 5 \cdot 6 \cdot 7 \ 1 \cdot 2$$

Since there are seven notes in the major scale, there are actually seven different musical worlds that you can create with this exercise. For each different note that you choose as your tonal center (which will serve as both the floor and the ceiling of your musical exploration), a completely different harmonic environment is created. And in each different harmonic environment, the seven notes of the major scale will give you different sensations. Of course they are really the same seven notes all along but they have the power to produce different sensations depending on the harmonic environment. So there is truly a whole universe of sounds and sensations to discover here. You should also practice creating these harmonic worlds all over your instrument by varying the starting note (Bb in our example) each time you do the exercise.

This is the perfect moment to add IFR Jam Tracks Level 1: Seven Worlds to your practice routine. These backing tracks were composed to give you the ideal musical accompaniment for your Seven Worlds practice. Each harmonic environment is provided in three different musical styles to help you make the connection between your IFR practice and the music you listen to in your daily life. And we composed each track to highlight the subtle differences that make each harmonic environment unique. So as you're jamming over these tracks, you will also be learning to recognize each harmonic environment by ear.

Sing the Map

There is no more powerful exercise for your overall musical growth than singing the notes of the major scale without the help of your instrument. Even if you never did any other exercise in this entire method, the simple practice of singing the major scale every day would eventually lead you to recognize the notes in every piece of music you hear. But it's important to understand *how* to sing the numbers, because executing the scale mechanically won't teach you anything.

First of all, I want to clarify that in the beginning you will probably need to use your instrument to help you get started with the exercise. In most cases you won't have any idea how the notes should actually sound, so you'll need to use your instrument as a reference. But you should only use your instrument to teach yourself the sound of each note. Once you are able to produce the notes correctly yourself with your voice, you should no longer use your instrument for this part of Exercise 2. It's important to be able to imagine and produce the sounds all by yourself. And once you learn the sounds by heart, this exercise becomes something that you can practice anywhere, anytime because you won't need an instrument to do it.

Here is a simplified version of the exercise that you can start with:

1. First play the major scale on your instrument in any key, and play close attention to how each note sounds:

$$1 \cdot 2 \cdot 3 \ 4 \cdot 5 \cdot 6 \cdot 7 \ 1$$

2. Now put down your instrument and sing the same major scale that you just played. You should actually sing each number out loud. (You will literally be singing, "one, two, three, four, five, six, seven, one.")

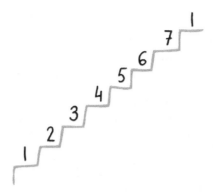

3. Now come back down the entire scale singing the numbers. (You will literally be singing, "one, seven, six, five, four, three, two, one.")

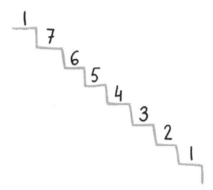

4. Now what we want to do is *wander freely* around the entire scale, singing each note by its number. We don't want to just go up and down the scale mechanically. The idea is to make music with these sounds and to really *feel* each note. It's important to get into a groove and activate the part of your brain that listens to and enjoys music. You might want to imagine a tempo and start moving your body in rhythm. Since I love percussion, I often tap a gentle rhythm with my hands to get the beat going. Then I start to sing melodies over this groove. In the beginning you might want to just pick a few notes and take your time to really master them. But eventually you should be able to include all seven notes of the scale in your improvisations.

Once you are confident with the exercise above you can move on to the full version of Sing the Map. In the full version, we practice the same exercise in all seven harmonic worlds of the major scale. To see an example, reflect again on the following drawing and remember that the major scale extends infinitely in both directions:

(etc.) 6 · 7 1 · 2 · 3 4 · 5 · 6 · 7 1 · 2 (etc.)

With that in mind, here's how the full exercise works:

1. Pick any note of the major scale (1 - 7) as your starting note. This will be our tonal center and it will serve as both the floor and ceiling of the musical range that we are going to study. As an example, this time let's choose note 5.

2. If you are not already familiar with the sounds that result from this particular view of the major scale, then play the resulting scale on your instrument so that you can hear how it sounds:

5 · 6 · 7 1 · 2 · 3 4 · 5

3. Once you have a very clear idea of how each note sounds, put away your instrument and sing the same scale that you just played, first in ascending order...

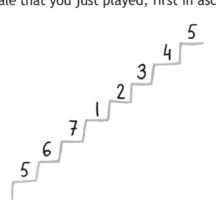

...and then in descending order:

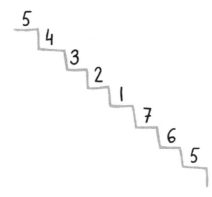

4. Now comes the creative part, when we wander freely around this region just as we did in the simple major scale starting on note 1. Be playful. Don't just sing the scale up and down. Pause on some notes and jump over others. Take time to "hang out" in

64

every little corner of this harmonic world. Enjoy each note deeply and appreciate its sound. You might want to make a drawing of the notes organized in this new way to help you visualize what you are singing:

$$5 \cdot 6 \cdot 7\ 1 \cdot 2 \cdot 3\ 4 \cdot 5$$

If you do this exercise every day with a different tonal center, soon you will find that you can imagine and produce the sounds all by yourself without even using your instrument first as a reference. That is when you begin to acquire a true personal mastery of the sounds. But don't rush. Just concentrate all your attention on enjoying whatever sounds you are working with today. Make your explorations musical. Feel the rhythm in your body and sing each note with feeling. Our goal is not merely to execute the notes accurately with our voice. Our real purpose is to discover their beauty and the meaning that each note has for us personally. So just relax and open yourself to their melodic possibilities. Each tonal center in the major scale produces a different harmonic world for you to discover and enjoy. And the best part is that you can explore them all with nothing more than your voice and your imagination.

This would be the perfect moment to add Sing the Numbers 1: The IFR Tonal Map and Sing the Numbers 2: Seven Worlds to your practicing. Sing the Numbers is IFR's own ear training program which is actually much more than just ear training. Each audio lesson is also a lesson in harmony and composition, using beautiful songs and melodies to teach you how you can truly make music in each of the harmonic environments. The result is that you'll not only learn to recognize all of these sounds by ear, but you'll also add this gorgeous library of sounds to your personal improvising vocabulary.

Free Your Imagination

It's also important to let your musical imagination out to roam freely sometimes. Remember that everything we study in music is for the purpose of expressing our musical imagination. So we don't want to get so carried away studying music that we let our imagination wither in the process. It's important to cultivate your imagination like a garden and give it plenty of water and sunshine. We do this in two ways: by *listening freely* and by *singing freely*:

Listen Freely: Make time in your life for sincere and full enjoyment of music with no thoughts at all in your mind. It should be music that you love and that holds your interest. Tune out all other sounds and submerge yourself completely in the world created by the music. You might even want to close your eyes or turn out the lights if you are listening at night. Really feel every sound and enjoy it completely. In this exercise you are absolutely forbidden from thinking about tonal numbers or trying to analyze the music in any way. Don't worry about identifying where those beautiful sounds are located on the tonal map. We already have plenty of exercises that help us to develop that ability. Right now we are doing something different, which is to nourish our imagination with the most beautiful music we know. So when you reach an especially powerful moment in the music, resist the temptation to analyze it. Instead, *memorize the sound.* Listen to it very closely and continue to imagine the same sound over and over again in your mind after the music has ended. In this way the sounds will enter very deeply into your musical memory. Then someday when you are creating your own music, this very same sound will be available to you at just the right moment when it fits perfectly with the music. And you will know how to play it because you can trust your ear to handle the translation for you in the moment. So take time to just listen and enjoy. It's more important than you think.

Sing Freely: Just as we need to listen deeply to music without making any attempt to analyze or name what we are hearing, we also need to create music in this same way. You can do this while playing a couple of chords on a guitar or piano, or you can do it over any type of recorded accompaniment. You can even do it along with the radio if you don't mind sharing the melodic space with the singer. But no matter how you do it, you should spend some time each week singing sounds freely, without trying to recognize where you are on the tonal map. If you have trouble getting started, try to clearly hear and sing a single note that appears in the music. Then just imagine the next lower note that seems to belong to the harmonic environment of the song. Then imagine the next note and the next, and keep going until you can hear a bunch of notes clearly. Now just let yourself flow with the music and gently move to whichever note seems to attract you most at each moment. If you really concentrate on the sounds that you are singing, the sounds themselves will tell you how to make music with them. But it doesn't really matter because this is not a performance. Singing "well" or producing an interesting improvisation is not the goal. The only goal is to imagine sounds and produce them, so there is no way to do this exercise "wrong". Just concentrate all your attention on the sounds in the music, and add additional sounds with your voice. This simple exercise will dramatically improve both your perception and your creativity over time.

Follow Your Voice

Now it's time to combine singing and playing at the same time. Wind instrument players will have to do this exercise on the piano but everyone else can do it on their main instrument. Just as in the other exercises, first we have to choose one of the harmonic worlds to study, and decide where to create this harmonic world on our instrument. Then we are going to improvise within this harmonic world by playing the notes on our instrument while simultaneously singing their sounds. When we sing and play at the same time, we do not actually sing the numbers out loud. You can just sing the sounds with whatever syllable you want ("la la la" or "mmm mmm mmm" or whatever).

What may surprise you about this exercise is how dramatically your musical ideas change when you sing along with your playing. When I first began to sing along with my own playing, I discovered that I had a lot more "pop music" and "R&B" sounds in my musical imagination than I had ever realized before. When I used to play jazz music from more of an artificial, theory-based approach, my solos were a lot more intellectual. I was always looking for the unexpected note or phrase that would be "interesting" and unusual. But my music lacked depth and humanity. It was only when I began to sing and include my musical imagination in my playing that I rediscovered the power and beauty of simple notes that I had been neglecting because they seemed too "obvious".

So the first step to playing from your imagination is simply to bring these two parts of your mind together. We need to connect our conscious mind (which moves our hands to play our instrument) with our subconscious musical mind (which enjoys and imagines musical sounds). A great way to create this connection is simply to sing while we play.

In the beginning, any way that you can achieve this connection is fine. But in the long run, it's important to understand who should be leading this dance. The idea is not to simply train the voice to follow along imitating the meaningless phrases that the hands execute without thinking. It's your *voice* that expresses your musical imagination. And so gradually, over time, the hands need to learn to express what the voice wants to sing. (Remember that this exercise is not called "Sing Whatever Your Hands Are Doing". The name of the exercise is "Follow Your Voice" because that's what we want your hands to do.)

Don't get too hung up on this in the beginning because the most important thing is just to get the connection going between your voice and your hands. But as you gain confidence, ask yourself whether you are really learning to play what you imagine, or just learning to sing the same mechanical phrases that you already knew how to play.

Follow the Melody (advanced)

Every one of the exercises above can be performed by an absolute beginner on his very first day of studying the IFR method. They are powerful exercises that give you direct hands-on experience working with the sounds of our musical system. You don't need to know anything in order to get started, and you can advance in these exercises at your own pace.

The two exercises that follow, however, require you to already have a certain level of personal experience with the notes of the major scale. If you are a total beginner, I would recommend that you don't go any further in this chapter until you have had a few months to enjoy working with the exercises above. You can still keep advancing in this book, and you can even move on to Exercise 3. But you shouldn't try to advance any further in Exercise 2 until you have a more solid foundation. Just set aside the more advanced levels of Exercise 2 until you're ready for them.

But if you already have a lot of confidence with the seven notes of our musical system, then you are ready to take the next step. This next exercise consists of listening to any piece of music and following along actively, visualizing each note of the melody on your tonal map of the major scale. You can even get out a sheet of paper and write out the melody using the tonal numbers 1 through 7 if it helps you to visualize it clearly. Basically you would be producing a tonal sketch of the melody similar to the ones I will show you in a later chapter, "Seeing the matrix".

Don't worry about trying to recognize everything that occurs in a song. Part of the learning process is to just get out there and try to find *something* that you recognize. You might listen to an entire song and only recognize a few notes. But that would be a great victory and a huge step forward. Once you get your first taste of your own ability to understand music by ear, it will awaken your curiosity and you will start to listen more actively all the time. In the beginning there will be a lot more sounds that you don't recognize than sounds that you do. But if you just keep doing the exercises in this chapter, particularly the most powerful one which is Sing the Map, little by little you'll start to notice these same sounds in the music all around you. And each new sound you recognize will serve as a foothold to help you recognize others. Soon they will all start to fall like dominoes.

Follow the Melody is also an important exercise because it helps you develop the attitude that your musical mastery is not limited to your instrument. Your real relationship with music is inside of you, and this is where your most profound discoveries will take place. You don't even need a source of music to practice Follow the Melody, because you can do it just as easily with songs and melodies that you *remember* in your mind. In fact Follow the Melody is really just the flip side of Sing the Map. Think of them as two complementary meditations:

In Sing the Map, we put <u>sounds</u> to the <u>numbers</u>.

In Follow the Melody, we put <u>numbers</u> to the <u>sounds</u>.

If you are looking for the most effective way to grow quickly as a musician, I will let you in on a secret. There is a lot more power in these two imagination exercises than in the exercises you do with your instrument. Just five minutes of this inner work will develop your skills more than an entire day of practicing your instrument. Keep that in mind as you decide where to concentrate your energy.

Follow the Melody also gives you way to escape your boredom whenever you find yourself stuck listening to music that doesn't exactly thrill you. Maybe it's your nephew's clarinet recital or maybe it's the background music at the dentist's office. But you can always turn the situation into a free music class. Simply by following the melody actively and visualizing where you are on your tonal map, you can use even the most silly or uninteresting music as a free ear training class. Not only is this a great workout for your ear but it will also give you an understanding of how songs actually work. One reason we practice following the numbers is so that we can learn these hidden lessons in the music all around us.

Exercise 2 - Mastery Level (advanced)

Now I want to show you the ultimate version of Exercise 2. It is something that you can practice for the rest of your life and it never becomes old or boring because it is a doorway to unlimited musical creativity and improvisation. It is also a very practical skill for anyone who enjoys sitting in at jam sessions or playing along with friends at a party. And it is the foundation for the most powerful improvisation practice of all, which is Exercise 5.

Have you ever wanted to play along with other musicians but couldn't find the right notes? Maybe you weren't able to recognize what key the song was in. This can be especially difficult with jazz music because the songs often contain one or more key changes. Maybe you tried fumbling for notes on your instrument looking for the ones that sounded good. Or maybe the chords were going by so quickly that you didn't even know where to start. This frustrating situation has happened to all of us. Even very advanced musicians will occasionally find themselves playing a tune that they are unfamiliar with, and it can be next to impossible sometimes to recognize the harmony by ear.

But now I want you to imagine a different scene in which everything flows effortlessly. Imagine that you arrive to a party or a jam session and a group of people are already playing music together. One of them offers to tell you the chords of the song so that you can play too. He says, "The first chord is a G minor seventh, then it goes to A seventh, and then D minor..." You reply calmly, "Thanks but don't worry about all that. Just let me listen for a minute and I'll follow you." When it's your turn to play, you start by playing just one single note on your instrument and then you pause for a moment. Then you go on to make a beautiful melodic solo that fits perfectly with the harmony of the piece and with what everybody else is playing. More importantly, you are expressing *your* music, exactly as you hear it in your mind. If the song contains key changes or other unexpected sounds, you pause for a split second at each of these moments and then you continue right on. You can do this just as easily over a song you have never heard before as you can over a song you know by heart.

Did you know that you already have the ability to do this? You just need to combine a few of the skills that you have been developing up to this point. This technique is not for beginners but once you have mastered the earlier exercises in this chapter you can put them all together to create a really powerful improvisation technique that allows you to make music effortlessly in any musical context. Here is how we use Exercise 2 - Mastery Level to immediately orient ourselves in any musical situation:

1. Listen to the music with your full attention for a moment.

2. Now mentally direct your attention away from the music. Sing the last note that you heard. Move up or down from this starting note to whatever seems to be the next note of the scale. Keep going until you can clearly imagine a whole range of notes.

3. Even if you are not aware of it, the notes that you are singing to yourself all come from the same major scale, and this is the key of the music. Keep moving around and singing these notes to yourself until you recognize that you are in fact singing a major scale. Come to rest on note 1 of this major scale.

4. You can strengthen your clarity of perception by continuing to sing all the same notes but this time putting numbers on them. You would literally be singing to yourself, "one...two.... three....four...etc."

5. Now that you are clearly feeling the tonality of the song, it's time to play just *one note* on your instrument. Listen to this note and ask yourself where this sound is located on your tonal map. Is it one of the seven notes of the major scale? Or is it one of the little black dots on our drawing?

6. If the note you are playing is one of the seven notes of the major scale, then you should already be able to recognize it by its sound. If it is one of the little black dots, then you just need to move up or down exactly *one half step* to enter the scale. Once you have entered the scale you should have no trouble identifying where in the scale you are.

7. Now that you know where you are, you also know where to find any other note you might want to play. So just start from the note where you currently are and begin to improvise freely along with the music. Don't forget to sing while you play if you want to really activate your musical imagination.

8. (Optional) If at some point your ear tells you that the key of the music has changed, just repeat the entire process again to feel the new tonality and locate yourself within it.

When you read the above exercise it may seem like a lot of steps but in reality it's almost instantaneous. Once you gain confidence with the exercise you will end up jumping directly to Step 5 without even bothering with Steps 1 through 4. If I want to play along with a group of musicians, all I do is play one single note on my instrument. Since I know the sound of every note of the major scale, plus the five little black dots outside the scale, I immediately know exactly where I am. The whole process doesn't even take a full second.

So the streamlined version of Exercise 2 - Mastery Level is even simpler:

1. Play one single note on your instrument.

2. Feel where you are on the tonal map.

If you have done your work with all of the exercises presented in this chapter, especially Sing the Map, then it will literally be this easy to orient yourself in any musical situation instantaneously. For many students, this is the level of mastery they have always dreamed of. Most people are drawn to musical improvisation by the simple desire to play along with friends and participate in jam sessions. If that is your goal as well, then with Exercise 2 you already have everything you need to enjoy playing with other people in any musical context for the rest of your life.

The key to this power comes from using your *ear* to understand the musical environment, and using your *imagination* to actually create the music. Notice how our entire paradigm is different from that of the person who tried to help us by telling us the names of the chords. The reason why beginners find improvising so difficult is that they are asking the wrong questions. Beginners always want to know the answers to two questions:

"What key is the song in?"

"What are the chords to the song?"

Both of these questions are wrong because they overlook the fact that our bodies are *already* feeling the key that the music is in. Even the most passive listeners in the audience can feel the key of the music! So we musicians don't need to start from scratch trying to deduce the key of the music as if we were solving some murder mystery. We just need to pause and notice what we are already feeling.

So the real question is not, "What key is the song in?" but rather, "Where in the key am I?" Any note you play must be located somewhere on your tonal map between 1 and 7. It might be one of the seven notes of the major scale, or it could be one of the little black dots. But what we know for sure is that it's somewhere on that drawing.

And to understand where you are on the drawing, all you have to do is listen to whatever note you are playing. Each note has a very particular and unmistakable sound. Even the five notes outside the major scale have their own particular sound, and in time you will come to know the sound of these notes as well. So no matter how many times a song changes key, if you just listen to whatever note you are playing at the moment you will always be perfectly oriented in the key of the moment.

Once you get good at this you will never again wonder what key a song is in, nor what chords are being played because it no longer matters. You won't have to guess what the other musicians are thinking because you will be connected with something much more powerful: what you are *feeling*. No matter how sophisticated a piece of music might be, at any given moment in time your ear will be feeling exactly one key, because that's what it's programmed to do. Once you learn to orient yourself relative to whatever key *you* are feeling, your ear becomes the only information you require.

To practice this technique you don't even need other musicians. All you need is a source of music to play with. You can do it over every song in your music collection, or just turn on the radio and improvise over whatever happens to be playing. The more you practice, the sooner you will find yourself using only the streamlined version, and you will be amazed at how easily you can instantly orient yourself in any song.

Summary

If there is one exercise in the entire IFR method that will accelerate your musical growth more than any other, it's Exercise 2. So no matter what instrument you play or how you would like to make music, I urge you to take the time to discover everything you can using each of the activities presented above.

Most of the work we do in Exercise 2 involves exploring the seven harmonic environments of the major scale. We call this set of exercises "Seven Worlds". In this chapter I showed you a number of ways to practice Seven Worlds with your instrument and your voice. This work is the essence of Exercise 2, and it is where you should concentrate your effort in the beginning.

Once you have developed a level of mastery with all seven harmonic environments of the major scale, you should begin to practice the two more advanced activities you saw in this chapter. Follow the Melody is the exercise of listening actively to any song or melody and trying to visualize where each note is located on your tonal map. And finally, Exercise 2 - Mastery Level combines everything you have learned until now to enable you to improvise with confidence in any musical situation for the rest of your life.

Here is a summary of the concepts and exercises we have seen in this chapter:

1. Seven Worlds

    a. Play the Map

    b. Sing the Map

    c. Free Your Imagination

        i. Listen Freely

        ii. Sing Freely

    d. Follow Your Voice

2. Follow the Melody (advanced)

3. Exercise 2 - Mastery Level (advanced)

Remember that your first priority should always be to enjoy yourself and have fun with whatever sounds you are using at the moment. Use these exercises as a pleasant, relaxing break from all of the other demands of your day. You have so many other areas of your life where you need to think and plan and struggle. Give yourself the gift of just a few minutes a day of relaxed musical contemplation with no goal whatsoever.

Think about how well any mother knows her own children's faces. Obviously she didn't come to know their faces through hard work and intense memory training exercises. She came to know them through loving contemplation under no pressure at all. And that's exactly how you should come to know the seven notes of our musical system.

Improvising for real

Musical improvisation is not a technical skill that one "learns to do". It is a natural spontaneous process that occurs in the imagination. It is not necessary to understand anything about harmony in order to improvise music. Even total beginners (including little children) can improvise beautiful melodies over any harmony simply by singing the first note that occurs to them, and then just letting the music flow wherever it wants to. The ear naturally gravitates toward the most pleasing sounds, so it's actually very easy to make music in this way if you just focus your attention on the sounds themselves.

Improvisation with the voice is the highest form of musical composition that exists because you are working directly with the sounds themselves. There are no phony techniques or theory to rely upon. For this reason it can be scary at first. It's normal to feel completely lost the first time you attempt to improvise with nothing but your voice. If you are accustomed to flying up and down your instrument with scales and arpeggios, trying to sing your way through the same song can be a humbling experience.

But I would argue that this experience is the single most important step that any improvising musician can take in his or her own artistic development. It is a test of one's sincerity. It requires absolute humility to say to oneself, "Okay, I know a lot of tricks that allow me to make music over this tune. But do I actually *feel* anything when I listen to the harmony? Are there any sounds here that I recognize? Do I have anything of my *own* to contribute?"

It doesn't matter what the answers to these questions are in the beginning. That's not the test. The real test is whether or not you are willing to reset your musical understanding to zero and start from scratch. If you can find the courage to put down your techniques and open yourself to the music with humility, you will find that you do in fact hear musical notes in your imagination, and lots of them!

These purely musical ideas that you express with your voice come directly from your musical imagination, or from what I call your "inner composer". Your inner composer is an absolute musical genius who can effortlessly resolve even the toughest harmonic problems. Remember, the ear *naturally* gravitates toward the most pleasing sounds in any musical situation. So no matter how difficult a chord progression might look on paper, for the ear it makes no difference. The ear always knows what it is feeling. It knows which notes are painful and which ones are relaxing. For the ear, there is no such thing as a "difficult chord progression" or an "awkward key". Simply put, the ear never makes mistakes. The mere fact that you imagine a sound is an absolute guarantee that it makes perfect musical sense.

But playing directly from your imagination is more than just a powerful way to make great music. It's also one of the most beautiful experiences you could ever know. There is nothing more exciting in the world than to begin a solo with absolutely no idea what you are going to play, nor where your ideas are going to come from. At a moment when most musicians would be nervously scrambling around looking for the sheet music, you will be trying to do just the opposite, to *empty your mind* and prepare for the adventure.

This is the essence of improvising for real. A truly musical idea is one which is born in the mind as *sound*. Even before knowing the name of the note, the true improviser *hears* the note in his mind. There is absolutely no theory involved in choosing the note. It is pure imagination.

We do study harmony and chord progressions very deeply in IFR, but we don't use our knowledge of harmony to decide what notes to play. That decision always comes directly from our imagination in the form of sounds. The reason why we are passionate about studying harmony is so that we will know *where* to find the sounds that we are already imagining.

In other words the question is not, "What are the correct notes to play over this Fm7 chord?" The real question is, "What is that *sound* I hear in my mind and where will I find it on my instrument?"

To answer this question we just need to understand two things:

- where each sound is located on our tonal map

- how to apply this tonal map to our instrument

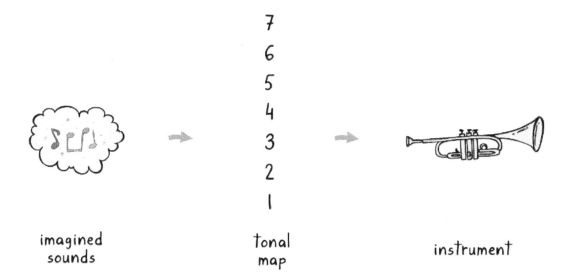

| imagined sounds | tonal map | instrument |

And so really, we study harmony in order to better understand ourselves. What we are really trying to do is understand the thinking of that great musical genius that lives inside of us. We can hear the notes that our inner composer wants us to play, but in order to play them we need to remember *where* we discovered these beautiful sounds. This is the question that leads us directly to the major scale as the origin of every musical sound in our culture.

When we discover the enormous creative capacity of our own imagination, we begin to lose interest in the tricks and formulas they teach us in music schools. Since every one of us is already blessed with a genius inner composer, the real goal of our musical study should be to learn to tap into that great treasure inside of us. And so we stop looking outside ourselves for rules and formulas to create music artificially, and we begin dedicating all of our time and energy to just learning how to play what we imagine. We stop thinking consciously about "right notes" and "wrong notes" and instead we concentrate all our attention on simply *listening* to that inner voice and expressing it on our instrument.

We also come to understand musical mastery in a new and more personal light. It's not about playing music that is faster, better or more sophisticated than the next person. It's about playing *our music*. The only mastery we care about is the ability to express the musical ideas of our inner composer. And so we begin to develop a kind of fascination for recognizing sounds. The organized work that we do in IFR eventually leads us to recognize almost every sound we hear. This is why many students of IFR are able to play any song they hear without sheet music, even after only hearing the song once. But it's not really our goal to impress our friends and family with this rather freaky ability. It's just a necessary skill in order to fulfill our real desire, which is to express the music that we imagine.

In fact, I believe that this is what a genuine comprehension of harmony really is. Music theory was never intended to replace your imagination.

Your vast musical knowledge

If you are a beginner to musical improvisation, at this point you might be thinking, "But how can I just *imagine* great music? I don't know the first thing about improvising!" Even very experienced improvisers are often just as scared to rely on their imagination to create music. After all, they may have invested many years in learning to improvise from a more mechanical or theoretical approach. Playing from the imagination sounds like going back to square one.

But no matter what level of formal music education you may have received, this is nothing compared to the *unconscious* musical training that you have been receiving all your life. It would take many large volumes to explain everything you have learned about composing from the thousands and thousands of musical examples you have been exposed to. Nursery rhymes, TV jingles, pop songs, Christmas carols, movie soundtracks, rock songs, jazz solos and classical music all work in the exact same way using all of the same harmonic materials. And through repeated exposure to this musical language, somewhere in your mind you formed a basic idea of how music is supposed to sound and what it can do. You also developed an unbelievably rich vocabulary of musical ideas and imagery. There is literally more musical knowledge stored in your subconscious mind than you could ever hope to use in a lifetime.

From the moment people begin to improvise, they immediately begin to unconsciously employ all the very same techniques that are studied in composition courses. They use meter, tonality and dynamics in very intentional ways. Their music has a coherent mood. They use repetition and variation to create form and poetry in their music. And there is always some kind of thematic development that gives the listener the feeling of going on a musical journey. Even children do all of these things *automatically*. We are so highly trained by the music of our culture that we simply don't know any other way of making music. And we do it all unconsciously, without having the slightest idea what any of these things are called.

The fact is that by the time we pick up our first instrument each one of us is already a very highly trained musician. Your real music education is not contained in whatever theory you might have studied in a classroom. It is in the music itself, the music that you have been listening to and enjoying all your life. Theory and formulas can't even come close to summarizing all of the subtle details you have picked up just from listening.

This subconscious musical knowledge is many times greater than the limited amount of information that can be memorized consciously. For example, a concert pianist who learns to perform a piece perfectly will have trouble remembering how to play the same piece just a few years later. But I'll bet that you can still remember perfectly the sound of melodies that you haven't heard since you were a little child. Our memory for written notes and chord symbols is very limited. But our memory for the sounds themselves is immense.

And so the first step to improvising freely is to understand that the music you want to express is already inside of you. The problem is that this enormous body of subconscious musical knowledge is stored in your mind as sounds and sensations, not as musical notes with names like F# and Bb. For this reason most people can't play or express in any way these remembered sounds. So instead they set about learning music as if it were something completely new and foreign. They buy sheet music and memorize songs one by one, or they study licks and phrases to use in their improvisations. But the greatest music library in the world is already available to you, stored deep inside your own mind. The fact that you can sing your favorite melodies proves that you already know what the notes are. You just don't know how to *name* the notes that you are remembering. The information is there but it's stored in a different format. The notes are stored in your memory as *sounds*, not as musical symbols.

What is needed is a translation. If you could translate the sounds in your musical imagination into notes that can be played on an instrument, then you could immediately begin to use this vast repertoire of sounds in your music. This is why I say that all musical knowledge is really self-knowledge. The improviser's path is a journey inward. Instead of looking outside ourselves for rules and formulas, we look within ourselves to understand and organize the sounds that make up our own musical imagination. You may not realize it yet, but this is exactly what you are doing in IFR Exercise 2: Melody.

Music theory is actually redundant

Interestingly, not all societies approach music the same way. There are places where children learn about rhythm by playing drums instead of by looking at little dots on a piece of paper. There are places where families dance and sing together in their homes, where all parties are accompanied by live music and where teenagers create elaborate choreographies to perform in the street for absolutely no reason at all. In these places where everyone seems to be so talented and musically active, there is one subject that never seems to come up: music theory. In these cultures music is not something for a chosen few to theorize about. It is something for everyone to create and enjoy.

I have always been fascinated by traditional African percussion. I'm no expert on percussion but I have had the good fortune to study with some great people in many places including Brazil, Senegal and Guinea Bissau. These experiences have influenced me a lot as a person and as a musician. I went to these countries innocently enough, just looking to learn some cool drum rhythms. But what I ultimately learned was a totally different way of relating to music, a different value system. Music serves a different purpose in these places. In my opinion, it serves a better purpose. Its function is not so much to entertain or impress but rather to heal and to connect people with their past, with each other and with nature.

They also have a completely different approach to teaching music. I was surprised when I found out that my percussion teachers had no way of writing down their music. Not only that, but in fact they didn't even have any way to *talk* about their music! The whole Western idea of half-notes, quarter-notes, rests and measures was completely unknown to them. And I'm talking about some of the most well-known and respected musicians in Brazil and West Africa. These guys are "masters" in the most austere sense of the word. They are incredibly precise and clear-thinking. They have complete mastery over the sound of their instruments and they know a seemingly infinite repertoire of compositions and arrangements. When you get a few of them together to play it's an awesome experience. Their music is thunderous, beautiful, joyful and frightening all at the same time!

When I discovered that they have no names or symbols for the rhythms they play, I figured that their music must be largely improvised, kind of like the hippie "drum circles" that are common in the U.S. and Europe but maybe with a higher skill level. This assumption also turned out to be wrong. In fact the pieces they play are very rigidly defined right down to every last little sixteenth-note. They have different sections with 1st and 2nd endings, codas and the like. And each section consists of multiple parts to be played simultaneously by several different drummers. There are even sections for call-and-response and improvisation. But these are all my words, my way of explaining how their music works. They don't use any of these terms. They don't even know what a measure is. Their music has triplets and eighth-notes, but the musicians themselves have no words to say, "triplets and eighth-notes".

What was most astonishing to me was the absolute perfection and simplicity in their use of time. I mean, if nobody has any concept of a measure or a time signature then probably there will be a few measures with extra beats, won't there? In fact there is nothing of the kind. They play in absolutely perfect 4/4 time, or 3/4 or 6/8 or what have you, with no deviation ever from the basic time signature.

It is actually very easy to notate their music with our Western music staves and symbols because their music is so extremely precise and well-ordered, despite the fact that they live their entire lives without ever analyzing it verbally. From my Western persepective, I was very impressed to discover that people could achieve so much despite the lack of theory. But the real story is about what they are able to achieve *as a result* of their lack of theory. Unencumbered by a parallel language, they can concentrate entirely on the language of sounds. They simply live inside this world of sounds and they get to know all of its elements so deeply that it never even occurs to them to *name* the elements that make up their music.

In our own culture we are obsessed with naming things. If we can't reduce something to words we feel like we don't really understand it. In music, this obsession has driven us to invent a staggering number of musical concepts that students are now required to read about and memorize. Every conceivable way to group notes together has been declared a "scale" and has been given some exotic name. Every possible type of harmonic movement has been painstakingly identified and catalogued. College music professors today are more concerned about our ability to correctly name all these techniques than they are about our ability to actually make music.

And yet, despite all our theory and all our names, almost nobody in our society has any idea how music really works. Most of us don't even understand the simple songs we hear on the radio. Paradoxically, we only begin to understand how music works when we stop asking the question. The question itself pulls us out of the world of sounds and throws us into the world of discussion about sounds. What we are really doing is shifting our attention to a parallel language alongside what was already a very highly organized language. This is why I say that music theory is *redundant*. Music itself is already so very elegant, so supremely well organized, that its mere contemplation leads one to comprehend it perfectly.

Sound, map and instrument

In this chapter I want to take a closer look at the work you are doing in Exercise 2, and show how this work will ultimately enable you to express any sound that you can imagine. As you saw in the chapter "Improvising for real", there are two quick translations that happen on the journey from imagination to instrument. When we imagine a sound that we want to play, first we need to recognize where this sound is located on our tonal map. Then we need to visualize the tonal map on our instrument so that we can play the exact note that we are imagining. This two-step translation sounds a lot more complicated that it really is. In practice it happens automatically and instantaneously for any sound that we really understand. In this chapter I'll try to show you what I mean by this.

The first part of this translation is to recognize the sounds we imagine and understand where they are located in the tonal octave we are feeling. Many people are intimidated by this part because they have never tried to recognize the sounds they hear, and they automatically assume that this ability is only enjoyed by "musical geniuses". But remember that relative to any tonal center, each note on your tonal map produces a very specific sensation in your mind and body. So learning to recognize these sensations is not as difficult as it may seem. You just need time to get to know them. Once you have had the opportunity to discover for yourself the sound of each note on your tonal map (including the five notes outside the major scale), you will have no trouble recognizing these sounds in the music all around you, and in the music you imagine.

Our journey begins with the simplest sounds that exist, which are just the seven notes of the major scale. Our first goal is to learn to recognize these seven notes by their *sound*. In Exercise 2, you have already begun to practice several very powerful ways to develop this ability. In time you will become so familiar with these seven sounds that you will recognize them instantly in any melody that you hear or imagine:

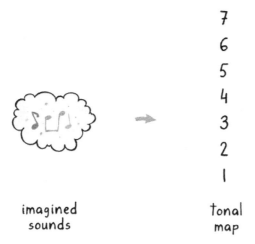

7
6
5
4
3
2
1

imagined   tonal
sounds   map

The other half of our technical challenge as improvisers is to be able to visualize this tonal map anywhere on our instrument so that we can actually play the notes we are imagining. By now I trust that you have played the major scale in several different keys on your instrument. Whenever you practice playing the major scale on your instrument, you are working on the second half of our technical challenge. Specifically, you are practicing the translation from the tonal map to your instrument:

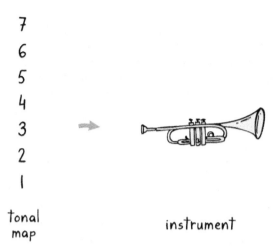

7
6
5
4
3
2
1

tonal
map

instrument

To improvise comfortably using the IFR method you will need to become an absolute master at visualizing this tonal map anywhere on your instrument. But I don't mean just running scales up and down your instrument. What we really need is the ability to *visualize* any portion of the tonal map anywhere on our instrument.

Here is an example. Let's say you are playing any random note on your instrument. But your *ear* tells you that this is note 2 of the key that you are currently feeling:

$$\{♪♫♪\} = 2$$

Now let's say that you imagine a new sound in your mind. This is a purely musical idea that comes into your mind as a *sound*. If you were a singer, you could just go ahead and sing this note without even worrying about having to locate or name it. But since you want to play this note on your instrument, you need to first recognize where the sound is located on your tonal map. Let's say that your ear tells you that the sound you are imagining is note 5:

$$\{♪♫♪\} = 5$$

Your technical challenge then is to move from note 2 to note 5:

2 · 3 4 · 5

Notice that it's not necessary to visualize the entire major scale in order to make this movement. We just need to understand clearly the tiny region that is relevant to our current musical idea. Ironically, people who practice playing scales up and down all day with a metronome never actually develop this clarity of vision. They may be able to execute the entire scale at lightning speed but when confronted with the simple challenge described above they don't even know where to begin. That's why I say that our goal is not to practice executing the major scale in its entirety. Our goal is to come to really *know* it, and to be able to visualize any part of it anywhere we want. This translation from tonal map to instrument is the second half of our technical work as improvisers.

The key to your success with Exercise 2 and everything that follows is to maintain an absolutely perfect integration between all three zones (sound, map, instrument). In other words, it doesn't do you any good to practice playing the notes if you can't recognize them by ear. And it doesn't do you any good to recognize the notes by ear if you can't find them on your instrument.

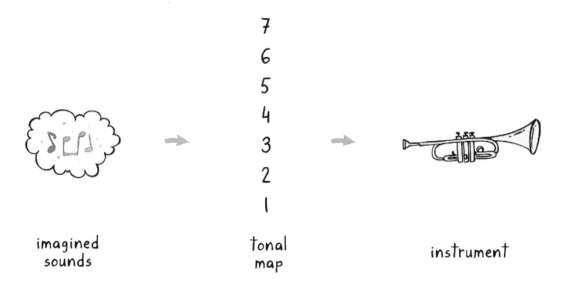

imagined
sounds

tonal
map

instrument

To create this solid integration, in the beginning it might be helpful to work with just a few notes until you develop so much confidence with them that you are incapable of making a mistake. For example you could start by declaring notes 1, 2 and 3 to be your area of focus. You could practice singing these notes to yourself, recognizing them by ear and of course playing them on your instrument in any key. After you have developed complete confidence with all three notes, then you could have a friend test you by playing a short melody made up of notes 1, 2 and 3 on a piano. If you have really come to understand these notes then you should be able to recognize the entire melody instantly without the slightest hesitation. You should also be able to choose any random key on your instrument and play this same melody perfectly the very first time you try, without having to fumble for the notes. If you could do that, then I would say that you have a real mastery of notes 1, 2 and 3. Your understanding of these three notes is perfectly integrated across all three zones: sound, tonal map and instrument.

At that point you could begin to include note 4 in your daily studies. But remember that we are in no hurry to move on. If all of Western music is based on just seven notes, then we can't really blame our difficulties on there being "too much material" to master. Our problem is really quite the opposite. There is so *little* material to master that most people can't see how they will ever use it, so they never bother to master it. Instead they just move on to the next thing, and the next, and so on without ever giving their full attention to the seven notes that make up everything in our musical culture.

"Moving on" is the wrong metaphor for musical study. Mastery comes not from moving on but from *digging in* and learning the lessons of each moment. So as you practice Exercise 2, remember to take it in at your own pace. You don't have to do my exercises exactly as I describe them. If an exercise feels like it gives you too much material all at once, then do less. Keep the spirit of the exercise but concentrate all its power on just two or three notes. Sing these notes every day, visualize them on your tonal map and improvise with them on your instrument. Over time you will expand your focus little by little until you have confidence with all seven notes of the major scale, plus the five "outside" notes represented by the little black dots on our drawing. After that you'll go on to study chord progressions, songs and the entire world of modern harmony.

But for every new idea that you want to add to your musical repertoire, take the time to really master it across all three zones of sound, map and instrument. If you stay faithful to this fully integrated approach to learning music, one day you will have a personal knowledge and mastery of our musical system that cannot be bought in any school.

Seeing the matrix

Just like the characters in the movie "The Matrix", we too live our entire lives surrounded by a matrix that we cannot see. We are so sensitive to the emotional content of music that we automatically look right past the notes and never even notice them. As soon as the music starts we find ourselves transported to a world of images, thoughts and feelings. This ability to assign a human meaning to sounds is really a sign of our inherent musical genius. But it prevents us from noticing the astonishingly simple matrix of notes from which all of this music is composed.

In this chapter I want to take you on a whirlwind tour of famous melodies from many different styles of music. I will show you exactly where each melody is found within the major scale so you can play it on your instrument. Some of these melodies also make occasional use of notes outside the major scale, so you will have an opportunity to hear what that sounds like as well.

As you look at the following examples I encourage you to get your instrument out and actually play through all of the songs that you know personally. The examples will be much more impactful if you play them yourself. Just pick any key in which you can comfortably play about two octaves of musical range. Play the major scale a few times to warm up and then play the melodies as I have written them out. I think you will be amazed to discover all of these famous songs right there inside your major scale. For most people, this is the moment of no return. Once you see for yourself the intimate connection that our music has with the major scale, you have truly begun to "see the matrix".

I don't expect you to know all of the following songs but my hope is that you will recognize a least a few of them. If you don't recognize a song by its title, probably it doesn't make sense to try to play it. But if you do recognize the title to the song, then the first thing you should do is to read the lyrics that I have written out and try to recall in your mind the sound of the melody. Then play the melody using the scale numbers that I have written above each word. Try to play the melody with the same intention and feeling that you recall from the original song. That's an essential part of this discovery process.

As you read each melody, pay special attention to the height at which each number is drawn. Just as in traditional sheet music, I use the height of the number to indicate whether the melody is going up or down. This helps to avoid confusion when the melody crosses the octave line. For example, if the melody is on note 7 and then goes *up* one scale degree to note 1 of the next octave, then I will draw note 1 higher on the page than note 7 (as in the drawing below on the left). If on the other hand the melody were to go *down* from note 7 all the way to note 1 at the bottom, then I would draw note 1 lower on the page than note 7 (as in the drawing on the right).

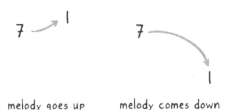

melody goes up   melody comes down

We'll begin with a selection of R&B classics. These songs are often overlooked by students of improvisation who are more interested in learning jazz standards. But they are an important part of the musical culture of many great jazz players. I lived for a time in Buffalo, New York which had an amazing music scene with dozens of active bands playing R&B, soul, blues, rock, jazz and even free improvisation. On any given night there were two or three different places where you could go to hear excellent live jazz music. This is a luxury that was hard to find even in much larger and wealthier cities. But the most beautiful thing I remember about the Buffalo jazz scene was the dignity and kindness of the musicians. Everybody was welcome to play regardless of age, color, gender or musical ability. Advanced younger players with a sophisticated, modern sound played right alongside elderly gentlemen who had more of a blues or gospel sound. Women were given special encouragement and plenty of room for soloing. Even little kids would step up and try a solo, and the whole room would cheer and applaud.

What united these ordinary working class people was much more than the desire to play jazz music. They shared a common need for friendship, respect and good times in a city that could be harsh and brutal much of the time. And even though every jam session began with the typical repertoire of jazz standards, somewhere around 3am you would begin to hear a different kind of music. The same guys who were playing Monk earlier in the night would now be playing the music of Marvin Gaye. Loosened up by several hours of playing, they would gradually relax into the music that was closer to their hearts and to their childhood memories. Here are a few examples of beautiful melodies from this style:

<u>Marvin Gaye - What's Going On</u>
(Written by Renaldo Benson, Alfred Cleveland and Marvin Gaye)

```
6         5   6   6     5   5  6
     3                        3   3   2
                                        1
```
Mother, mother, there's too many of you crying.

```
  1
     5  6        5   6   5     6   5  5   6
           3                          3   3   2
                                              1
```
Brother, brother, brother, there's far too many of you dying.

<u>Bill Withers - Lean On Me</u>

```
3    2   1   3   3    2   2   1
```
Lean on me, when you're not strong.

```
1    1   7   6   5       1   2   3    3  2   2
```
And I'll be your friend. I'll help you carry on.

<u>Ray Charles - Hit the Road Jack</u>
(Written by Percy Mayfield)

3
  | 2 | | 2 2 | 2
              6   6   6
Hit the road Jack, and don't you come back.

                6   6 | | 6
    3   3
  |
No more, no more, no more, no more.

3
  | 2 | | 2 2 | 2
        6   6   6   6   6
Hit the road Jack, and don't you come back no more.

<u>Stevie Wonder - As</u>

      3 3 3 3 2 | | |
5 5   5 6
As around the sun the earth knows she's revolving

      3   3   3   4   3   2 2 | 2
5   5
And the rose buds know to bloom in early May

      3   3   3   4   3 2
5   5
Just as hate knows love's the cure

   | 6   6 | | 6   6
You can rest your mind assured

      6 6 6 7   7 6
4   3
That I'll be loving you always.

85

<u>Al Green - Let's Stay Together</u>

```
            7
3   3 4 5      5   5
```

I'm so in love with you.

```
                6                       b6
3    3 4   5        4   4    4   4   4     5 4
                        |               |
```

Whatever you want to do is alright with me...

Did you notice the note b6 toward the end of the second line? On your drawing of the major scale, this note is the little black dot in between notes 5 and 6. It is located one half step above note 5, and you can play it just as easily as you play the seven notes of the major scale. This is the only note in the whole song that falls outside the major scale. But as you will see when you get to IFR Exercise 4: Mixed Harmony, the *explanation* for this note actually comes from the major scale even though the note itself is outside the scale. It's an example of mixing metaphors from the major scale. Literally a sound has been "copied" from a different place in the major scale and "pasted" here. So even though the note itself is outside the major scale, the overall sound of this phrase is one that you will discover within the major scale. Once you become an expert in the sounds of the major scale, you will be able to recognize them even when they are mixed up or out of place. This is the subject of Exercise 4, and it is at this level that you will begin to recognize and understand every note in every piece of music you hear.

Now we'll look at some famous melodies from pop and country music. Jazz players sometimes consider this music too simple or too "white" for their taste. Unfortunately it's all too common among jazz musicians to adopt an attitude of superiority toward popular music. But this is an ignorant attitude that prevents musicians from enriching themselves with the beauty and sentiment expressed in this music. In fact the sweet simplicity of popular music is probably the best education that a free improviser could ever receive.

A great example is Charlie Haden. When we listen to his playing alongside Ornette Coleman on albums like "The Shape of Jazz to Come", it would never occur to us to accuse Haden of sounding too "white". What you hear between the musicians on that album is a collective search for beauty and meaning that transcends all boundaries, both musical and social. But what many people don't realize is that Charlie Haden's earliest musical education came from singing country and folk songs on the radio with his family. I believe that it was precisely the sweetness and lyricism of country music that taught Haden how to make musical sense even in an avant-garde free jazz context.

So let's look at some simple melodies from pop and country music without judging them as good or bad. They are all just melodies, and if they have become popular then they must contain something that is inherently beautiful.

The Righteous Brothers - Unchained Melody
(Written by Alex North and Hy Zareth)

| 2 | 2 ^{3} 2 | | 7   2   3 |
                              5

Oh, my love, my darling, I've hungered for your touch

2 |

        3 ^{4} 5

A long lonely time.

Sting - Every Breath You Take

3 ^{4} 3   2
                | |

Every breath you take

      3 ^{4} 3   2
    | | |

And every move you make

        3   4   4   3   2
  | | | | |

Every bond you break, every step you take

2 | 3 | |

I'll be watching you.

Freddie Mercury - Bohemian Rhapsody

3 3   2 3 3
Mama, just killed a man.

3 3 4 5 4   3   2
Put a gun against his head.

2   3   4 5   4   3   2
Pulled my trigger, now he's dead.

5   7   6 6
3 3 3
Mama, life had just begun

I   I   I   I   I
6   6   4
                          3   2 2
But now I've gone and thrown it all away.

Hank Williams Sr. - Your Cheatin' Heart

I
5   6 6 5   5   6   5   4
          2 3
Your cheatin' heart will make you weep.

I   I   I   7   5   6   4   3
You'll cry and cry, and try to sleep.

I
5   6   6 5   5   6   5   4
          2 3
But sleep won't come the whole night through.

I   I 2 I   7   5   6
Your cheatin' heart will tell on you.
7 I

<u>Johnny Cash - I Walk the Line</u>

                    4
1 1 1 2   2   2   3   2   1

I keep a close watch on this heart of mine.

1 1 1 2   2   2 3 3 2 1

I keep my eyes wide open all the time.

                      6
       3 4   4   4   5 4
1 2   3

I keep the ends out for the tie that binds.

                2
1 7   1 7 1
      6
        5

Because you're mine I walk the line.

Even the melodies from punk, heavy metal and modern rock are based on the major scale. This is surprising to many people because the grungy sound effects of rock music fool us into thinking that the melodies couldn't possibly be based on the same harmony used by Mozart. But below are several examples that prove that even the most rebellious rock music is as well-behaved as a choirboy in its respect for the major scale:

<u>Ozzy Osborne - Crazy Train</u>
(Written by Ozzy Osborne, Randy Rhoads and Bob Daisley)

                  1 1 1   5
5   6 5   6 5 5   4   4 3
  3 3   2   1 1 2 3   1

Crazy, but that's how it goes. Millions of people, living as foes.

                  1 1   1 1
5   6 5 5   5 6   5 5   4   4 3
  3 3   2   1 1 2 3   1

Maybe it's not too late to learn how to love and forget how to hate.

<u>The Ramones - I Wanna Be Sedated</u>
(Written by Joey Ramone)

                            6
5 5   5 5   5 5   5   5   6 5 4 3 4 3 3   2   2 3
                                        1

Twenty twenty twenty-four hours to go.   I wanna be sedated.

3 3   3 3   3 3   2 3 2 4 3 3   2   2 3
                                        1

Nothing to do, nowhere to go.   I wanna be sedated.

Guns N'Roses - Sweet Child O'Mine

5 5 5 5   4 3 4 5   3   4 3   4 4 4 3
                                            2

She's got a smile that it seems to me, reminds me of childhood memories.

4 3 4 3   4 3   4   4 4 3

Where everything was as fresh as the bright blue sky.

Nirvana - Smells Like Teen Spirit
(Written by Kurt Cobain, Krist Novoselic, Dave Grohl)

3   5 6   6 5 4   3   4   3   2 3 2   7

Load up on guns. Bring your friends. It's fun to lose and to pretend.

3   5 6   6 5 4 3 4 3   2 3 2   7

She's overboard and self-assured. Oh no I know a dirty word.

Red Hot Chili Peppers - Otherside

3   3   2   2   3 2   7 6 7 6

How long, how long will I slide? Separate my side.

6   3   2   7

   3 3

I don't, I don't believe it's bad.

Another fact that surprises many people is that even the sophisticated sounds of jazz music have a very direct relationship with the major scale. Most jazz standards are based entirely on the major scale with only occasional use of outside notes. For this reason, standards offer a tremendous education in basic harmony and composition. Just as R&B and country music served as an important education for the jazz players I mentioned earlier, it's clear that playing simple jazz standards in all twelve keys was an invaluable education for musicians like John Coltrane.

A lot of people focus on the innovative aspects of Coltrane's later music. But what we forget is that *everybody* was using those new innovative sounds at that time. He may have had some innovations that were particularly his own, but that doesn't explain why Coltrane's music has endured whereas we can't even remember the names of most of his contemporaries. What set

Coltrane apart was not the cleverness of his innovations but the power and the depth of the music he created with them. Music schools today are cranking out musicians by the thousands who can all imitate Coltrane's exotic sounds. But these exotic sounds were not the source of his genius. They were merely the raw materials that Coltrane enjoyed working with. His mastery in using those sounds to tell a human story is something he learned over the course of decades playing the very simple songs we call jazz standards.

These songs, most of which were composed for musical theater and are sometimes called "show tunes", are wonderful teaching examples in basic tonal harmony. Many of them almost seem to have been designed purposely just to illustrate how the sounds of the major scale can be used in surprising and lovely ways.

Many musicians who come from a rock or pop background are intimidated by jazz standards. But even long and fairly complex jazz standards are very easy to play in any key if you understand the origin of their sounds, which is always the major scale. And as you will see for yourself in Exercises 3 and 4, the chord changes that go with these melodies are also based entirely on the major scale. So playing the chords in any key is just as easy as playing the melody. This is why students of IFR are able to play the jazz standards they know in any key. Here are a few examples of standards based entirely on the major scale:

Summertime
(written by George Gershwin)

3   3 2   2 3
  1   1   1
            6
              3

Summertime, and the livin' is easy.

3   2 2   1   1   1 7
  1   6   6

Fish are jumpin' and the cotton is high.

My Romance
(written by Richard Rogers and Lorenz Hart)

                 6 7 1 1 7 6
     5   5   5
3 4   3 4
My romance doesn't have to have a moon in the sky.

              5 6 6 5
   2 3   2 3 4   4 3
1   1
My romance doesn't need a blue lagoon standing by.

There Will Never Be Another You
(written by Harry Warren and Mack Gordon)

₅ ₆ ₇ | ₂ ₃ ⁵ ₂ | ₂

There will be many other nights like this

₃ | ₂ ₃ ⁵ ⁶ | ⁶ ₅ ⁶

And I'll be standing here with someone new.

Stella by Starlight
(Victor Young)

| ₇ ₆ ₇ | ₅ ₅ ₆ ₅ ₅ ₆

The song a robin sings, through years of endless springs.

₂ ⁴ ₃ ₂ | ₃ #4 ⁶ ₅ ₅ ₆ | ₇ ₆ ₅ ₆ ₇ | ³ ₂ ₂

The murmur of a brook at evening tides, that ripples through a nook where two lovers hide.

You Don't Know What Love Is
(written by Gene de Paul and Don Raye)

₇ ₇ ₆ | | ₇ ₆ ₇ | ₂ ³ ₂ | ₇ ₆

³
You don't know what love is, until you've learned the meaning of the blues.

₆ ₇ | ₂ ₃ ⁴ ₃ ⁵ ⁴ ₃ ₃ ₂ ₂ | ₇ ₇

Until you've loved a love you've had to lose, you don't know what love is.

If you happen to know this last song, you know that it is one of many beautiful jazz ballads that have a very dark and minor mood. Other examples are "Beautiful Love", "Autumn Leaves" and "My Funny Valentine". But the idea that these songs are based on a "minor scale" or that they are in a "minor key" is a myth. There are many dark and mysterious sounds within the major scale. When you begin to study the seven different chords of the major scale, you will be astounded by the variety of moods and feelings that these seven background colors produce. Some of them don't seem to resemble the sound of the major scale at all, but they are all right there on your drawing, waiting to be discovered.

Up to now most of the examples have been from American music. So let's finish our tour with some songs from Latin American countries. We will look at a Jamaican reggae song, a Mexican bolero, a Cuban bolero, a Brazilian bossa nova and finally an Argentine tango:

<u>Bob Marley - Redemption Song</u>
(Written by Edward R. Hawkins and Bob Marley)

6   5   5 5   6   6 6 5
       4   3   4   4   3   4

Old pirates, yes, they rob I, sold I to the merchant ships.

3   2   4   3   3
       1 1   1   1   1 1   2   2

Minutes after they took I, from the bottomless pit.

<u>Bésame Mucho</u>
(written by Consuelo Velázquez)
                                                #5 6 7
              3   2 2 2 2   3   3 3   4   4 4   3
6 6 6   6 7 1

Bésame, bésame mucho, como si fuera esta noche la última vez.

6 6 6   6 5   6
            4   3   2   3   3   6   6
                         1   1   6   7   6 7 6   #5 6

Bésame, bésame mucho, que tengo miedo a perderte, perderte después.

<u>Toda Una Vida</u>
(written by Osvaldo Farres)
                         3 66   6 6
3   2   #1 3   4
      1 7 7   6

Toda una vida me estaría contigo.

       4   6   6   6 #5 6
2   3   5 4 3
                          3   3 3 3 3   7 7
                       1   7   7

No me importa en qué forma, ni cómo ni cuándo, pero junto a ti.

93

Wave
(written by Antonio Carlos Jobim)

6   1   7   5   b6   7   2   4   3   5
            3   4

Vou te contar, os olhos já não podem ver,

5   5   6   5   4   4   3   4   3   4   5   3

Coisas que só o coração pode entender.

Malena
(written by Lucio Demare and Homero Manzi)

   6 6   1 1 1 7 7   7 6 6
3   4
           2

Malena canta el tango como ninguna,

        4 5 4   #5
3 3   3   3   2 3
               7 1

Y en cada verso pone su corazón.

I hope you are beginning to grasp the power of our tonal point of view. By looking beyond the names of the notes and instead focusing on each note's *position* in the major scale, we begin to see how simple all Western music really is.

You should also understand that not every song is so perfectly clean in this sense. Obviously composers can also use "outside notes" any time they want. A lot of people get nervous when I mention that, because they assume there must be hundreds of "outside notes" and it must be impossible to learn them all. So let's be clear. There are exactly five. (There, now that wasn't so bad, was it?) And in fact you already know right where these five outside notes are located, because they are nothing more than the five little black dots on your drawing of the major scale. Learning to recognize these five outside notes by ear is every bit as easy as learning to recognize the seven notes of the major scale. Each has its own distinctive sound that you will come to recognize in time.

So now I want to show you a different Brazilian bossa nova that illustrates almost the exact opposite of what I have been telling you all along. As you look at the following tonal sketch of a line from "Garota de Ipanema" (translated in English as "Girl from Ipanema"), notice how many outside notes seem to occur:

Garota de Ipanema
(written by Antonio Jobim and Vinicius de Moraes)

1   b2   1   b7   1   b7 b6 b7   b3   3   b3   b2   b3   b2   b2
                                                  7

Ah, porque estou tão sozinho? Ah, porque tudo é tão triste?

94

What a mess! The sight of so many flat symbols seems to contradict our belief that all of our music comes from the major scale. But this is only a visual illusion. The fact is that even these notes come from the major scale as well, but a *different* major scale from the one in which the song is rooted. This is another example of "copying" sounds from one part of the major scale and "pasting" them in another place. This is the concept that we will study in IFR Exercise 4: Mixed Harmony. For now all I want you to understand is that even the outside notes always have a logic that is rooted in the major scale. And as you grow in your ability to feel and use the major scale in your music, you will have no trouble improvising even over music that includes passages from other keys.

The seven harmonic environments

Some things are hard to explain but easy to understand. No amount of words can explain the color blue, for example, to a person who has never seen it. We don't teach kids about colors with long explanations about optics theory. We simply point out various blue objects and say, "That's blue."

As it happens, the concept "blue" is not a particularly hard one to learn. We all know exactly what it means, even though nobody seems to be able to put it into words. That's because when we talk of the color blue we don't really care about the exact scientific definition. What we are really talking about is a shared human experience, the sensation we feel in the mind when blue light strikes the retina.

When we talk about chords, we are also talking about a shared human experience. The exact details of a chord's construction are not really the most important thing. Modern music courses flounder because they get caught up in the microscopic details of how to name every possible grouping of musical notes. But the origin of all Western harmony is found in just seven fundamental chords. These seven chords are created in a very simple way from the seven notes of the major scale. The reason most people never learn to recognize harmony by ear is that they never got the chance to experience the *sensations* produced by these seven chords. Our teachers show us how to correctly construct a G minor 9th chord with a flatted 13th. But what we really needed was for someone to tell us, "That's the 6 chord."

Your first job as a student of harmony is to get to know personally these seven essential chords. A chord is not merely a group of notes to be played now and then. A better way to think about chords is that they are the musical *environments* in which our melodies take place. If you think of the melody as an actor on a theatrical stage telling a story, then you can think of the chord as the background behind this actor.

Since our first goal is to learn to recognize these environments for ourselves, we are going to use a very simple formula to create them. We're not going to use a bunch of complicated names for all the many variations that can occur in a particular chord. It's not that the differences don't matter. Of course they matter, the same way that a particular shade of blue might be very important to a great painter. But the painter is not helped by having to memorize five hundred different names for five hundred different shades of blue. His attention to detail is infinite but his need for vocabulary words is not.

So let's define each of the seven chords in a simple way that lets us produce them and start getting to know how they sound. The chords are built on the simple idea of starting on the root note and then just adding higher notes that are separated by two steps of the scale. A basic four-note chord will have the following notes:

root   (This is the starting note and it's also the name of the chord.)

3rd (2 steps up from the root.)

5th (2 steps up from the 3rd.)

7th (2 steps up from the 5th.)

That's it. That's all you need to know to create all seven essential chords, the entire foundation of Western harmony. Let's go ahead and build them now. The first chord is called the "1 chord" and it is made up of the notes 1, 3, 5 and 7:

① 2 ③ 4 ⑤ 6 ⑦

The case of the 1 chord is obvious because the root, 3rd, 5th and 7th of the chord are literally just notes 1, 3, 5 and 7 of the major scale. But now let's look at the 2 chord. Now note 2 is the root, and the four notes of the chord will be 2, 4, 6 and 1. (Remember that the major scale doesn't stop when we get to note 7. We just keep right on going into the next octave):

② 3 ④ 5 ⑥ 7 ①

Simple, isn't it? All we're doing is taking the root of the chord and then jumping up two notes, then another two notes and then another two notes. All of the chords are built in this same simple way. The notes of the 3 chord are 3, 5, 7 and 2:

③ 4 ⑤ 6 ⑦ 1 ②

The notes of the 4 chord are 4, 6, 1 and 3:

④ 5 ⑥ 7 ① 2 ③

The notes of the 5 chord are 5, 7, 2 and 4:

⑤ 6 ⑦ 1 ② 3 ④

The notes of the 6 chord are 6, 1, 3 and 5:

⑥ 7 ① 2 ③ 4 ⑤

And the notes of the 7 chord are 7, 2, 4 and 6:

⑦ 1 ② 3 ④ 5 ⑥

That's all there is to it. These are the seven essential chords on which all Western music is based. In IFR Exercise 3: Pure Harmony, you'll have a chance to create all of these harmonic environments for yourself and experience improvising in them. But first I want to give you a glimpse of why this tonal vision of the chords is so powerful.

Knowing which notes make up these chords is not only useful for producing them. It also enables us to quickly orient ourselves in the music. The notes of each chord (indicated by the circles in the above drawings), represent the most *consonant notes* for anybody improvising a solo. For example, imagine that a piano player friend of yours is accompanying you by playing the 6 chord on the piano. Literally what your friend is doing is putting the notes 6, 1, 3 and 5 into the air. As you improvise, you will notice that whenever you also happen to be on any one of these notes (6, 1, 3 or 5), the result is a very relaxed and consonant sound. Literally your note "harmonizes" with the environment and produces a sensation of relaxation. On the other hand, whenever you play one of the other notes of the scale (for example note 4), you will feel a kind of tension in the air as your note clashes with the backdrop of your friend's chord.

Now it's not that the consonant notes are any "better" or more correct than the dissonant notes. That's not the point. We actually need both halves of our musical vocabulary in order to tell a story. But seeing clearly where the chord notes are is helpful because it orients us and helps us to find whatever note we are imagining. It's also a great learning tool for beginners because it makes it so much easier to find the "pretty notes" that beginners often long for.

You can even create a map of these consonant notes in any piece of music. Since every note in the above drawings is just one of the seven notes of the major scale, the first step to understanding how harmony flows through a piece of music is to see for yourself *where* these notes are actually located. To do this we just need to look at the chords we defined above, but in a drawing of the major scale as it really is, in its proper order from 1 to 7:

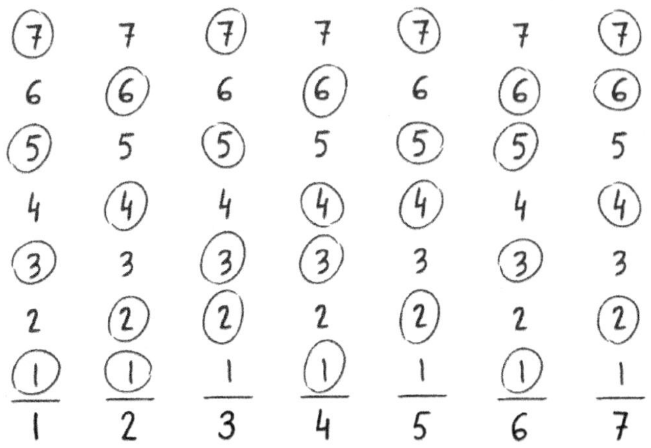

The first column shows the notes of the 1 chord. The notes are 1, 3, 5 and 7. The next column shows the notes of the 2 chord (2, 4, 6 and 1). Remember that we built this chord by starting on note 2, then used our pattern of jumping up two notes, then two more, etc. This is what led us to the notes 2, 4, 6 and 1. But notice in this new drawing *where* these notes are actually located. Note 1, which was the last note we added to the 2 chord, is actually *below* all the others in the major scale. This "tonal vision" of the notes of each chord is tremendously powerful because this is how your ear actually feels the flow of harmony. For your ear, chords have no beginning and no end. Your ear simply feels a natural attraction toward several different places in the octave. These consonant notes that attract the ear are the ones that are circled in the drawing above. So the power of our tonal map is that it allows us to visualize exactly where the harmony is flowing at any given time. In each of the seven musical environments above, the circles represent the most consonant notes that naturally attract the ear.

So now I can give you a preview of how we use this tonal vision in our playing. You don't need to do anything with this musical example. Just follow along for now. But imagine that you are playing a song that consists of the following chords:

Most beginning improvisers (and even many experienced ones) would look at the chord symbols above and immediately ask themselves two questions:

What kind of minor scale should I play over the Cm7 chord?

What kind of major scale should I play over the Dbmaj7 chord?

These are actually the wrong questions to be asking. But to make matters worse, many improvisation teachers will actually give students *answers* to these mistaken questions. So then the poor student goes off trying to make music by manipulating one scale in one moment and a different scale in the next. In fact some people even think the very definition of a great improviser is a person who can smoothly switch from one scale to another without interrupting the music. But if we really understood the song in the first place we wouldn't have any need for such mental acrobatics.

The chords in the above example are nothing more than the following:

You don't yet have all the information necessary to make this observation for yourself. But soon you will. And when you are able to recognize this for yourself, you won't have any need to superimpose artificial scales over these chords because you will be connected directly with the *origin* of the chords. You will see the entire harmonic environment at once, and you will visualize effortlessly the notes that surround you at all times. You will recognize the harmony above as being nothing more than a simple alternation between the 3 chord and the 4 chord:

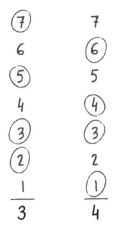

99

What's even better is that you won't even have to use this information in any conscious or mechanical way. You'll just relax and play whatever notes you imagine. But you will feel perfectly oriented because you will understand what's going on around you. At each moment you will literally *feel* an attraction toward the circled notes in the above drawing. You don't necessarily need to *play* them. That's up to you. If you want to gently flow with the harmony of the piece you can let all your melodies come to rest on the notes inside the circles. But you can also create tension against this natural harmonic flow whenever you want, simply by playing the notes outside the circles.

The important thing is to let all of this occur naturally. Theory will never tell you what notes to play. The actual melodies will always come from your musical imagination. But what we can achieve with theory is an understanding of the harmonic environment of any piece of music so that we know where to find the sounds that we imagine. We should never resort to applying artificial scales over each chord. Any piece of music worth playing is worth understanding. By connecting with the true harmony of the piece you can liberate yourself from all those mental acrobatics and just concentrate on saying what you want to say.

Fortunately it's not difficult to recognize the major scale in the harmony all around us. Remember that all of our music actually comes from the major scale in the first place, so spotting the connection is a lot easier than you might think. The key is to first develop your confidence with the seven chords of the major scale without even worrying about how you will apply them in a live playing situation. Remember the example of a child learning to name the colors. By starting with very basic and clear examples the child develops a personal idea of each color, and later has no difficultly recognizing endless variations or mixtures of these basic colors. This is exactly how you are going to learn to recognize the harmony in the music all around you. You will begin this work in IFR Exercise 3: Pure Harmony.

Piano for everyone

If you are enjoying our journey together and you are excited about mastering harmony and musical improvisation, at this point I would encourage you to think seriously about incorporating a piano or keyboard into your musical study. It can be an inexpensive one, as long as it has an enjoyable sound and a comfortable feel. Even if you have never played a piano before in your life, I will show you how to immediately begin using it to make music with the very same concepts you have been learning. The ease with which a total beginner can begin to enjoy playing the piano is one of the most fun and rewarding fringe benefits of the IFR method. So even if your main interest is some other instrument, I encourage you to seize this opportunity to expand your horizons as a musician. You will find the piano to be an incredible learning tool and an unlimited source of pleasure.

If you cannot afford to get a keyboard right now, don't despair. There are many other ways to experience harmony and I will give you lots of ideas throughout the rest of this book. Many of the activities in Exercise 3 can be done on any instrument, so there is no reason you cannot continue to grow as a musician using whatever materials you have available. But if you do have access to a keyboard, then this chapter is for you. You are going to learn how to use what you already know about harmony to begin making music immediately on your keyboard or piano.

The key is to remember that the very same method that you are using to learn to improvise on your own instrument can just as easily be applied to the piano or any other instrument. In other words, you already have all the tools you need in order to learn to improvise on the piano. These tools are the Five Exercises. Starting with Exercise 1, as you progress through the exercises you will develop the same level of comfort on the piano that you have with your own instrument. You may decide someday to take lessons from a piano teacher in order to work on the physical aspects of playing the instrument properly. But in the beginning it's not strictly necessary to take such a formal approach. The only thing you need in order to start making music on the piano is an understanding of the physical layout of the keyboard. It's actually very simple and intuitive. Take a look at the following drawing showing the names of the piano keys in any particular section of the piano keyboard:

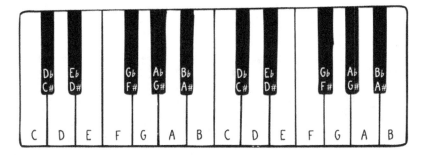

Just as you did with your own instrument, the first thing you should try to understand is the order of these notes from lowest to highest. In other words, you need to visualize the unbroken chain of half steps across the entire range of the piano. Follow the dotted line in the drawing below to trace this path for yourself:

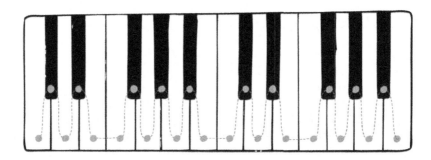

What surprises many beginners is that there is actually no difference between the black keys and the white keys. As you follow the dotted line from left to right, each new key you play moves you up a half step, regardless of whether the new key is black or white. If you visually follow the path of the dotted line in the above drawing, each dotted line segment represents an upward movement of one half step. It makes no difference whether this movement occurs between a black key and a white key, or across two consecutive white keys. So the first step in understanding the piano is to set aside the whole question of "black keys and white keys" and learn to see the entire keyboard as one long unbroken chain of half steps. If you want, take a few minutes right now to practice Exercise 1 on the piano. Try it first with half steps and then with whole steps. This simple exercise will help you gain confidence with the basic geography of the keyboard before moving on.

Once you are clear about how the notes on the piano are connected, you can easily visualize the major scale anywhere you want. All you need to do is combine your new understanding of the piano keyboard with what you already know about the major scale:

$$1 \cdot 2 \cdot 3 \; 4 \cdot 5 \cdot 6 \cdot 7 \; 1$$

Let's look at an example using Eb (also called D#) as our note 1. The first thing we need to do is simply locate this note on the piano and play it. This is the note on the left hand side of the drawing below that I have labeled with the number 1. Moving upward from this note 1, notice how the path of the dotted line leads us along the unbroken chain of half steps, and how we can easily select the notes of the major scale along this path:

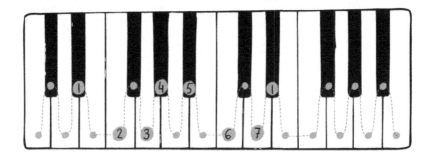

Can you see the half step movement between notes 3 and 4 in the above drawing? And can you see the other half step movement between notes 7 and 1? Notice that all other movements are whole steps. The drawing may appear confusing at first, but just be patient and trace the dotted line of half steps with your eye until you can see how it works.

Here is a different example using the note B natural as our note 1. This time I have removed the dotted line. Can you still see the unbroken chain of half steps underlying the major scale?

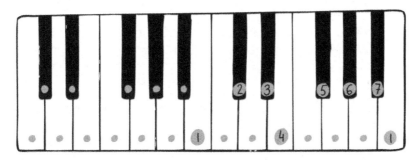

(Playing activity)

Now you are going to practice this on your own. I want to lead you through the activity the first time because the thought process is very important.

1. Select any random key on the piano and play it. This will be note 1.

2. Pause to enjoy this moment. Don't worry about visualizing the entire major scale. Don't even worry about where note 2 is. Just allow yourself to be on note 1, and allow yourself to *not* know where you'll go next.

3. Now let's calmly begin to think through the movement to note 2. From your tonal map, you know that there is a whole step between notes 1 and 2. So that means you'll need to skip over the very next half step you see on your piano, and play the one after that. Take as much time as you need to study the piano keyboard until you can see these two half step movements clearly.

4. Now execute this movement and play note 2.

5. Once you have arrived to note 2, I want you to clear your mind again. Allow yourself to be on note 2 without worrying about where you'll go next. But this time there's something else we need to let go of. Now I want you to allow yourself to *forget* where note 1 was located! Clear your mind of everything except for the fact that you are currently on note 2. With just that one piece of information, you already have everything you need in order to find any other note you want. So don't try to memorize the notes of the scale as you figure them out. Let go of each note as you move away from it. If you decide later you want to return to it, you'll know how. This is the real skill we are trying to learn.

6. Whenever you're ready, think about the interval that you need in order to go from note 2 to note 3. From your tonal map drawing, you know that this interval is a whole step. So skip over the very next half step that you see on your piano keyboard, and play the note just after that. This is note 3.

103

7. Continue on in this way, pausing on each note to just relax and remember where you are. For each new movement, first picture your tonal map drawing and then visualize this movement on your piano keyboard.

Practice this on your own in several different keys. Remember, don't make any attempt at all to memorize the actual sequence of keys that you are playing. Memorizing the notes of all of the different major scales is not our goal, because practicing scales from memory won't give you the visualization skills that you will need later for totally free improvisation. In IFR, the way we practice is to play one note at a time, *imagining* every new movement required.

This will seem slow in the beginning but that's the point. Our goal is not to simply finish the exercise but to actually notice what we are doing in each moment. If you play with this consciousness, every single note you play will increase your confidence with the *entire* piano keyboard. So just try to relax and focus all of your attention on moving around the piano the same way you learned to move around your own instrument in Exercise 1. If you take the time to visualize each interval as you go, you will build a solid foundation for unlimited musical growth. In no time at all you will be able to visualize any type of movement instantly. You should never resort to playing memorized scales in order to gain speed. It might feel more satisfying in the moment but it will lead you down a long lonely road of playing with fear and uncertainty. Take the time to see each movement clearly. Exercise 1 will help you to practice this.

Once you have gained the ability to visualize the major scale anywhere on your piano, it would be a good time to go back to Exercise 2 and do the Seven Worlds exercises on the piano. Take time to enjoy improvising single-note melodies in all seven harmonic environments all over the piano. To make your practicing more meaningful, remember to sing while you play. All of these experiences will make it a lot easier for you to create the chord accompaniments that you are going to learn in IFR Exercise 3: Pure Harmony.

Exercise 3: Pure Harmony

<u>Objective</u>: To continuously improve in your ability to...

Recognize the seven harmonic environments and create your own music within them.

Exercise 3 is the most exciting exercise for most students because it opens so many doors right away. This is where our tonal approach to studying harmony begins to really pay off. Without any new theory at all, you will soon be improvising beautiful melodies over an incredible variety of chord progressions and music styles.

Our goal in Exercise 3 is to gain experience making music in each of the seven harmonic environments. There are two important benefits that you are going to get out of this work. One is that you will discover for yourself the possibilities that each environment offers for creating melodies. Through practice you will gain experience and confidence making music in any harmonic situation. But there is a more subtle benefit which may ultimately be even more powerful. This is a "free benefit" because you always receive its full value, even on days when you feel like your improvisations are uninspired or when you feel that you are not discovering anything new at all. By the simple act of spending a half hour or so in one of the musical environments, an imprint is left on your subconscious mind of how that particular musical environment *feels*. Over time, the repeated exposure to these seven environments will give you the ability to instantly recognize them in the music all around you. Just like a house with seven rooms, if you spend enough time in each room you will eventually have no trouble telling them apart from one another. The only difference is that in our case, in order to experience these seven rooms we first have to *create* them.

At several points in this book I have made a comparison between musicians and painters. But there is an important difference. We musicians work with materials that do not actually exist in the physical world. Students of the plastic arts can sit and contemplate the color red for hours if they want to. But the only way we can contemplate the sound of a particular chord is to produce it ourselves in the moment. By putting the right sounds into the air, we get to hear and feel the chord for a brief moment. But as soon as the vibrations die down, the chord literally disappears out of existence. This is why we make so much use of repetition and calm, meditative improvisations. Since our materials don't actually exist in the physical world, we need to be constantly bringing them into existence in order to get to know them.

In this chapter I will give you some ideas about how to do this. No matter what instrument you play, you can use your own primary instrument to investigate these seven harmonic environments. Actually, you already began this process in Exercise 2. In the Seven Worlds exercises you experienced improvising in all seven *modes* of the major scale. This was one way to experience the seven different harmonic environments. You had no chords accompanying you, but you could still get the feel of each environment just by limiting yourself to one particular octave. By using a particular note as both the floor and ceiling of your musical range, you essentially created a new scale that has its own particular sound and feel. For example, by using note 6 as the tonal center you created the scale shown in following drawing:

$$6 \quad 7 \ 1 \quad 2 \quad 3 \ 4 \quad 5 \quad 6$$

Notice that although the notes themselves are nothing more than the major scale played in a different order, the *shape* of the above drawing is very different from the shape of the major scale in its original order from 1 to 7.

In Exercise 3 we are going to take this practice to the next level in two ways:

- We will take a closer look at the role of each note in the resulting scale.

- We will learn to make a musical accompaniment that we can solo over so that we can move outside a single octave without losing the feel of the harmonic environment.

To begin with, we need to sharpen our awareness of the notes that make up the "chord" in each of these seven resulting scales. There are infinite ways to practice this consciousness with your instrument. But one of the most powerful ways is simply to alternate between experiencing the chord and experiencing the entire scale. We call this exercise Seven Worlds Expanded and we practice it in three different ranges.

Seven Worlds Expanded (modal range)

1. Choose one of the seven chords to work on. To continue with the above example, let's choose the 6 chord. Pick any starting note on your instrument and make this note 6 of the major scale. Play the entire scale from this note 6 to the next note 6, one octave higher, just as you did in Seven Worlds from Exercise 2. Improvise within this scale for a couple of minutes:

$$6 \quad 7 \quad 1 \quad 2 \quad 3 \quad 4 \quad 5 \quad 6$$

2. Now limit your improvisation to just the notes of the 6 chord. Remember that each chord is made up of the root, 3rd, 5th and 7th. So now the only notes that we can use for improvising are notes 6, 1, 3 and 5. These notes are shown in circles in the drawing below. Improvise for a few minutes with just these notes. Pay special attention to the feeling of resolution that you get when you come to rest on note 6, at either the top or the bottom of the scale.

$$⑥ \quad 7 \quad ① \quad 2 \quad ③ \quad 4 \quad ⑤ \quad ⑥$$

3. Now alternate between steps 1 and 2. Spend a couple of minutes improvising with the entire scale, and then a couple of minutes just working with the notes of the chord. Keep going back and forth between the scale and the chord. After a while you should be able to maintain your awareness of the chord even when you are improvising with the entire scale. Notice the feeling of relaxation that you get whenever you come to rest on one of the chord notes. The other notes of the scale produce a kind of tension that can be very beautiful, but they cause us to expect an eventual return to one of the notes of the chord. When you are improvising with the entire scale, notice how you can *use* this dynamic of tension and relaxation to inspire the musical story that you are telling.

Seven Worlds Expanded (tonal range)

1. Pick any starting note on your instrument. This will be note 1 of the major scale. Play the notes 1 through 7. Do not play note 1 again at the top of this range. We are going to work with exactly seven notes as in the drawing below. This is important because your entire range can be understood as simply a repetition of these seven notes. So we want to develop an awareness of where the notes of each chord actually "live" in this musical universe. Improvise with all seven notes for a couple of minutes.

1   2   3   4   5   6   7

2. Choose one of the seven chords to work on. To continue with our previous example let's choose the 6 chord. Play only the four notes that make up the 6 chord. These are notes 1, 3, 5 and 6 of the major scale. Look at the drawing below and notice where each of these notes is actually located within the major scale. Improvise for a few minutes with just these four notes. The feeling of the chord is probably not quite as clear to you as it was in the last exercise (modal range). But can you still recognize that these are the same notes you were playing before? The only difference is that now the notes are out of their natural order because we want to focus on where they are actually found in the tonal octave from 1 to 7.

①   2   ③   4   ⑤   ⑥   7

3. Alternate between steps 1 and 2. Spend a couple of minutes improvising with the entire scale, and then a couple of minutes just working with the notes of the chord. Keep going back and forth between the scale and the chord. Just as you found with the previous exercise, after a while you should be able to maintain your awareness of the chord even when you are improvising with the entire scale. It will probably be more difficult for you to really *feel* the 6 chord, because now you are playing its notes out of order. But this is an important exercise because it teaches us where these notes are actually located in any octave.

1   2   3   4   5   6   7

①   2   ③   4   ⑤   ⑥   7

Seven Worlds Expanded (unlimited range)

1. Choose one of the seven chords to work on. Let's continue with the example of the 6 chord. Pick any starting note on your instrument and this will be our note 6. Starting on this note 6, play the major scale over the entire range of your instrument. Go up to the very highest

note you can play and down to the very lowest note. Improvise in this key over your entire instrument for a few minutes.

$$4\ 5\ 6\ 7\ 1\ 2\ 3\ 4\ 5\ \textcircled{6}\ 7\ 1\ 2\ 3\ 4\ 5\ 6\ 7\ 1\ 2$$

2. Now limit your improvisation to just the notes of the 6 chord. You can still use the entire range of your instrument but now the only notes that exist are notes 6, 1, 3 and 5. Play the notes of this chord over your entire range and improvise freely with these notes for a few minutes.

$$5\ 6\quad 1\quad 3\quad 5\ 6\quad 1\quad 3\quad 5\ 6\quad 1$$

3. Now alternate between steps 1 and 2. Spend a few minutes improvising with the entire scale, and then a few minutes just working with just the notes of the chord. Keep going back and forth between the scale and the chord, and keep extending both concepts over the entire range of your instrument.

$$4\ 5\ 6\ 7\ 1\ 2\ 3\ 4\ 5\ 6\ 7\ 1\ 2\ 3\ 4\ 5\ 6\ 7\ 1\ 2$$
$$5\ 6\quad 1\quad 3\quad 5\ 6\quad 1\quad 3\quad 5\ 6\quad 1$$

Guided only by the simple concepts presented here, Seven Worlds Expanded can take you on many different adventures. You will not only discover a different set of sounds and sensations in each of the seven harmonic worlds that you explore, but you also have unlimited freedom to create whatever kind of experience you want to have in each world. Here are a few examples of what practicing Seven Worlds Expanded might look like on any given day:

Practice Day: Monday
Harmonic World: The 4 chord
Range: Tonal
Mood: Meditative

Practice Day: Tuesday
Harmonic World: The 5 chord
Range: Unlimited
Mood: Funky

Practice Day: Wednesday
Harmonic World: The 7 chord
Range: Modal
Mood: Spooky

Practice Day: Thursday
Harmonic World: The 2 chord
Range: Tonal
Mood: Jazz

Practice Day: Friday
Harmonic World: The 6 chord

Range: Modal
Mood: Melancholy

These suggestions are all interchangeable. You can play just as funky in the 1 chord as you can in the 5 chord. And the 3 chord can be just as meditative as the 4 chord. In other words, it's not really the harmonic material that dictates the emotional impact of the music. What really determines how the music sounds is the emotional energy and attitude that *you* bring to the music. So don't just use Seven Worlds Expanded as a harmony exercise. Use it as a daily *creative exercise*. Challenge yourself every day to make your music say something, to make it express something about what you are feeling in the moment. Forget about the notes. Get yourself into a particular state of mind and play from that feeling.

IFR Jam Tracks

To master the seven chords of the major scale, it's especially valuable to practice with the IFR Jam Tracks because they provide the complete harmonic accompaniment behind your improvisations. This lets you hear the chord notes in their proper harmonic context, bringing out the important differences between each chord of the major scale.

The IFR Jam Tracks series also helps you learn to recognize chords and chord progressions by ear, because of the step-by-step way that the learning path has been designed. For your Exercise 3 practice, you can now begin using IFR Jam Tracks Level 2: Pure Harmony Essentials and IFR Jam Tracks Level 3: Pure Harmony Advanced. You'll find both at ImproviseForReal.com.

Seven Worlds Expanded - Mastery Level

Once you have gained a level of confidence with Seven Worlds Expanded in all three ranges (tonal, modal and unlimited), for a really advanced workout you can put down your instrument and do the entire exercise using only your voice. By singing the numbers instead of playing them on your instrument you will increase your understanding and perception tremendously. This goes not only for the above exercise but for any musical exercise you encounter. Always look for ways to internalize the exercise and make it more personal. Any time you can shift your focus inward, from your instrument to your voice and ultimately to your imagination, the exercise becomes more powerful. So try to do the above exercise about half of the time with your instrument and the other half of the time with just your voice.

Melody Paths

After you have studied all seven chords thoroughly with Seven Worlds Expanded, the next step is to combine these chords into chord progressions so that we can discover the relationships between the chord notes. We do this with the IFR exercise Melody Paths. This exercise will enable you to visualize the musical paths that wind their way through any chord progression, no matter how difficult the chord progression may look on paper. It helps us to see the "big picture" and understand how all of the different chords relate to one another.

Here's how the exercise works. As you're discovering in Seven Worlds Expanded, in any harmonic environment there will be a few notes that attract your ear especially (the chord notes) and some others that seem unresolved or tense. But when a song involves more than one chord, the notes that attract your ear will change from one chord to the next. With our visual approach to harmony, we can see this movement of chord notes on our tonal map, and these connections are what we call "melody paths".

Take for example the following simple chord progression:

By now you should feel totally at home in each of these three chords. But now let's look at how the harmony flows *across* the chords. We'll start by drawing a tonal map of all three chords, and then we'll look at just one of the many available paths through the harmony.

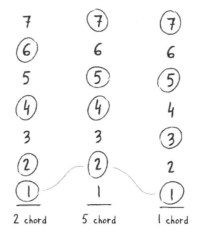

Sing the numbers of this melody path out loud while playing the chords on a piano or listening to one of our jam tracks. (I'll show you how to create the piano accompaniment later in this chapter.) In this example you would literally sing "one.....two.....one" as you play the three chords. Do this over and over again until you can literally *hear* this melody in the chords themselves. Then move on to the next path. Focus on very simple horizontal paths first, since these are the easiest to hear and imagine. Let's look at the next path:

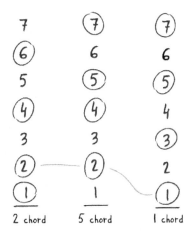

Sing this new melody several times. Then go back and sing the first melody a couple of times. Go back and forth until you can clearly hear both melodies in the chords themselves.

When you are totally confident with notes 1 and 2, then you can move on to include note 3 in your melodies. This opens up two new melodic possibilities:

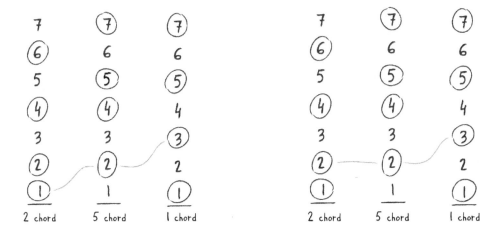

Our work really is this simple and methodical. We just keep going, exploring every possible melodic path across the three chords. As you can see, even if you limit yourself to just very horizontal melodies with no large jumps, there are still quite a lot of possibilities:

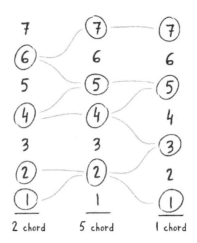

Keep working with these chords until you can sing every one of the melody paths in the drawing above. And don't forget about melodies that cross into the next octave. These paths are not as easy to see on my drawings but they are just as attractive to your ear. Here is a simple example:

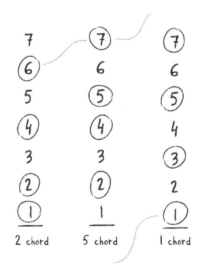

The drawing is a little confusing but what I'm trying to show is that the final note 1 is actually *above* note 7. After singing note 7 in the 5 chord, you move up a half step to land on note 1 of the next octave. Don't forget to explore these possibilities to move freely across the octave line with your melodies. Remember that your ear doesn't know where the octave line is. So for your ear, these melodies that cross the octave line are just as simple and melodic as the melodies that occur within a single octave.

Why do we spend so much time investigating every little corner of these chord progressions? Remember that an artist can't get by with second-hand explanations. An artist needs to have direct personal experience with the materials of his art. The purpose of this exercise is not merely to practice executing these melodies. You could probably do that very easily right off the bat. But the reason we spend so much time investigating each melody path is to give you a chance to decide what *you* think about each of these melodies. Is there anything here that you actually like? Are there any melodies that you find especially beautiful? Give your full attention to each melody that you sing, and just notice how it sounds and how it feels to you. The sensations you discover in this exercise are yours alone. They can never be taught to anyone else because they cannot be explained in words or theory. But it is this personal knowledge that is the essence of mastery.

I should make a slight correction to my earlier comment that we are studying the melodic paths across this chord progression. To be more exact, what we have really been studying is how *consonance* itself flows through the chord progression. We haven't even considered the melodic possibilities of the notes that fall outside the four basic notes of each chord. This is intentional because first we want to get to know the notes that are in the very center of the harmony. But once you have learned to flow with the harmony in this way, you can also begin to practice your ability to stand out against the harmony. This just means having the freedom to sing notes outside the chords. Here is an example that is especially pretty, even though every single note is outside the chord of the moment:

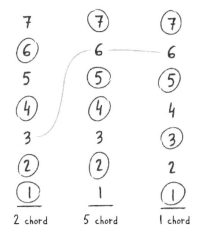

In time, you can learn to feel just as connected to the harmony even when you choose to remain on these more ambiguous or unresolved notes. When you get to the point where you feel equally comfortable on any one of the seven notes in all three chords, you have truly mastered the chord progression.

Think of Melody Paths as a technique for studying chord progressions the same way you have been using Seven Worlds Expanded to study individual chords.

Home Chords

This next technique for piano is both a powerful visualization exercise and a useful technique for fast and simple chord accompaniment. The name comes from the fact that your right hand never leaves the "home" position covering one single octave of the major scale. Remember that in any single octave we have all the notes we need to create any one of the seven chords. So by leaving the hand centered over the octave we can play all seven chords in a very easy way. Here's how the technique works:

Pick any starting note on the piano to serve as note 1, and play the entire major scale from 1

113

to 7. We'll represent these notes by the following drawing:

$$1 \quad 2 \quad 3 \quad 4 \quad 5 \quad 6 \quad 7$$

Now play just the four notes of the 1 chord, all at once:

$$1 \qquad 3 \qquad 5 \qquad 7$$

Now play just the four notes of the 2 chord. Remember that your right hand never leaves "home" but rather it stays centered over the tonal octave playing the notes of the 2 chord in the order that they appear in the octave (1, 2, 4 and 6):

$$1 \quad 2 \qquad 4 \qquad 6$$

Notice that there is one place in the chord where you have a pair of "neighbors" (notes 1 and 2). The rest of the notes are separated but you have two notes touching each other, at the left side of your hand.

Now play just the four notes of the 3 chord. Notice again that there is one place where you have two neighboring notes touching each other. In this case they are notes 2 and 3, again at the left side of your hand:

$$2 \quad 3 \qquad 5 \qquad 7$$

Now play just the four notes of the 4 chord. Notice where the neighbor notes are now. This time they are in the middle of your hand:

$$1 \qquad 3 \quad 4 \qquad 6$$

The neighbor notes are also in the middle of your hand when you play the 5 chord:

$$2 \qquad 4 \quad 5 \qquad 7$$

When you play the 6 chord, the neighbor notes are now on the right side of your hand:

$$1 \qquad 3 \qquad 5 \quad 6$$

The neighbor notes are also on the right side of your hand when you play the 7 chord:

$$2 \qquad 4 \qquad 6 \quad 7$$

Once you get the hang of the above technique for expressing any of the seven chords, you can add a bass accompaniment with your left hand to make things sound more full and musical. If you are a beginner you can just use the classic bass accompaniment of simply alternating between the root and fifth of the chord. Let's take the example of the 1 chord. Choose a nice slow tempo and play half-notes in the bass, alternating between notes 1 and 5:

While your left hand provides a steady background with this alternating bass line, use your right hand to play the 1 chord that you learned above. Don't worry about trying to integrate your two hands together in a sophisticated way. Just try to get into a comfortable groove with your left hand gently rocking between the two different bass notes, and play the chord with your right hand once in a while. If you are new to the piano this will seem strange at first but just take your time. Think about the different places that you can work the chord in with the bass line. For example you could play the chord on beat one, precisely when you play note 1 with your left hand:

Or you could play the chord on all of the off-beats, in between the moments when your left hand plays:

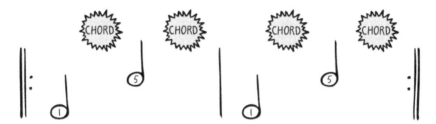

With practice you will eventually get comfortable playing with both hands at once, and you will be able to make up your own rhythms like this one:

To change to a different chord with this technique, you just need to do two things:

1) Select the appropriate shape with your right hand.

2) Physically move your left hand to play the root and fifth of the *new* chord.

Just to be clear, here is a list of the root and fifth notes of every chord:

For the 1 chord, the root and fifth are notes 1 and 5.
For the 2 chord, the root and fifth are notes 2 and 6.
For the 3 chord, the root and fifth are notes 3 and 7.
For the 4 chord, the root and fifth are notes 4 and 1.
For the 5 chord, the root and fifth are notes 5 and 2.
For the 6 chord, the root and fifth are notes 6 and 3.
For the 7 chord, the root and fifth are notes 7 and 4.

So your left hand will be alternating between the two notes indicated above for each chord. Your right hand will be immobile, hovering over the tonal octave between notes 1 and 7. Here are the notes that your right hand will be playing for each chord:

1 chord: right hand plays notes 1, 3, 5, 7
2 chord: right hand plays notes 1, 2, 4, 6
3 chord: right hand plays notes 2, 3, 5, 7
4 chord: right hand plays notes 1, 3, 4, 6
5 chord: right hand plays notes 2, 4, 5, 7
6 chord: right hand plays notes 1, 3, 5, 6
7 chord: right hand plays notes 2, 4, 6, 7

Home Chords serve two different purposes. For beginners, they are an easy way to play all seven chords of the major scale. With this technique you can instantly create a simple accompaniment for any song or chord progression. Once you get used to the *shapes* of the seven chords presented above, switching between them becomes almost effortless. Try it for yourself. Pick a couple of chords and try switching between them. Your right hand should remain centered in the "home position" (covering one single octave of the major scale from 1 to 7). But your left hand will physically move in order to play the root and fifth of each new chord in the bass. Do you see how powerful the piano is? With very little practice you can learn to create a solid accompaniment for any number of chords in all 12 keys.

The deeper purpose of the Home Chords exercise is that it gives you practice visualizing exactly *where* the notes of each chord are found in the tonal octave. Every time you play the piano in this way, you are getting a visual refresher course in basic harmony, because the piano keyboard itself shows you exactly which notes participate in each chord. The clarity of vision that results from practicing the piano in this way will help you in every aspect of your music.

Accompanied Singing

Once you have developed a level of comfort with the piano, Accompanied Singing could become your favorite exercise in the whole IFR method. It is creative and interesting, and it will very quickly give you a powerful command over the sounds in all seven harmonic environments. It consists of improvising with your voice using the entire major scale, while using the piano to create a harmonic backdrop. The exercise is very simple to describe:

1. Pick any starting note to use as note 1 of the major scale.

2. Play the entire scale and sing each number. Pay close attention to each sound because you will need to remember these sounds and use them in your vocal improvisation.

3. Use Home Chords to create a quick chordal accompaniment in one particular chord of this major scale.

4. While playing this accompaniment, sing the seven notes of the major scale saying their numbers out loud. (You will literally be singing, "one.....two.....three....etc.") Improvise melodies with these seven notes, playing around with them any way that you like.

Variations:

*   For a more guided experience, you can use our audio course Sing the Numbers in which we sing each melody to you in tonal numbers and then you sing it back. Through singing these beautiful melodies you will discover the sounds of all seven harmonic environments, plus countless beautiful Melody Paths that appear when we combine these chords into chord progressions.

*   You can also combine this exercise with Seven Worlds Expanded - Mastery Level. Continue using Home Chords for your accompaniment but this time alternate between singing the entire scale and singing just the four notes of the chord. This is a tremendous exercise that will greatly strengthen your perception of harmony.

*   Another variation is to combine Accompanied Singing with Free Your Imagination from Exercise 2. Keep playing the chord on the piano but now improvise freely with your voice, singing any sound that comes into your mind. Don't sing the numbers anymore. In this activity you are not required to know where you are on the tonal map. In fact you should try to do just the opposite, to *forget* where you are on the tonal map and just concentrate on imagining sounds. Remember that your musical imagination is your greatest treasure. Don't forget to cultivate this part of your talent.

*   One of my favorite exercises is to sing the seven notes of the major scale while alternating between two *different* chords on the piano. Here is an example using the 6 chord and the 2 chord:

    1. Use Home Chords to create an accompaniment in the 6 chord. Don't forget to include the left hand bass accompaniment since this is what gives the music all its groove and power. With your voice, sing the entire major scale over this accompaniment. Notice how your voice blends in perfectly with the piano when you sing notes 1, 3, 5 or 6. And notice the feeling of tension that occurs when you sing any of the other notes.

    2. After you have thoroughly investigated the 6 chord, now change to the 2 chord in your piano accompaniment. Don't forget to change your left hand bass accompaniment as well. Again, sing the entire major scale and notice that this time the notes that blend in with the piano are notes 1, 2, 4 and 6.

    3. Keep going back and forth between steps 1 and 2 until you are completely clear about the sounds in each chord. (Take as much time as you want in each chord.

Give yourself time to get comfortable in each harmonic environment before trying to combine them.)

4. Once you are totally clear about all of the sounds in these two harmonic environments, it's time to combine them. Imagine a simple song that alternates between the 6 chord and the 2 chord:

5. Create this accompaniment using Home Chords to alternate between the two harmonic environments. Once you have your piano groove going, improvise with your voice using the entire major scale. Now you can sing any note you want at any time. There are no wrong notes. You may notice that some notes blend in more while others stand out more. But you don't have to worry about trying to consciously keep track of which notes belong to which chord. Just listen to each note and hear for yourself how it sounds. Don't be alarmed if the note you are singing is quite dissonant against the backdrop of the current chord. Enjoy the dissonance, knowing that you can move away from this note whenever you want to. If you listen very closely to each note you sing, the note itself will tell you what you should do next. So just allow yourself to sing whatever note is most enjoyable to you at any given moment, and your music will flow naturally and beautifully.

Follow the Harmony (advanced)

Just as we have been practicing Follow the Melody since Exercise 2, we can now begin practicing Follow the Harmony as well. This means listening actively to the music all around us and learning to recognize the chords by ear.

Remember to approach this new practice with a sense of humor and a lot of patience, because at first there are going to be a lot more sounds that you don't recognize than sounds that you do. But most people are surprised by how much they *can* recognize so easily. It's a lot of fun and I urge you to try it!

Here are some tips to help you:

1. Start with *very* simple music. Folk songs, children's songs and country music are the best place to develop your skills. Choose a recording of a song that seems like a good candidate to analyze by ear. Listen to the recording and use the technique that I showed you in the chapter, "Understanding begins with listening" to connect with the tonality of the song and clarify which of the sounds is note 1.

2. Once you are oriented in the key of the music, listen to the bass. In most popular music, the bass is almost always playing the root of the chord at all times. So just listen to the bass part and analyze it the same way you do in Follow the Melody from Exercise 2. But it's even *easier* because the bass line isn't going to be anywhere near

as complicated as the melodies you have been analyzing. In a typical pop tune there are usually only three or four chords, and they don't go by very quickly. So it's very easy to follow what the bass player is doing, and this will tell you the chords to the song.

3. Sketch it out on paper. Human beings have a very limited ability to visualize many things at once. So it's critical to get out a piece of paper and a pencil so that you have someplace to capture everything you figure out. The first step should always be to sketch out the *form* of the song. By this I simply mean the number of measures in the tune. If you did jigsaw puzzles as a child, you know that the first step is to try to put the border together. The same strategy works just as well here. Once you get the structure of a tune outlined on a piece of paper, you can start to "fill in the blanks" with the chords you recognize until you have the entire song figured out. And even if you don't recognize *any* of the chords you can still at least count the measures going by, right? So put that down on your piece of paper. Draw a little box for every measure that you count until you get to the point where the tune starts repeating itself.

4. At this point I would go back to the beginning of the song and sketch out the melody to the song. Even though our main focus now is the harmony, I always like to sketch out the melody anyway because it helps me keep track of where I am in the song. Remember the techniques that you learned in Exercise 2 to feel the tonality of the song and locate any particular note within the major scale. You don't have to capture every last detail if you don't want to, but at least write out enough of the melody so that you can see the form of the song when you look at the page.

5. Now go back and listen to the song again, following along visually in the sketch you have just made. This time apply the same techniques from Exercise 2 to recognize the bass note of each chord. With most songs you should be able to recognize at least some of the chords just by following the bass player.

6. Don't get hung up on exceptions or difficulties. Remember that there is much more to come in this book. What you have learned up to now is important and it represents a good part of what you hear in the music you listen to. But it doesn't cover everything. When you hear sounds that you don't recognize, don't kill yourself trying to figure them out. We probably just haven't got to those sounds yet. So just move on and try to find *something* that you do recognize. Remember that you are taking your first steps into the fascinating world of recognizing both melody and harmony by ear. This is an awesome skill that even most professional musicians do not have. So be patient and celebrate every little victory along the way!

As an example we'll look at the song "My Heart Will Go On" recorded by Celine Dion for the movie Titanic. I would encourage you to get a copy of this tune and listen to it so that you can follow the rest of the discussion in this example. You should also have your instrument on hand to actually play the melody as we transcribe it.

To understand the harmony of this song, the first thing I would do is listen to the entire song and just make a note of how many measures are in each section:

Intro - 8 bars

Verse - 8 bars (repeated twice)

Chorus - 8 bars (repeated twice)

After completing these sections, the song repeats itself by going back to the intro, then the verse again and finally the chorus. So we only need to analyze these sections once. The first step is simply to create this space on a piece of paper, putting the right number of measures in each section:

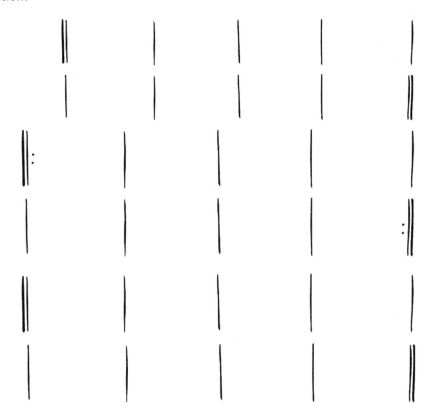

We can approach these three sections one by one. In each section I would first sketch the melody and then go back and listen to the harmony. Here is the melody to the intro:

Don't be confused by the little note stems rising up above each number. That's just my attempt to make the numbers look more like musical notes. It lets me show the difference between an eighth-note and a quarter-note, for example. As you play through the melody above, pay attention to the height at which each number is drawn. Just like standard sheet music notation, the higher notes are drawn higher on the page than the low notes.

At this point, if the chords were difficult to hear I would just keep going, sketching the melody to the verse and the chorus so that I can see the entire song on the page. Then I would go back and try to pick out some of the chords to the song, filling in the blanks until the mystery is solved. But in this case the harmony is very easy to recognize because there are just a few chords and the bass note can be heard very clearly. So before moving on I would go ahead and fill in the chords to the intro. There are only three chords in the entire intro. They are the 6 chord, the 5 chord and the 4 chord.

Intro:
| 6 | 5 | 4 | 5 | |
| 6 | 5 | 4 | 5 | |

At this point, if you want to check my work you could try playing the above intro on a piano. Play the melody with your right hand, and using your left hand play just the bass note of each chord. I think you will recognize the sound of the song immediately.

The words begin with an eight bar phrase that is repeated. I would write this line one time only and use repeat symbols:

Upon going back to listen to the chords behind this melody, I notice that the harmony is not exactly the same for the two times that this melody is repeated. The first time through the harmony is a little ambiguous. It basically stays on the 1 chord and uses some suspended notes to create the harmonic movement instead of actually changing to a different chord. These are subtleties that have more to do with the specific arrangement than with what I would consider to be the essence of the song. In a live playing situation these subtleties are really up to the individual musicians' taste. So I wouldn't get hung up on trying to capture such small details from a specific recording. What I would write out is the basic harmonic flow that I feel when I listen to the melody. This harmony can be heard very clearly in the bass part the second time the melody is sung. This time the chords are 1, 4 and 5.

Now we can move on to the chorus, which is the last section in the song. This is another 8 bar melody which is repeated twice with a slight variation. The basic melody is the following:

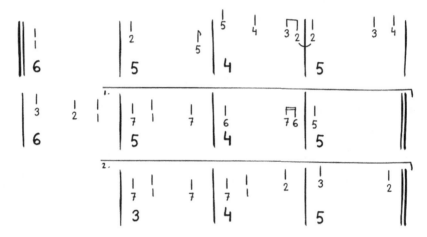

But even though the melody is almost exactly the same both times, I can't use simple repeat signs because there are some important differences between the first and second time, especially in the harmony. So I need to use first and second endings to show the correct harmony for each line:

Just after this section, the chorus ends with the melody on note 1, just as the flute comes back in to play the intro again. I will draw one more line after the chorus to show this. So here now is the completed tonal sketch of "My Heart Will Go On".

My Heart Will Go On - James Horner, Will Jennings

Intro:

(flute plays intro again)

As you can see, this is an especially simple song. There is not a single note outside the major scale in the entire song. And there are only five chords, all of which come directly from the major scale. You may not have such good luck with the first few songs you try to analyze in this way. Most songs will have at least one or two chords that you may not be able to recognize. But just write down as much as you can and you'll see that with practice you will improve rapidly. Don't worry about the measures you aren't sure about. Just put a question mark in each measure you can't figure out. Over time, more and more of those question marks will turn into chord symbols.

Chord Comping on the Piano (advanced)

With the piano we can easily extend our earlier concepts into a more interesting technique for chordal accompaniment, or what is commonly called "comping". I recommend this exercise even for advanced piano players because although you may have lots of other resources for creating chordal accompaniments, the real purpose of this exercise is to strengthen and clarify your vision of tonal harmony on the piano keyboard. So it's an important exercise for both beginners and professionals alike. Here's how it works, using the 1 chord as an example.

1. Choose any key on the piano to use as note 1 of the major scale. Using your right hand, play the major scale from 1 to 7 and improvise in this scale for a couple of minutes to get accustomed to the notes in this key.

    1   2   3   4   5   6   7

2. Again using just your right hand, now play the notes of the 1 chord all at once. These notes are 1, 3, 5 and 7, as shown in the following drawing.

    ①   2   ③   4   ⑤   6   ⑦

3. Now we are going to raise this chord by what is called an *inversion*. It's very simple. All we are going to do is drop the note 1 that is at the left side of your hand, and replace it with another note 1 that is one octave higher, to the right of your hand.

    ~~1~~   2   ③   4   ⑤   6   ⑦   ①
                                        ↑

4. You will need to physically move your hand to the right in order to play the new set of four notes. Play this new chord and think of it as just another way to express the 1 chord.

    ③   4   ⑤   6   ⑦   ①

5. Now take this 1 chord up another inversion by dropping note 3 from the left and adding note 3 an octave higher to the right. Again, you will need to move your hand to the right in order to play the new set of four notes.

    ⑤   6   ⑦   ①   2   ③

6. Now take the chord up another inversion by dropping note 5 from the bottom (left) and adding note 5 to the top of the chord one octave higher.

    ⑦   ①   2   ③   4   ⑤

7. Finally, move up one final inversion by dropping note 7 from the bottom of the chord and adding it to the top. With this final movement we return to the original voicing of the chord, but the entire chord has been moved one octave higher.

$$①\quad 2\quad ③\quad 4\quad ⑤\quad 6\quad ⑦$$

8. Keep moving the 1 chord up the entire length of the keyboard by cycling through these four inversions. Then come down the entire length of the keyboard. Practice moving around freely and notice how the shape of your hand changes for each different inversion.

Once you are comfortable moving the 1 chord all over the piano with your right hand, you can add a bass accompaniment with your left hand just as you did with Home Chords. At first you might feel clumsy trying to integrate your two hands together. But it's really the same thing you did earlier. The only difference is that now your right hand has the freedom to play any one of the above chord inversions, or voicings, anywhere on the piano. This opens up all kinds of new expressive possibilities for your accompaniment.

Once you can do this comfortably, you have an excellent beginning technique for accompanying any musician with the piano. Since you have unlimited freedom of movement in your right hand, you have an extensive vocabulary of sounds that you can use to develop a story and make your accompaniment interesting. And with your new understanding of tonal harmony, you have all the tools you need to improvise accompaniments over all seven chords in all twelve keys.

I'll leave the investigation of the remaining chords mostly up to you but let's think through one example together, just to make sure you know exactly how to do it. Let's think about how we would create a piano accompaniment in the 2 chord:

1. First choose a key to play in. Pick any random note and we'll make this note 1 of the major scale. Play the major scale from 1 to 7 and improvise for a couple of minutes in this key in order to get used to the notes.

$$1\quad 2\quad 3\quad 4\quad 5\quad 6\quad 7$$

2. With your right hand, now play just the four notes that make up the 2 chord. The notes are 1, 2, 4 and 6:

$$①\quad ②\quad 3\quad ④\quad 5\quad ⑥\quad 7$$

3. Practice moving this chord up through all of its inversions exactly as you did before:

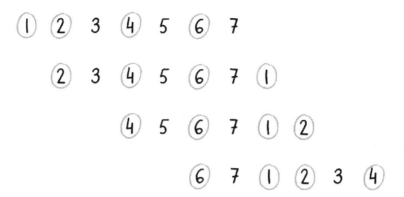

4. For your left-hand bass accompaniment, you can use the same technique of alternating between the root and fifth of the chord. But in this case the root note is note 2, and the fifth of the chord is note 6:

Just as you did before, try to create a slow gentle groove with your left hand alternating between these two notes in the bass. Whenever you feel like it, let your right hand drop a chord in place. Choose any inversion of the chord you want. Notice how you can create melodies within your accompaniment by moving around between different inversions of the chord. Your ear will naturally hear the highest note of the chord as the melody note.

Once you are comfortable improvising piano accompaniments in all seven chords, the really exciting thing is to combine two or more chords together to form a progression. Just as you did with the simpler Home Chords, you can alternate between two different chords to make a much more interesting harmonic environment for piano comping. Here are a few chord progressions you might try. I think you'll enjoy them:

| 1 chord | 1 chord | 5 chord | 5 chord |

| 6 chord | 6 chord | 4 chord | 4 chord |

| 4 chord | 4 chord | 3 chord | 3 chord |

These are just a few combinations to get you started. Invent your own combinations! And there's no reason to stop at just two chords. You can make longer progressions if you want to. Use your imagination and follow your ear. You can use this technique to compose simple harmonic backgrounds for your own compositions, to accompany other musicians or just to enjoy playing the piano. And if you want more ideas for improvising with chords on the piano, you'll find many more exercises like this one at ImproviseForReal.com.

Chord Comping on the Guitar (advanced)

Needless to say, our tonal vision of the seven chords can also be applied to the guitar, and this can be the inspiration for a complete approach to comping chords on the guitar. Since the guitar is my own primary instrument, this subject has been a lifelong fascination of mine. The way that the notes are arranged on the guitar makes it possible to develop an entirely visual methodology for applying tonal harmony to the guitar. Using this vision it's possible to play chords on the guitar just as freely as piano players do. A comprehensive approach to improvising tonal harmony on the guitar is too big to fit within this book. But what I can offer you right now are two things.

First I can offer you what I believe to be the best advice for you right now. I encourage you to investigate this subject on your own using nothing more than your guitar and the ideas presented in this chapter. Think about how you would adapt the Chord Comping exercise to the guitar. Obviously it's not practical to be so rigid in creating the different voicings because the guitar doesn't allow you to play consecutive notes as easily as the piano. But there are countless other ways that you can group the notes together. For example, just think for a moment about the 1 chord. The 1 chord contains notes 1, 3, 5, and 7. If you consider the entire range of your guitar from the very lowest note (the open low E string) to the highest note you can reach, do you have any idea how many different places you can find notes 1, 3, 5 and 7 in any particular key? The answer is *dozens*. Your guitar neck is literally peppered with notes of the 1 chord all over the place. Take a look at how many notes of the 1 chord we find in the key of F, using just the region between the 1st and 12th frets:

What we need to develop on the guitar is a systematic method for exploring these possibilities and incorporating them into our musical vocabulary. As you investigate interesting ways to group these notes together, you will notice many patterns. Some of the shapes will change slightly in other keys, due to the irregular tuning of the guitar. The shapes will also be slightly different for other chords of the major scale (the 2 chord, the 3 chord, etc.) because the notes of these chords are separated by different intervals than the notes of the 1 chord. We will study this more deeply in later chapters. But for now, I would encourage you to just enjoy playing with the notes of the seven basic chords and pay attention to the shapes that result on your guitar neck. This will teach you many important lessons about harmony and the guitar. If you just keep going with this line of thinking, you will eventually make all the same discoveries that I have, and I promise it will be an amazing journey filled with many surprises.

The other thing I can offer you are the video courses and workshops that we have created just for guitarists. These courses follow the same methodology presented in this book, with an extensive exploration of soloing, comping and chord melody playing on the guitar. Together they form a complete framework for mastering harmony and improvisation on the guitar. You'll find all of these resources at ImproviseForReal.com.

Summary

In Exercise 3 we learned several new ways to begin studying the chord notes running through each of the seven harmonic environments:

1. Seven Worlds Expanded (modal range, tonal range and unlimited range)

2. Melody Paths

3. Home Chords

4. Accompanied Singing

5. Follow the Harmony (advanced)

6. Chord Comping on the Piano (advanced)

7. Chord Comping on the Guitar (advanced)

Over the next few chapters I'll give you even more ideas that you can begin to investigate immediately using the techniques you have learned in Exercise 3. I hope you enjoy countless hours of musical discovery with this material.

Composing your own music

Now that you know about the seven basic harmonic environments, you have a nice beginning set of materials to start composing your own original pieces. Composing music is a lot of fun and it can be a great source of personal satisfaction. It offers you the same creative freedom that you enjoy when you are improvising, with the added luxury of *time*. You can take as much time as you want to put each note in just the right place, and you can change your ideas as many times as you want. Best of all, composing gives you a way to create music in a form that lasts. When we are improvising, each moment is unique and can never be repeated again. The music that is created is something private, shared only by the few people who happen to be there. Composing is our attempt to catch these beautiful moments and preserve them forever.

Composing, like improvising, is a very personal thing. There are so many ways to compose that I can't even begin to imagine what your process will eventually look like. The one thing that is sure is that it will be *your* process, and nobody can tell you how you should do it. But since a lot of people are intimidated by the idea of taking their first steps as composers, I want to offer you some ideas that might help you to get this part of your creative life going.

Here are a few quick tips before we get started:

What matters is the process, not the product. Our goal is not to produce a hundred great compositions, nor even a single good one. We just want to begin to enjoy the art of organizing sounds into compositions. It's actually great fun to arrange sounds on a page or in a computer program and watch as your composition slowly takes shape. If you approach composition with a relaxed and open mind, it's extremely addictive. Focus on having fun, and the rest will take care of itself.

Don't judge yourself. There are no rules and there is no such thing as cheating. You are free to plagiarize, imitate, fantasize, calculate or even just put random notes on a page without even knowing how they will sound. Some techniques might be less fulfilling than others, but you'll figure all that out on your own. Over time you'll gravitate toward the style that is most rewarding to you personally. So don't worry about whether you are composing the "right way". Do whatever you want, since that's what composing is all about.

Don't wait for a complete idea. Many people think that the way inspiration works is that an entire musical composition just appears in your head. And since this has never happened to them, they assume they don't have the "gift" of composing. But it doesn't work that way. Inspiration is nothing more than becoming fascinated by a particular sound or idea. Maybe while you are doing one of the activities in Exercise 3 you are drawn to the sound of a particular note in a particular chord. Develop that idea! Write that note down and build a composition around it. Maybe in the moment you can only compose one or two measures because that's all it takes to express that one simple idea. But write it down anyway. If you write down the melodies, chord progressions or compositional ideas that occur to you each day, soon you'll have a wealth of raw material that you can combine to make very beautiful compositions.

Make each finished composition tell exactly one story. Don't try to fit all of your musical knowledge into every composition. You have plenty of time to make all the compositions you want. So try to let each composition be just one special thing. Say that one thing and be done with it. Then let go of your idea and move on to the next one.

These are some of the insights that have helped me overcome my own fears and difficulties with respect to composing. I hope they can also be of some help to you. Now let's look at a couple of simple ways to start making your own music. Over the course of your life you will go on to compose music in much more sophisticated ways. But even with the simple techniques presented in this chapter you could enjoy composing for years.

To get started, you basically need three things:

1. Some way to produce the seven chords of the major scale. For most people this would be a piano or simple keyboard. But it could also be a guitar or even a piece of software on your computer.

2. The ability to record this accompaniment and play it back so that you can imagine melodies and hear how they sound over this harmonic background. You could use a tape recorder, a digital recorder or a piece of recording software on your personal computer.

3. Some way to write down or otherwise capture your musical ideas (both melody and harmony) in order to work with them or save them for a later date. This could be as simple as a pencil and some paper or it could be as sophisticated as a MIDI editing program on your computer.

If you have these three elements covered then you already have everything you need to begin composing your own music. To show you how easy it is to get started, let's make a couple of compositions together. For the first one, we'll choose a chord progression first and then think about melodies later.

Starting with the harmony

One way that you might compose a piece of music is to start with a series of chords that you especially like. A great technique for beginners is simply to alternate between a couple of different chords from the major scale, because this almost always produces an attractive backdrop for simple, pretty melodies. For example let's say we choose the 2 chord and the 6 chord. You can sketch out a simple form on paper and use these two chords any way that you want. Here is an example:

Composition Idea #1

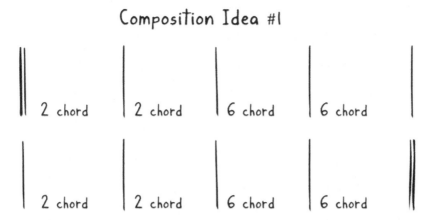

With your piano or keyboard, you can use our Home Chords technique to create a simple but solid accompaniment that alternates between these two chords. (If you want to save yourself the hassle of trying to visualize the major scale across black keys and white keys, just play in the key of C for now. The seven notes of the C major scale are just the seven white keys, so playing Home Chords in the key of C is especially easy.) Once you can play your accompaniment reasonably well, make a recording of yourself playing these chords on the piano. Later you'll play this recording in the background as you imagine melodies, so be sure to make the recording long enough so that it gives you plenty of time to investigate melodies before the recording ends.

Now we are going to create the melody. You might do this any number of ways:

Imagine a musical fantasy. This is one of my favorite ways to compose music. Imagine that you are on a stage in front of an enormous audience. There is complete silence and the lighting is just right. How does the music start? What kind of mood does it create? What other instruments are in the band? If you start your composition with this moment in mind, sometimes all you have to do is listen to the concert in your mind to know how your composition needs to go.

Sing freely. Another way to create melodies is to just relax into the music and let yourself imagine whatever melodies occur to you. You can do this entirely in your mind or you can sing the melodies with your voice. You might spend an entire morning singing melodies to yourself and never quite find that perfect melody. But often, later that same day, a particular hook from one of your melodies will come back to you. *That's* the precious idea that you should develop.

Improvise with your instrument. You can also get out your instrument and jam over your recorded accompaniment for as long as you like. If you set up a second recording device, you can capture your improvisations and listen to them later. When you listen to the recording, you might be surprised at the beauty of some of the lines you played. Often when we are improvising we are so busy trying to create music that we don't fully appreciate the value of our own ideas. But hearing them played back to us lets us judge them more objectively. Using improvisation as a technique for composing is a little bit like the practice of "brainstorming" in the business world. You just throw out as many ideas as you can without judging, and then later you go back and mine this material for ideas of value. If you try this technique, here is a tip that may help you. Try improvising lines with very few notes. Most people have a tendency to ramble on with their improvisations, using hundreds of notes when just a few would be more interesting. If your goal is to produce a composition worthy of repeated listening, it is especially important that you be very economical with your notes. Don't feel you need to spell out everything for the listener. Ambiguity creates mystery and allows the listener to project his or her own feelings onto the composition. Don't be afraid to be mysterious or unresolved.

Sculpt your ideas. This is really the essence of what differentiates composition from improvisation. The techniques above may be helpful to get your creative juices flowing, but once you have some interesting ideas together you will want to work and rework these ideas to create a story that flows exactly the way you want it to. The nice thing about this part of your work is that it doesn't need to be connected in time with your moment of inspiration. If you wake up one day in the mood to compose, it doesn't matter whether you have any particular musical inspiration that day. You can just get out your notes and recorded ideas from earlier sessions and select a few ideas that seem especially interesting to you. If you have done a good job of capturing your musical inspirations in the moment, then you should always have tons of raw material lying around that you can sculpt whenever you are in the mood to do some composing.

To continue with our example, now imagine that through some combination of the above approaches you finally settle on the following melody for the chords we decided earlier:

Composition Idea #1

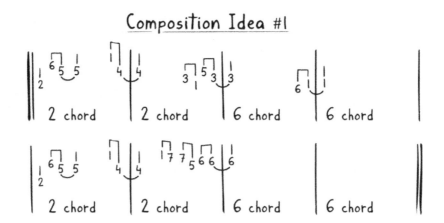

You might not be satisfied with this piece of music as a finished composition, but it's pretty catchy and could serve as a small section of a larger tune someday. This is already a big accomplishment for one day. Remember that we have our entire lives to compose music, and we won't always know in the moment exactly what to do with a particular fragment that we compose. So just enjoy the process and keep capturing your best ideas for future use.

Starting with the melody

Now let's look at the opposite approach to composing simple tunes, which is to start with a melody that you find beautiful. As before, a good first step is to write this melody out so that you can see the form of the piece clearly. Let's say for example that you stumble onto a melody that you like while you are practicing Exercise 3 over the 1 chord:

Composition Idea #2

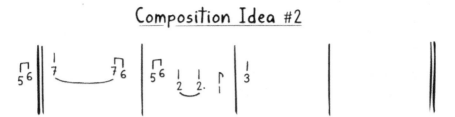

This short little phrase can serve as the inspiration for a much longer melody, and could even be the basis of an entire song. Often when we are improvising our ideas won't be much longer than this example. But then later when you sit down to turn this idea into a composition, you can imagine how the rest of the melody should continue. For example you might extend your idea a few measures more to create the following:

Composition Idea #2

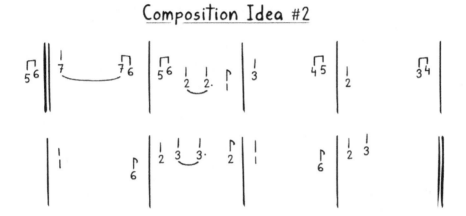

Now comes the fun part. The fact that you imagined the original melody over the 1 chord doesn't mean that this is your only option. You could also give your song a much richer harmonic background. If you are good enough at the piano to play this melody and some basic chords at the same time, then you can try all different combinations of chords to accompany your melody. If that is beyond your current ability level with the piano, then you can just do exactly what we did earlier but in reverse order. You can make a recording of your melody and then play the recording back while you try different chordal accompaniments on the piano. You might finally settle on something like the following:

Composition Idea #2

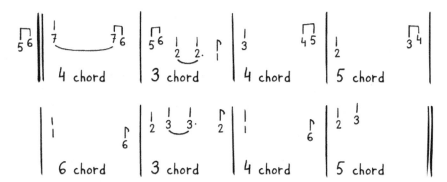

With these new chords, our melody now sounds much more beautiful and interesting. But our song is still very pleasant and melodic to the ear because every sound in our final composition comes from the same key. In the future we will remove this limitation but I encourage you to spend as much time as you can (years, even) composing with just the seven notes and the seven basic harmonic environments of the major scale. The skills you learn here are precisely what will enable you to make musical "sense" even when you are working with much more abstract materials later on.

I hope that these examples have given you some ideas that will help you get started with one of the most rewarding activities for any musician, which is composing original music. As with anything that you create over time, the best part is that everything you create stays created forever. Every new idea or bit of effort moves you forward. At first you probably won't feel that your work is amounting to much. But one day you will look back with great satisfaction at a whole collection of your own creations. So just take your time and enjoy yourself every step of the way.

And remember...

What matters is the *process*, not the *product*.

Don't judge yourself.

Don't wait for a complete idea.

Make each composition tell exactly one story.

Family jam sessions

One of the great pleasures that music offers us is the chance to play with other people. The joy and fun of improvising collectively with other musicians is unlike anything else in this world. And being able to participate in these informal "jam sessions" is one of the most rewarding benefits of understanding harmony.

In Exercise 2, you learned all the skills you needed in order to participate in these jam sessions. You learned how to orient yourself instantly using only your ear, and you learned how to improvise freely no matter what key the music is in. As an individual player, this is all you need to improvise with confidence in any musical situation for the rest of your life.

But now that you have begun Exercise 3 you have entered a whole new territory. Now you can actually *create* these jam sessions and give this wonderful experience to other people. And it doesn't even matter whether the other musicians understand anything at all about harmony. It's not necessary for them to see the "big picture". They just need a simple way to understand where to find the notes that will sound good to their ears. So with your understanding of harmony, you can easily give each musician what little orientation he or she needs to make music with the group.

The title of this chapter is inspired by the image of a family playing music together. It makes no difference whether they are serious musicians, hobbyists or if they have no musical experience whatsoever. There is no minimum age requirement either. In fact sometimes the most surprising and beautiful moments come from little children. But whether you imagine yourself playing with friends, family or just other musicians, the ideas in this chapter are all intended for an intimate social context like a party at your house.

The key to creating these magical moments has to do with creating the right kind of atmosphere. This is far more important than the technical skill level of the participants. While it helps to have people who are positive and open, don't make the mistake of assuming that they will automatically know what to do. A few words from you can go a long way toward putting everyone in the right frame of mind for an experience that everyone will enjoy and remember for a long time.

In this chapter I will try to give you some ideas about how to use what you have already learned to create jam sessions for any number of participants. First we'll look at the personal aspects of getting people together and creating the right kind of situation, and then we'll talk about different kinds of musical games and activities that you can use to get people playing.

Bringing people together

Here are some things to consider about what tends to make jam sessions "work" and be fun for everyone. These are just my observations. Think about how these ideas might apply to your own style and your situation.

> **Time and place.** If you want to have a jam session as part of an evening party, I suggest you start early and keep an eye on the clock, especially if you have neighbors that might be bothered by noises late at night. It's much better to have many jams that end at a

reasonable hour than to have one spectacular all-night jam that gets you kicked out of your neighborhood. Try to set up the space in such a way that even the people not playing are included. Some people will want to tag along just to listen and enjoy, and the positive energy they contribute is just as valuable as the music itself. (After you have played music for a few years you will start to realize that good listeners are much more rare and precious than good players.) So make sure these people are just as comfortable and just as included as the players.

Whom to invite. This is a delicate subject that is worth thinking about. Personally I feel that music should be democratic in the sense that everybody deserves an equal right to play music as a means of enjoyment and personal growth. But that doesn't mean that everybody plays music for these reasons. For some it's an ego trip and an opportunity to show superiority over others. Now I could tell you that part of your mission in life is to bring these lost sheep into your fold and help them find their happiness in life. But the reality is that some people are so overbearing that their presence is destructive. Only you can make the decision whether to be patient and supportive with these people or whether to send them packing so that the other people in the jam can express themselves without conflict. Since it's not always easy to predict which people will contribute to a positive environment, one nice solution is to propose each jam as a one-time event. That way you can just enjoy each person for what he or she brings, and you don't have to feel obligated to invite all the same people to the next jam session. Remember that a key ingredient in making music is *space*. If any musician consumes too much space, the rest have no room to work. So don't be shy about restricting invitations. It's actually a big part of your responsibility.

Values. Don't assume that just because you feel non-judgmental toward others means that they automatically know this about you. Many people are terrified by the idea of improvising in public. They are afraid that they won't know what to do, that they will become blocked or simply that nobody will like what they play. Your job as a host is to make sure everyone "gets it" that this is about having fun and listening to each other, and not about showing off or comparing one person to another. You can say this explicitly or just weave it into your conversations. But one way or another, make sure everybody knows that this is a safe place for playing, experimenting, expressing ourselves and making mistakes.

Making music

Here are a few musical games and activities to get you started. Once people get comfortable they often start inventing their own ways to make music together. When that starts to happen, you can let go of whatever agenda you had coming in. Think of these ideas as nothing more than optional ice breakers and use them only when people are stuck or unsure about how to get started.

Sound Sketches. This is a very simple musical game in which we gradually create a very full sound environment together. It starts with a single musician repeating a single short phrase. The phrase could be as simple as one single note, or it could be a short melody. But the phrase needs to be played repeatedly in rhythm for the entire duration of the game. Then the next musician can add his own short phrase to this environment. Now two musicians are playing together, and the musical environment is more interesting. Each of these two musicians must continue repeating his musical phrase for the entire game. Then the next musician enters with his own contribution, then the next and so on until all musicians are playing. The final result can sometimes be so amazing that people will be laughing out loud. Here is a tip: the sound space fills up very rapidly. So each musician should be careful not to add too many notes to the environment. In fact some of the very best results happen when each musician adds just a single note. As more and more notes fall into place, a very rich environment is created.

Improvisation with Sound Sketches. This is similar to the last game but each musician starts his contribution by playing a brief free improvisation before settling on a repeated phrase. The first musician would improvise freely for a minute or two and then decide upon a short phrase to repeat. When he or she begins repeating a phrase, this is the signal for the next musician to begin improvising freely over this repeated phrase. When the second musician is done improvising, he or she settles on a short phrase to repeat, and adds this phrase to the one still being played by the first musician. This is the signal to the third musician that he or she can now enter, and so on. This goes on until all musicians have done their improvisations and are contributing their short repeated phrases to the overall environment.

Extended improvisation with Sound Sketches. The last game works for any number of people but it will be very short if there aren't many players. But we can keep going with this game even after all of the musicians are in. Once the last person has finished his improvisation and is now playing a repeated phrase, the very first player could simply abandon his or her original repeated phrase and improvise freely again. After improvising, he or she would then invent a new short phrase to repeat and add to the group. Then the second musician can do the same, etc. In this way we can all keep taking turns indefinitely, and the musical background over which we are improvising also keeps changing and evolving continually. This is an especially great game for just two or three people because the changes to the environment are very dramatic whenever anyone changes his part.

Sound Sketches to free improvisation. By simply giving each musician the freedom to *change* his repeated phrase whenever he wants, we open the door to the fascinating world of free improvisation. The difficult thing about free improvisation for beginners is *control*. Since there are so many possibilities, we become paralyzed by our own freedom and we start playing randomly, without ever developing a coherent idea. For this reason, using Sound Sketches is a good way to focus players' attention on a simple musical idea that they can develop and work with however they want. To convert Sound Sketches into a platform for totally free improvisation, all we have to do is give each musician the permission to vary, expand or abandon his repeated phrase whenever he wants. Some people may change their repeated pattern only occasionally whereas others will change their pattern so often that in fact no pattern exists any longer. What they are really doing is freely improvising in a group context. Both extremes are fine as long as everyone is listening to one another and working to make the overall sound beautiful.

True free improvisation. This is just what it sounds like. Every musician can play whatever he or she wants at any time. Each person also has the freedom to *not* play, and this is a critical component of keeping the music interesting. If all musicians are playing all the time, then the overall texture of the music never changes. But simply by dropping out, a musician can dramatically change the sound of the overall group. Then when the musician comes back in, the sound of his instrument will be much more powerful because it is new again. This helps to divide the music into "chapters" and give it a sense of form. The most common stumbling block to free improvisation is getting started. A good way to begin is to let one musician start improvising freely with no accompaniment. By really *listening* to that first musician, we begin to have all sorts of ideas that we can contribute. All you need is a brave volunteer to be the first to start playing. Then others can gradually enter as they begin to have ideas.

Improvisation in a key. This is not a musical game but simply a guiding principle that we can apply to any musical game. Up to now we haven't imposed any restrictions on the notes that people can play. This leads to many wonderful and exotic sounds, since the final result will almost always include notes from all different keys. But it can also be a lot of fun to produce more conventional sounds, similar to what we hear in pop music. To accomplish this, all we need to do is decide on a key and agree to all play using just the notes from that key. Try this variation with any of the exercises above, and you'll notice that the resulting sound is very different. One thing to be aware of is that not all instruments assign the same note name to a given sound. For example when the piano plays the note Bb, this exact same note is called C on the trumpet. But each musician will most likely already know how to handle this translation for his or her instrument. And in any case it's simple enough to check for misunderstandings by having everyone play the agreed upon scale before beginning. If all the scales do not sound the same then there is some confusion somewhere, and it's probably related to these differences in the names of the notes for each instrument. But once everyone is clear about the key in which we are going to improvise, we can play any of the musical games above and the result is guaranteed to be melodic and sensible to the ear.

Improvisation over a chord. This is where the music really begins to sound like the kinds of things we hear on the radio. You are going to use what you learned in Exercise 3 to create a coherent musical environment for everybody to solo over. To create the backdrop of a particular chord, we just need to designate a "rhythm section" to provide the harmonic environment. These might be two or three horn players or they might be the more traditional harmonic instruments like guitar, bass and piano. But in any case, the way that these musicians can create the feeling of a particular chord is simply to restrict their playing to just the notes of that chord. The nice thing is that it's not necessary for them to understand where chords come from as you do. You can just tell them what notes they are allowed to use. For example, let's say we have agreed to play in the key of C and you propose an improvisation over the 2 chord. You would just think through the notes of the 2 chord in the key of C (the notes are D, F, A and C). Tell the members of your rhythm section that their job is to create an accompaniment that uses just these four notes. They can build this accompaniment together using the very same principle we saw in Sound Sketches. When they have their accompaniment together, the other musicians can take turn soloing over this accompaniment. The soloists don't have to know anything about the notes of the 2 chord. Their job is to use all seven notes of the key of C to improvise freely by ear.

Improvisation over a chord progression. This is the same idea, but instead of having the rhythm section maintain a single chord, now we might imagine alternating between two different chords or even compose a short line that involves many different chords. It all depends on the skill and comfort level of the musicians that will make up the rhythm section. For the soloists, these new chords don't represent any additional complexity since they don't have to know anything about the chords. Their job is just to solo freely in the key of the music. But for the rhythm section the job can get complicated quickly, so you might want to stick with just a couple of chords in the beginning. A simple alternation between two chords can be a fantastic backdrop that is very inspiring to solo over.

Playing popular songs. If your jam includes a guitarist or piano player, they may know the chords to one or more popular songs. If you are able to recognize what key these songs are in, then you can explain to the other musicians how to find the key so that they can improvise along with the music. This is an idea that you may not be able to take advantage of right now. But soon you will be an expert in recognizing chord progressions and keys by ear, and you can use this knowledge to help everyone else make music together.

Playing jazz standards. If the musicians in your jam session are more advanced, they may already have experience improvising over jazz standards. Any standard that is based mostly in the same key is very easy to solo over. All you have to do is tell people which notes belong to the key of the song. But many jazz standards involve several key changes. For musicians who already have a certain level of skill, this makes jazz standards a lot of fun to play. But for a beginner it can be very frustrating. If you have some people who want to play standards and others who simply can't follow along, you could propose to the beginners that they take a break and let the jazz players have their fun. The other option is to insist that all musical games be inclusive of everyone. But usually people are more than happy to take a break and let others shine, especially if they've already had lots of opportunities to shine themselves. You'll know what's best in the moment.

I hope these ideas have stimulated your own creativity. We could go on inventing musical games for a long time and I encourage you to do that on your own. Also don't underestimate the people you invite to your jam. Once you get them started they will probably invent their own games that are even better than the ones presented here.

I will leave you with one final thought. It has to do with keeping the magic alive while everyone is playing. The most important contribution you make to a jam session is not in the musical games you propose, nor in the notes you play on your instrument. It's in what you are doing while *other* people are soloing. When someone else is taking a solo, listen to every single note they play. When we are improvising we very often feel unsatisfied with our own playing, because we are not quite able to express what we want to. There may be just one precious moment in which we have a beautiful idea and we execute it perfectly. You need to be present for that moment, both for your own enrichment and so that the player has someone with whom to celebrate that victory.

Sun and Moon

Of the seven harmonic environments that you have been exploring, there are two that are so important in our music that they overshadow all the others. In fact almost every song in the world is built around one of these two tonal centers. They are as fundamental to our music as are the Sun and the Moon to our poetry.

One represents warmth, light and happiness. The other represents darkness, mystery and melancholy. Together they offer such an enormous range of feelings that many musicians do not realize that they are simply two different chords of the major scale. And these two tonal centers are so famous that even non-musicians are perfectly familiar with the technical words we use to describe them: Major and Minor.

These two tonal centers are the 1 chord and the 6 chord. You can appreciate the differences between these two harmonic environments by comparing them side by side:

1 · 2 · 3 4 · 5 · 6 · 7 1

6 · 7 1 · 2 · 3 4 · 5 · 6

Using the first scale as a reference, notice how the shape of the second scale is different. Look closely at the exact places where the two scales are different. Notice that there are three notes that fall in different places:

For the next few months, I want you to pay special attention to these two tonal centers in your practicing. Of course you should continue your investigation the other chords as well. All seven harmonic environments are beautiful and important, and each one has a very specific lesson to teach you. But try to set aside a little bit of time each week to pay special attention to the two most important tonal centers in our music.

I am now going to show you a wonderful exercise that will teach you more about these two tonal centers than all the theory in the world. It is really just a very specific way to do Exercise 3. The exercise is called Sun and Moon and we'll do it in two parts. Once you get accustomed to this simplified version you can move on to the full version.

Sun and Moon (beginner level)

1. Pick any starting note at random on your instrument and we'll make this note 1.

2. Using all of the techniques you learned in Exercise 3, practice making music in the 1

chord. Remember that you can use Seven Worlds Expanded, Home Chords and Accompanied Singing, as well as any other musical game or exercise that you invent yourself.

$$①\quad 2\quad ③\quad 4\quad ⑤\quad 6\quad ⑦$$

3. Once you have thoroughly investigated the musical possibilities that the 1 chord offers, it's time to flip the tonal center to minor and see how that changes things. Go back to your original starting note, the one that you have been using as note 1. Now we are going to consider this very same note to be note 6 instead of note 1. Play the entire major scale from this note 6 to the next note 6 one octave higher. Improvise for a minute in this new key to get used to the new notes. Then use all of the same techniques from Exercise 3 to practice making music in the 6 chord.

$$⑥\quad 7\quad ①\quad 2\quad ③\quad 4\quad ⑤$$

4. Now alternate between steps 2 and 3. Improvise for a while in the 1 chord, with your starting note representing note 1 of the major scale. Then improvise for a while in the 6 chord, with your starting note representing note 6 of the major scale. Notice exactly which notes change when you switch between the two environments. Notice how the overall *mood* of your music changes as well.

You could spend several weeks playing around with the above exercise in all keys. Don't rush. Remember that your goal is not merely to master the technical details but to make your own important personal discoveries. In terms of theory, the shift from major to minor is a simple one. A few of the notes move to new places and there isn't much more to the story. On a purely technical level you'll probably have the above exercise mastered on the first day. But the way that these changes affect your mood, and the hypnotic effect that these two environments have on the *emotions* in your music, is something very profound.

There is something that we haven't talked about very much yet, but I would like to say a few words about it now. When we began this practice, we started by using very light words about musical games, wandering around freely and being playful. I began this way on purpose because some people are intimidated by words like "free improvisation". It's scary enough to journey out into that dark and mysterious world of harmony for the first time. We don't need the additional pressure of having to put on a show or make something that sounds musical.

But you're not a beginner any longer, and hopefully the world of harmony isn't feeling so dark and mysterious anymore. So as you continue to grow in your daily practice, you might want to take a step back and reflect on what it is that you are actually doing. Your practicing can still be light and fun, but I think you probably already have a sense that you are no longer just playing games. You are creating music, and your music expresses something. Every time you sit down to practice the IFR method, what you are really practicing is your ability to create music spontaneously. So I encourage you to really take your time with the above exercise. Don't just walk through it as a technical exercise. Use it as a *creative exercise*. Every note you play is a challenge to bring out your best, to express something personal and beautiful. There are no unimportant notes. So don't be satisfied with mastering the material on a technical level. The real challenge is to see what you can express with this material.

Sun and Moon - Mastery Level

When you get to the point where you can instantly visualize both harmonic environments (major and minor) in any key on your instrument, and their differences have come to have a personal meaning for you, then you are ready to create actual song forms based around these two tonal centers. This is what we do in the full version of Sun and Moon.

1. Pick any starting note at random on your instrument and we'll make this note 1.

2. We are going to practice improvising over a very simple song form. We will use the 1 chord as the tonal center, and we will use just one other chord as a departure from the 1 chord. Every time you do this exercise you should choose a different chord to contrast with the 1 chord. This time, as an example let's choose the 4 chord. Imagine a simple song based on these two chords:

3. To better understand the harmony of this simple song, make your own tonal map that shows the flow of the consonant notes between these two musical environments:

4. Using all of the techniques you learned in Exercise 3, practice making music over this simple song form. Remember to investigate both chords using Seven Worlds Expanded, Melody Paths, Home Chords and Accompanied Singing.

5. Once you have thoroughly investigated the musical possibilities that this pair of chords offers you, it's time to flip the tonal center to minor. Go back to your original starting note, the one that you have been using as note 1. Now we are going to consider this very same note to be note 6 instead of note 1. Play the entire major scale from this note 6 to the next note 6 one octave higher. Improvise for a minute in this new key to get used to the new notes.

6. Now we are going to reproduce the same song form we used earlier, but this time the entire song will be based around the minor tonal center, which is the 6 chord. The

first chord in the song will obviously be the 6 chord, but we need to figure out what the other chord needs to be. What we want to preserve is the *relationship* between the two chords. In our earlier example, we alternated between the 1 chord and the 4 chord. One way to clearly see the relationship between these two chords is simply to imagine yourself walking up the scale from note 1 to note 4:

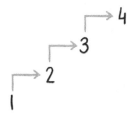

This is the exact same movement that we need to preserve in the new tonal center:

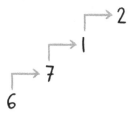

As you can see, if we want to reproduce the same harmonic movement in the minor tonal center, we need to go up to the 2 chord. So here is what the original song would look like if it were based around the minor tonal center of the 6 chord:

7. Again, you can draw your own tonal map of these two chords to see clearly how the harmony flows across the two harmonic environments.

8. Now use all of the techniques you learned in Exercise 3 to practice making music over this song form. On a purely emotional level as a listener, notice what this song has in

common with the earlier song you created using the 1 chord and the 4 chord. Notice also what is different about the two songs.

9.   Go back and forth between steps 4 and 8. Spend ten minutes in the major tonality using chords 1 and 4. Then spend ten minutes making music in the minor tonality using chords 6 and 2. Notice how the scale itself changes when you switch between major and minor, and how this affects the sound of your music.

Sun and Moon is a pretty advanced way to practice Exercise 3. You shouldn't attempt this exercise until you have mastered all seven harmonic environments by themselves. But once you have become totally comfortable making music in any one of the seven harmonic environments, from that point on you could use Sun and Moon as your primary technique for studying pure harmony. Each time you do it you will select a different starting note to use as your tonal center, and a different chord to contrast with the 1 chord. The consequence of these two simple variables is that you will eventually end up studying every possible harmonic relationship in every possible key, in both major and minor tonality. This makes Sun and Moon - Mastery Level an incredibly compact exercise that allows you to practice everything you have seen in the IFR method up to now.

I want to end this chapter with some thoughts about pacing. You may have noticed that every time I rattle off one of these exercises for you, I am giving you perhaps *months* of work to keep you busy. Try to remember that they are not homework assignments and there is no "due date". They are just ideas for a rainy day. Whenever you feel like immersing yourself in the world of harmony, my hope is that you will open up this book and quickly find an activity that sounds fun and interesting. So please remember that IFR is not something that you can ever actually finish. You don't even need to personally experience every exercise that I show you. They are all just ideas and possibilities. The most important guiding principle is what I told you in the very beginning of this book. This entire musical practice is exclusively for your own enjoyment. Our only goal is for you to learn how to use your instrument as the doorway to your own personal paradise. If you have already found that doorway for yourself, then the truth is that it really doesn't make any difference what you study from here on. *Everything* you do in your private world of harmony will cause you to learn and grow. So just take in new harmonic concepts according to your own appetite. Go off and have fun with whatever you know currently. When you're hungry for more, come back and we'll look at something new.

Tension and Release (in melody)

One of the defining characteristics of Western music is the constant interplay of Tension and Release. In our music barely a second goes by that doesn't involve this little story playing itself out in one way or another. In fact our music is so filled with this interplay that it would be literally impossible to count all of the times that we feel these two sensations during the course of a typical song.

Whenever you work on IFR Exercise 3: Pure Harmony, one of the areas of awareness that you are developing has to do with the difference between the "chord notes" in any harmonic environment and the "other notes" of the scale. For example in the first harmonic environment, the chord notes are 1, 3, 5 and 7 and the other notes are 2, 4 and 6. Actually, my definition of the 1 chord as being just the notes 1, 3, 5 and 7 is kind of an oversimplification. But it's a useful one, especially in the beginning. For the beginner trying to make sense of this immense world of sounds and sensations, a good first step is just to lump all of the notes together into two broad categories: chord notes and other notes.

Think for a minute about this dynamic between chord notes and other notes. When you are improvising in Seven Worlds Expanded and you are using all seven notes of the scale, do you notice how the chord notes *continue* to be the most consonant notes? In other words, can you feel the sensations of Tension and Release in your music as you move from one of the "other notes" to one of the chord notes? If not, go back and practice this very slowly and pay attention to what you feel.

The next time you listen to your favorite album, I want you to try to notice these same sensations of Tension and Release in your body. Don't think about it too much. Remember that it's not about guessing how the music works or trying to figure out what the individual musicians were thinking. It's about *noticing* what the music actually does to you. Just direct your attention inward, and see if you can find a few moments that you can clearly identify as moments of great tension followed by a pleasant relaxation in your body.

But also remember that these concepts are subjective and they are only metaphors. You can't literally label every single note as either Tension or Release. A note might seem relaxed when compared to the previous note but tense when compared to the notes which follow it. So you shouldn't try to label every single moment as either Tension or Release. I just want you to become aware of these feelings in your body when they arise.

Now we'll look at an exercise that could be thought of as the mastery level of Exercise 3. At this level we have awareness of every single note in the chromatic scale and we practice using all of these notes in our music. It may help you to continue to mentally organize these notes into separate categories, but now there are *three* categories:

- the *chord* notes (the four notes that make up the chord)
- the *other* notes (the remaining three notes of the scale)
- the *outside* notes (the five notes outside the key, or the little black dots on our drawing of the tonal map)

Playing outside notes is not difficult. What is difficult is maintaining control of your music while doing so. As you do the following exercise, make a constant effort to keep the harmonic environment alive by spending most of your time in the chord notes and the other notes of the scale. Save the outside notes for special moments, at least in the beginning. This will help you get to know them without destroying the overall coherence of your music.

Exercise 3: Pure Harmony - Mastery Level

1. Choose a starting note on your instrument and choose one of the seven harmonic environments in which to work. Make drawings of the three different categories of notes in this environment: chord notes, other notes of the scale, and outside notes. In our example, we'll use the 2 chord.

(2)   2

            1#

(1)   1

7   7

            6#

(6)   6

            5#

5   5

            4#

(4)   4

3   3

            2#

(2)   2

2. Using Seven Worlds Expanded or Accompanied Singing, improvise with all three categories of notes. In your first experiences with the outside notes, you might try resolving these notes directly to the nearest scale note. In other words, don't abandon the musical problems you create. Don't leave an outside note hanging there in the air and then go off to some other place to start a new idea. Create the tension and enjoy it for as long as you want but then *resolve* this tension before moving on.

3. Once you have come to really know the sound of all five outside notes, try to incorporate them into your improvisations with Accompanied Singing as well. It will take a lot of concentration in the beginning, but remember that you don't need to master all 5 outside notes on the first day. Just start to include them one at a time in your playing and then little by little strive to also imagine them when you are singing.

4. In general, from now on whenever you practice Exercise 3, try to be aware of all three categories of notes. Include these notes in your consciousness and in your music. When the day comes that you can easily imagine the sound of all twelve notes of the chromatic scale in all seven basic harmonic environments, you can declare yourself to be an absolute master of Pure Harmony.

Tension and Release (in harmony)

In the last chapter we saw how individual notes can create a sensation of tension or relaxation against a particular harmonic backdrop. But in any piece of music, this same drama of Tension and Release is also playing itself out on the level of the harmony itself. As a dissonant chord flows into a more relaxed chord, it produces the exact same sensation of Tension and Release as we have been learning to feel in our melodies.

You can perceive this on some level between any two chords. But there is one particular combination of chords that produces such a clear sensation of Tension and Release that it has become the very engine of harmonic movement in all of our music. This combination is the 5 chord (representing Tension) and the 1 chord (representing Release).

To experience this for yourself, use the techniques you learned in Exercise 3 to study the following simple song form:

To feel the flow of tension and relaxation that occurs in the harmony, try to stay very close to the chord notes in both environments. Don't use a lot of outside notes trying to produce tension *against* the chord of the moment. Just play the chord notes and maybe occasionally the other notes of the scale. In other words, when you are in the 5 chord try to bring out the sound of the 5 chord as clearly as possible. That way when you flow into the 1 chord, you will really feel how the tension of the 5 chord is relaxed in the 1 chord.

On a purely emotional level, notice how the above harmony works. The line begins in tension, and ends in relaxation:

This gives the line a sense of completeness. It gives you the feeling that this could be the very last line of the song. If the song did continue, we could repeat this same line again or we could move on to a different idea. But the current musical statement feels complete when we arrive to the 1 chord.

Now look at what happens if we reverse the order of the two chords:

Emotionally, now we are left in suspense at the end of the line:

Notice how you can feel this tension in your body. When you reach the end of the line you know instinctively that another line must follow. You know that there is no way in the world that the song is going to end on that 5 chord. It just doesn't sound right. It is begging for a resolution.

If you can feel these sensations when you play the chords above, then you already understand these two chords perfectly. We aren't going to go much further with this type of analysis because ultimately what we need to do is return to the world of sounds and just listen to each chord as it really is. But since these two chords play such an important role in creating a sense of harmonic movement in our music, I want to show you some ways we might use them.

Notice from the example above that when we end a musical line in tension (the 5 chord), it has the effect of opening a conversation, as if somebody were asking a *question*. And notice that when we end a musical line in relaxation (the 1 chord), it has the effect of closing the conversation, as if somebody were *answering* a question. What this means is that we could easily structure this dynamic of Tension and Release into a larger form of Question and Answer:

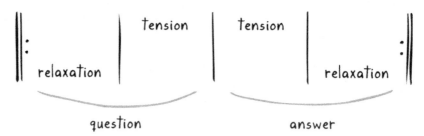

The way we would express this form musically would be with the following harmony:

And sure enough, if you play the above song form you will notice that this is exactly how it feels. Any melody you play across the first two measures will sound like a question. And any melody you play across the final two measures will sound like the answer to this question.

To sharpen your own awareness of Tension and Release in harmony, you should practice improvising over all of the song forms shown in this chapter. These simple exercises will give you a solid grounding in the art of improvising in complete sentences. This lyrical approach to making music will be invaluable to you later on, when you are improvising over much more abstract material.

In addition, when you get to Exercise 4 you will learn how to use these concepts to create a sense of direction and movement *anywhere* in our musical system. In preparation for that, there are just a few key ideas you need to understand from this chapter:

- The 5 chord produces tension, but not just any kind of tension. It produces a very specific kind of tension that causes your ear to expect a resolution to the 1 chord.

- With some sleight of hand, we can use this same technique to cause listeners to feel a very strong attraction toward *any* tonal center.

- This is the concept that we will explore fully in IFR Exercise 4: Mixed Harmony.

Musical shapes

In this chapter we are going to look at the four basic chord shapes that appear in the major scale. You will learn to recognize them by ear, to visualize them on your tonal map and to create them anywhere on your instrument. Mastering these musical shapes is the key to your next step forward as an improviser. It is by altering these shapes that we will create all of the rich and exotic sounds of Mixed Harmony.

The first chord shape is called "major". It has the following form:

$$1 \qquad 3 \qquad 5 \qquad 7$$

You are so familiar with this chord shape that we don't need to do anything special to investigate it any further. This is the chord shape you are using every time you improvise in the 1 chord. So the only new information here is that this type of chord is called "major".

The next chord shape that we find in the major scale has a flatted seventh. We will call this chord shape "dominant". A dominant chord has the following four notes:

$$1 \qquad 3 \qquad 5 \qquad b7$$

To hear the difference between a major chord and a dominant chord, get out your instrument and play both chord shapes. Pick any starting note and make that note 1 of your major scale. Play the entire scale if it helps you orient yourself. Then play just the notes 1, 3, 5 and 7 and improvise with these notes for a minute or two. What you are playing is a major chord. Now lower note 7 by a half step to play the note b7. On our drawing of the major scale, this is the little black dot between notes 6 and 7. As with any altered note, you can visualize exactly where b7 is located by imagining our drawing of the entire major scale:

Improvise for a couple of minutes with just the notes 1, 3, 5 and b7. This is the sound of a dominant chord. Go back and forth between the major chord and the dominant chord until you can feel the difference between them.

The next chord form we find in the major scale is called "minor". It has both a flatted third and a flatted seventh:

$$1 \qquad b3 \qquad 5 \qquad b7$$

Again, you can visualize both of these altered notes using our drawing of the major scale. The new note b3 is just the little black dot between notes 2 and 3:

To get to know this sound for yourself, improvise for a few minutes with just the notes 1, b3, 5 and b7. This is the sound of a minor chord. Compare it to the major chord by switching between the two. Compare both to the dominant chord. Notice how the mood of your music changes when you switch between chord shapes.

The last chord shape we find in the major scale is called "minor flat 5". In this chord shape, everything is flatted except note 1.

1   b3   b5   b7

The new altered note is b5, which is located in between notes 4 and 5 of the major scale:

Improvise for a few minutes with just the notes 1, b3, b5 and b7. This will probably sound strange to your ear. The minor flat 5 chord shape has a very beautiful and mysterious sound, but it's not used very often in popular music except as a transitional chord. So your ear is probably not accustomed to spending a lot of time in this chord. But take your time to enjoy its exotic sound. Remember that anytime a sound strikes your ear as unusual, that means that you are learning something new. Don't shy away from these moments! Embrace them and enjoy the new discovery.

In summary, there are four chord shapes that are found within the major scale:

major	=	1	3	5	7
dominant	=	1	3	5	b7
minor	=	1	b3	5	b7
minor b5	=	1	b3	b5	b7

I haven't shown you *where* these shapes appear yet, but we'll get to that in the next chapter. But before moving on, you should take the time to become an expert in these four chord shapes. It's not enough to just understand them intellectually. Remember the example of Michael Jordan practicing free throws. Mastery takes time. You should study these chord shapes until you learn to hear them, recognize them, imagine them and play them anywhere on your instrument without a moment's hesitation. Here are some ideas that will get you thinking about ways to develop this level of mastery.

Rock Jumping

This exercise reminds me of trying to cross a stream by jumping from one rock to the next. It requires you to visualize clearly the distances between the notes of each chord shape.

1. Choose one of the four chord shapes to study. (For example major.)

2. Pick a random starting note on your instrument and imagine it to be note 1.

3. Now play just the notes of the chord shape you selected (in our example the notes would be 1, 3, 5 and 7). But instead of imagining the entire major scale in order to locate these notes, use what you know about the *distances* between the notes in this chord shape. These distances are shown in the following drawing:

Look closely at this drawing and notice the distances between the chord notes:

- There are 2 whole steps between notes 1 and 3.

- There are 1½ steps between notes 3 and 5.

- There are 2 whole steps between notes 5 and 7.

- There is just a half step between note 7 and the following note 1.

Study this drawing and learn these distances deeply so that you no longer need to visualize the entire scale in order to find the notes of this chord shape. Learn to trust your knowledge of the distances between the notes of the chord so that you can jump directly to each note as if you were jumping from one rock to another in a stream:

4. Improvise with these five notes (notes 1, 3, 5, 7 and note 1 of the next octave) for a few minutes. Relax and take your time to enjoy the sound of this chord. Try to visualize the distances between the notes but also try to really listen to the sound of each note. Be playful and make melodies in every little corner of the above drawing.

But what if you had chosen one of the other three chord shapes to study? Here is the complete set of drawings to help you visualize the jumps between the "rocks" in each chord shape:

Major

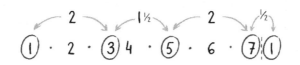

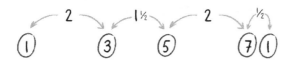

Dominant

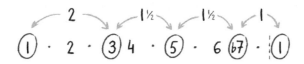

Minor

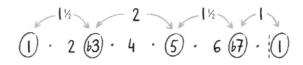

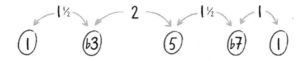

Minor b5

If you have difficulty making the jumps from one note to the next, remember that you already know a very powerful technique for learning to visualize any kind of movement across your musical range. That technique is Exercise 1. So if you find yourself struggling with the rock jumping exercises above, you might want to go back to Exercise 1 and use it to practice the four types of interval jumps that you need in order to make all of the above chord shapes. These four intervals are half steps, whole steps, minor thirds (1½ steps) and major thirds (2 whole steps). Use Exercise 1 to become an expert in moving all around your instrument using these new interval jumps. Then when you come back to the exercises in this chapter you will find them much easier.

Singing the Shapes

Just as I showed you in Exercise 2, the most powerful way to master any musical concept is to study it with nothing but your voice and your imagination. Practicing your instrument is important, but you will grow much faster as a musician if you practice your ability to clearly imagine all of these sounds with no help from an instrument. A good first step is to sing the following two melodies to yourself:

You can use your instrument to hear the sounds first if you need to. But then put your instrument down and create the sounds purely with your voice. You should literally be singing the numbers out loud ("one, three, one.......one, flat three, one").

Now sing the following two melodies:

The two examples above push you to imagine for yourself the difference between major and minor. The difference is in the third, which is flatted in a minor chord.

Now sing the following two melodies. These might be a little harder:

I think you can see where this is going. You can (and should) continue on your own by inventing your own exercises to compare and contrast all of the sounds in all four chord shapes. As with everything else that we have studied, remember that the real power is always in going *deeper*. We are always looking for ways to sharpen our focus so that small differences begin to seem large and obvious. On paper the difference between note 5 and note b5 might seem unimportant. But if you really concentrate and focus on the sound when you sing the two melodies above you will notice a *world* of difference between them!

Naturally we should extend this investigation to the 7th. We could begin by comparing a major chord to a dominant chord, since the only difference between them is that the seventh is flatted in the dominant chord:

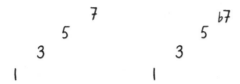

Also, don't forget to practice moving in the other direction. For example, sing the following two melodies for a different perspective on the difference between note 7 and note b7.

And don't forget to start in other places. For example, sing any random pitch and imagine to yourself that this is note 5. What would the following two melodies sound like:

We could go on all day inventing ways to imagine ourselves inside each of the four basic chord shapes. Take your time, improvise freely and enjoy yourself. Get to know every little corner of each one of these chord shapes. Practice them with both your instrument and your voice until you feel just as comfortable with them as you feel with the major scale itself.

And if you want to *really* master these sounds, you can even combine the notes in ways that *do not* appear in the major scale. Here are a couple of examples that you should try to sing for "extra credit". These shapes do not appear anywhere in the major scale, but as an exercise they are a wonderful way to prove to yourself that you really are beginning to understand all of these sounds. Try the following combinations just for fun. You'll notice that their exotic sound is a dead giveaway that these shapes are not found directly within the major scale:

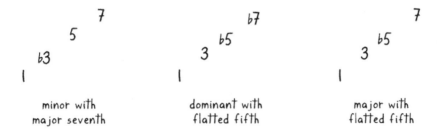

Extended Rock Jumping

In this exercise we take our rock jumping practice to the next level. We now learn to see each chord shape just as we have learned to see the major scale, as an infinite pattern with no beginning and no end. We will extend each chord shape across our entire musical range.

1. Choose one of the four chord shapes to study. (For example dominant.)

2. Choose one of the four notes of this chord shape. (For example flat 7.)

3. Pick a random starting note on your instrument. (For example C#.) Play this note for a moment and imagine that you are on the flatted seventh of a dominant chord. Don't worry about where the other notes of the chord are located. Most people instinctively become anxious at this point. They think they need to know where the root of the chord is in order to feel oriented. But as improvisers we need to get accustomed to feeling at home no matter where we might be. So just hang out here for a moment and try to get used to the idea that you are playing the flatted seventh of a dominant chord. This is the only orientation you need:

4. Now instead of imagining yourself in a stream, I want you to imagine that you are in the middle of a vast ocean. You are standing on a rock named b7. An infinite series of rocks stretches out both in front of you and behind you. The rocks are the notes of this dominant chord stretched across your entire musical range:

b7   I   3   5   (b7)   I   3   5   b7

5. Begin moving in either direction and go as far as you like. For each movement, all you have to do is visualize clearly the distance required for each jump.

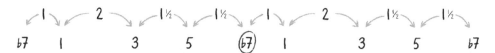

6. When you arrive to each new note, take a minute to rest and reflect on exactly where you are in the chord. Just hang out on this new note for a minute and don't worry about how you will make your next jump. It's important to realize that the only piece of information you require is simply the knowledge of where you are. Just knowing which note you are on gives you all the information you need to make the next jump upward or downward.

7. Once you are comfortable making these jumps across your entire musical range, take time to improvise with these notes. You will find that there are many new melodic possibilities available now that you can cross into different octaves.

Floating Arpeggio Studies

This is by far my favorite way to study musical shapes on any instrument. It's very reminiscent of Exercise 1. It's actually a lot easier than the previous exercise. But even so, for me personally this is the most powerful exercise I have ever discovered for developing a deep personal mastery of these musical shapes.

1. Choose one of the four chord shapes to study. (For example minor b5.)

2. Choose one of the four notes of the chord shape. (For example b3.)

3. Pick a random starting note on your instrument. (For example G.)

4. Play this note (G in our example) and imagine that you are currently on the flatted third of a minor b5 chord. (G = b3).

5. Close your eyes. Relax and try to enter your most meditative state of mind. Don't think about completing the exercise or trying to "learn" anything consciously. We're just going to relax here and enjoy making some very simple movements.

6. Play your starting note several times and really listen to it. Remember that we decided that this starting note is b3 of the chord:

$$b3$$

7. Now we're going to move up to the next note of this same chord. In our example, you would move up 1½ steps to the note b5. But before going further, we are going to just play with these two notes for a couple of minutes. Enjoy the relationship between b3 and b5 and notice how this interval sounds. Think to yourself the names "flat 3" and "flat 5" as you play each note.

$$b3 \qquad b5$$

8. Now move up another level and add the next note of the chord. In our example you would need to go up 2 whole steps to the note b7. And then stay here to improvise for a couple of minutes with all three notes b3, b5 and b7.

$$b3 \qquad b5 \qquad b7$$

9. Here is where the exercise takes a different turn. We are not going to expand our focus any more. Three is the perfect number of notes to let us contemplate and compare distances. So just enjoy these three notes for a couple of minutes more, and notice their separations. Notice how the distance between notes b3 and b5 is slightly smaller than the distance between notes b5 and b7.

10. Now what we will do is *shift* our focus upward to the next set of three notes. We are not expanding our focus as we did in Exercise 1. Instead we simply want to direct our attention upward, to the next group of three notes. To do so, we are going to drop

the lowest note and add a new chord note on top. In our example, we would let go of the note b3 and add note 1 on top. Improvise with these three notes for a few minutes and notice the distances between them as you play:

$$♭5 \qquad ♭7 \qquad 1$$

11. Continue to shift your focus upward or downward as you like, but always maintain your focus on exactly three notes of the extended chord. This practice of paying special attention to just one small part of a musical shape is a tremendous way to develop your understanding of the entire shape. It's also an important experience for your ear, because it introduces you to a wide variety of special sounds that are found within each of these musical shapes. If you can just relax and take the time to improvise freely with each set of three notes, you can lose yourself in this exercise for hours.

I suggest you practice these exercises for a few weeks or even months before moving on. The four basic chord shapes that appear in the major scale are the raw material of all modern harmony. So if you want to keep growing as an improviser, this is the place to concentrate all of your energy. A good goal to set for yourself is to be able to pick up your instrument, pick any random note and start playing any of the four chord shapes immediately without any hesitation. You should also be able to do the same with your voice. From any starting pitch you should be able to imagine and sing the notes to any one of the four chord shapes.

This can be a long term project that you can practice in parallel with all of the other things that you are doing in your musical life. But I don't recommend going any further in this book until you have really made these chord shapes your own. Be patient and find ways to enjoy making music with these four simple shapes. There is no hurry to advance to the next chapter. You'll go much farther as a musician if you take the time to get to know each of these chord shapes intimately. Once you have them mastered, you will be amazed by how simple Mixed Harmony really is.

Measuring distances

Now that you are an expert (or at least on your way to becoming one) in the four basic chord shapes, it's time to discover where these musical shapes are found within the major scale. To do this, I want to present a new concept to you. It has to do with a different way to use our drawing of the major scale. Up to now we have been using it as our *map* of the musical terrain in any key. No matter what note or chord we might have been playing, we always oriented ourselves relative to this map. But now we are going to use the exact same drawing in a very different way, almost as if it were a *tape measure*. We will use it to measure the distances between notes. This will lead to many profound observations that will help you to understand where Mixed Harmony really comes from.

A word of caution before we begin: you might need to read this chapter more than once to understand everything. It can sometimes be confusing when we start using the same drawing of the major scale in two different ways at the same time. But if you remember the two metaphors of a map and a tape measure, it will help you avoid getting confused.

First let's lay our map on the ground. We need to use a large map of two full octaves so that we can analyze all seven chords of the major scale:

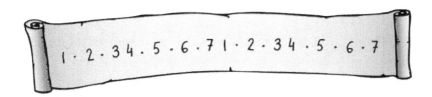

Now imagine another copy of the major scale floating above this one. This floating major scale will serve as our tape measure. It lets us see the dimensions of each chord and decide which chord shape each one is. If we place our tape measure directly over the 1 chord in our map, aligning note 1 on our tape measure with note 1 on our map, we see that obviously both drawings are the same. In the case of the 1 chord this doesn't show us any new information. The 1 chord is by definition a major chord:

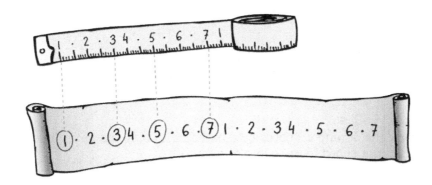

But now let's use our tape measure to analyze the 2 chord. We do this by lining up note 1 on our tape measure with note 2 on our tonal map:

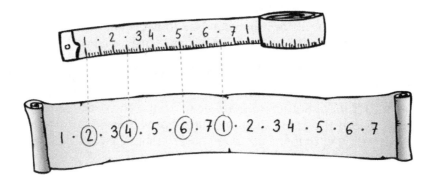

If you look closely at this drawing you'll notice that the notes of the 2 chord (notes 2, 4, 6 and 1 on the tonal map) do not all line up perfectly with notes 1, 3, 5 and 7 on our tape measure. This means that the 2 chord is of a different *shape* than the 1 chord. The distances indicated by our tape measure tell us what shape the 2 chord is. Look at where the dotted lines intersect with the tape measure. Can you see that the distances marked are 1, b3, 5 and b7? What this means is that the 2 chord is a minor chord, because the shape of the 2 chord corresponds perfectly to our definition of a minor chord (1, b3, 5, b7).

Don't be in a rush to understand how you will eventually use this observation. Just keep following along. Later you will do exercises in which you learn to internalize, visualize and *hear* all of this material.

(Playing activity)

You can confirm the above observation for yourself using your instrument:

1. Pick any starting note. (For this example, let's choose the note F.)

2. Make this note 1 of your scale, and play the entire major scale from this note 1 to the following note 1, an octave higher:

$$1 \quad \cdot \quad 2 \quad \cdot \quad 3 \quad 4 \quad \cdot \quad 5 \quad \cdot \quad 6 \quad \cdot \quad 7 \quad 1$$

3. Now improvise for a moment with just the notes of a major chord where F is note 1:

$$1 \qquad 3 \qquad 5 \qquad 7$$

4. Now lower the 3rd and 7th notes by a half step to play the notes b3 and b7. Improvise with this minor chord for a couple of minutes:

$$1 \qquad b3 \qquad 5 \qquad b7$$

5. Now erase this scale from your mind and go back to your original starting note (the note "F" in our example). This time "F" is going to be note 2 of the major scale, and we are going to play the entire major scale from this note 2 to the following note 2 one octave higher:

$$2 \cdot 3\,4 \cdot 5 \cdot 6 \cdot 7\,1 \cdot 2$$

6. Play this scale a few times and then improvise for a couple of minutes with just the notes of the 2 chord:

$$2 \qquad 4 \qquad 6 \qquad 1$$

7. As both your ears and your hands will recognize, you are playing the exact same notes you played earlier in step 4. This is all I want you to realize. The notes themselves are really just notes 2, 4, 6 and 1 of the major scale. But now we are learning to see the *distances* between them. And the way that we summarize all of the distances found within a particular chord is to notice its overall chord shape (major, dominant, minor or minor b5). Later we will do more exercises to gain confidence with these two different ways to visualize the notes. But for now I just want you to understand that neither of the two points of view is "correct" or better than the other. They are simply two different ways to understand where the notes are, and we need both of them.

Now let's measure the distances between the notes of the 3 chord:

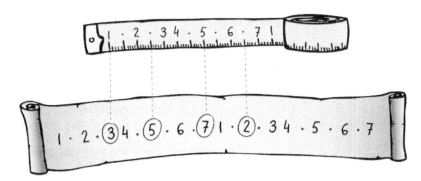

If you look closely you'll see that the notes of the 3 chord line up with notes 1, b3, 5 and b7 on the tape measure. This means that the 3 chord is a minor chord also, just like the 2 chord. In other words, while the notes themselves are different, the *separations* between the notes in the 3 chord are the same as the separations between the notes in the 2 chord. They both have the same chord shape.

Now let's look at the dimensions of the 4 chord:

161

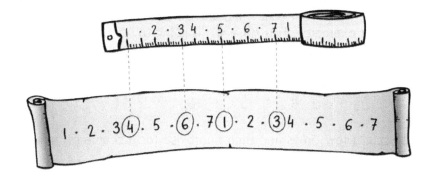

The notes of the 4 chord line up perfectly with notes 1, 3, 5 and 7 on our tape measure. This means that the 4 chord is a major chord, just like the 1 chord.

Now let's measure the 5 chord:

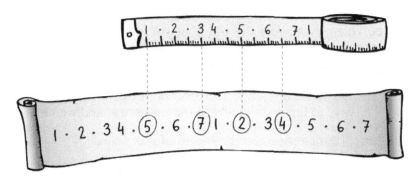

The notes of the 5 chord line up with the notes 1, 3, 5 and b7 on our tape measure. This means that the 5 chord is a dominant chord.

It's time to analyze the 6 chord, but you already know what the answer will be. You learned in the chapter "Sun and Moon" that the 6 chord is the most important minor chord in our music. Our tape measure analysis confirms that the 6 chord is indeed a minor chord:

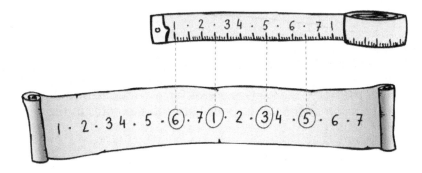

There is only one more chord left to analyze. Let's take a look at the 7 chord:

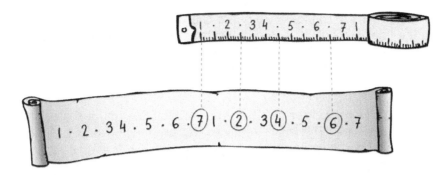

The notes of the 7 chord line up with notes 1, b3, b5 and b7 on our tape measure. And so finally we discover where the chord shape "minor b5" is found within the major scale. It is the 7 chord that has this strange and exotic sounding shape.

So let's summarize all of these observations:

I chord = major
2 chord = minor
3 chord = minor
4 chord = major
5 chord = dominant
6 chord = minor
7 chord = minor b5

Now I can finally show you the real symbols that we use in IFR to describe the seven chords of the major scale. These symbols will seem redundant at first but you will understand their usefulness when we begin altering chord shapes to create the sounds of Mixed Harmony.

For major chords we don't use any additional symbol. The two major chords in the major scale are the 1 chord and the 4 chord. So these will be written as simply the numbers 1 and 4:

1   4

For minor chords we use a hyphen after the number to indicate that the chord is minor. The minor chords in the major scale are chords 2, 3 and 6. So these chords will appear as follows:

2-   3-   6-

We will indicate dominant chords by using the letter D. The only dominant chord in the major scale is the 5 chord, which we will write as follows:

5D

163

And finally we need a symbol to indicate a minor chord with a flatted 5th. We will use a hyphen combined with the "b5" symbol. It is the 7 chord that has this chord shape:

$$7-b5$$

So here now is the final chord chart of all seven chords of the major scale, using the correct symbols for each chord type. This chart replaces the preliminary drawing that I showed you earlier in the chapter "The seven harmonic environments".

⑦	7	⑦	7	⑦	7	⑦
6	⑥	6	⑥	6	⑥	⑥
⑤	5	⑤	5	⑤	⑤	5
4	④	4	④	④	4	④
③	3	③	③	3	③	3
2	②	②	2	②	2	②
①	①	1	①	1	①	1
1	2-	3-	4	5D	6-	7-b5

Right now you don't need to do anything with these new symbols. But please take a minute to look at the drawing above and get comfortable with these new written names for the seven chords of the major scale. We can still refer casually to the chords as the "1 chord", the "2 chord", etc. when we are talking about them. But I will use these new symbols whenever I need to write the chords out in a tonal sketch or in a musical example.

If you're feeling a bit confused at this point, don't worry. It's perfectly normal at this stage to feel uneasy. First of all you might find it hard to follow my explanations above with the tonal map and the tape measure. And secondly you're probably wondering what the heck you are supposed to do with this information. But just be patient. The answers are coming. Once you've had a chance to work with this material, you'll come back to the drawings in this chapter and you'll understand them perfectly. In fact they will seem so obvious to you that you will probably have trouble remembering what the big deal was all about.

Cutting and pasting musical shapes

You are about to take the biggest leap forward of our entire journey together. With just one simple new concept you are going to multiply your capabilities by a hundred. And in the process, you will finally have all the tools you need to comprehend and play *every* song you have ever heard.

The secret to this new ability lies in understanding where Mixed Harmony really comes from. The origin of Mixed Harmony (as the name implies) is the mixing and rearranging of the basic sounds that we studied in Pure Harmony. By simply cutting and pasting these sounds to other important locations, we can produce all of the rich and sophisticated sounds of Mixed Harmony without any new theory whatsoever.

The reason I didn't show you this concept earlier is that it wouldn't have done you any good without a deep personal mastery of the major scale. You need to be something of an expert in seeing musical shapes before you can begin to imagine them in other locations. But now that you have had some time to work with the four basic chord shapes, it's time to start using them to create new sounds within the tonal landscape.

The most important metaphor in all of Mixed Harmony is that of Tension and Release. You have already learned how the 5D chord and the 1 chord produce these sensations to create the sense of direction and movement in a piece of music. Your first activity in Mixed Harmony is to see how these same concepts can be used to create a sense of movement *anywhere* in our musical system.

The key to this movement is the 5D chord. Its dominant shape creates a very particular kind of tension that is perfectly resolved in the 1 chord. Just hearing the 5D chord is enough to make us subconsciously expect and want a resolution to the 1 chord. So if we want to create this same sense of attraction toward *any* location in our musical system, we just have to put a temporary 5D chord in the right place. This "right place" is easy to visualize if you look at where the 5D chord actually sends you.

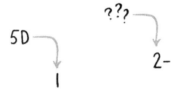

Look at the above drawing and ask yourself this question: if a dominant chord placed at note 5 causes your ear to expect the 1 chord, then where would we have to place a dominant chord in order to cause the ear to expect the 2- chord?

If you guessed note 6 you are correct. By placing a dominant chord at note 6 we create the *illusion* of a 5D chord at this location. This causes the ear to crave a resolution to its beloved 1 chord. But since we have placed this artificial dominant chord at note 6, we actually trick the ear into feeling an attraction toward the 2- chord.

The way we do this is to simply alter the shape of the 6- chord so that it becomes a dominant chord. We will call this new chord "6 dominant" and we will write it as "6D". The 6D chord causes the ear to expect and desire a resolution to the 2- chord.

But what does this look like in practice? What are the actual notes that make up the harmony of this moment? The answer to this question lies in understanding that these altered chords are nothing more than a *temporary deformation* of the basic harmonic environment. They do not represent a change of key, which is an error that is commonly taught in modern improvisation courses. Genuine key changes do exist and we will talk about them a little later. But the vast majority of Mixed Harmony has nothing to do with changing keys. It has to do with making slight alterations to the original harmonic environment in order to suggest different feelings.

If you understand that this is the true origin of Mixed Harmony, you'll never have to wonder what "scale" to play over a particular chord. The question itself becomes irrelevant because you already have all of the notes right there on your tonal map. All you have to do is make whatever adjustments are necessary to accommodate the new chord shape.

If my explanation sounds complicated, don't worry. In practice, the application of this concept is the simplest thing in the world. To see how it works, take a look at the following chord progression which is very common in American pop and jazz music:

```
 (7)    7      7     (7)
  6    (6)    (6)     6
 (5)   (5)     5     (5)
  4     4     (4)    (4)
 (3)   (3)     3      3
  2     2     (2)    (2)
 (1)   (1)    (1)     1
 ___   ___    ___    ___
  I    6-     2-     5D
```

Since we know that the 6D chord creates a strong feeling of attraction toward the 2- chord, it shouldn't surprise us to find that one of the most common variations on the above progression is to replace the 6- chord with 6D. The new chord progression is the following:

I   6D   2-   5D

Now the question becomes, "Which notes do I need to modify in the 6- chord in order to make it a dominant chord?" If you remember our analysis of the 6- chord, we saw that the notes of 6- are arranged in a minor chord shape. That is to say, the four notes of the 6- chord (notes 6, 1, 3, and 5) are in the positions of 1, b3, 5 and b7 relative to note 6:

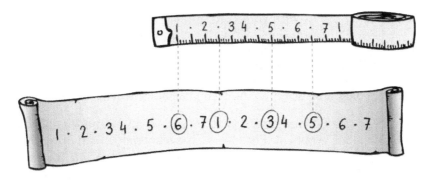

But the notes of a dominant chord would be 1, 3, 5 and b7 relative to the starting note. The difference is in the 3rd of the chord. A minor chord has a flatted 3rd and a dominant chord has a natural 3rd. So in order to create a dominant chord we need to raise the 3rd of the chord by a half step:

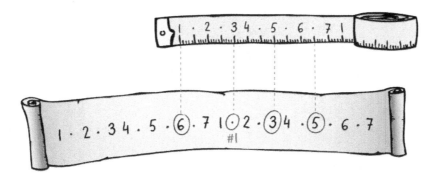

That's it. All we need to do to create the 6D harmonic environment is replace note 1 with note #1. The rest of the notes remain unchanged:

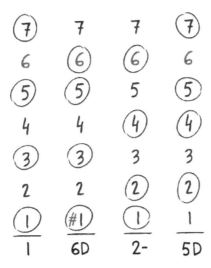

You'll begin to work with these Mixed Harmony environments in Exercise 4. But just to get a sense of how easy it can be to create these sounds in your music, you can take a few minutes now to play through the above chord progression. You can study it using any of the techniques you learned in Exercise 3, either with your own primary instrument or with a piano.

What I want you to notice about this approach to studying harmony is how much information can be reduced to such a simple final result. The only new information here is really just the altered note #1. In other words, the entire harmonic environment of 6D can be summarized by remembering that the only alteration to the basic harmonic environment is the note #1.

And through our daily practice we can learn to integrate all of these concepts together and turn them all into one giant synonym. For me, #1 is synonymous with 6D which is synonymous with pushing the ear forward to 2-. Most importantly, I have come to know these sounds personally so that I can recognize them and use them without even consciously thinking about their names. Through the daily practice of Exercise 4, you too will develop this ability.

Exercise 4: Mixed Harmony

<u>Objective</u>: To continuously improve in your ability to...

Recognize and create temporary deformations to the basic harmonic environment.

Exercise 4 is a simple and personal approach to studying modern harmony that will give you the freedom to continue learning and growing on your own for the rest of your life. Instead of using theory to try to explain unusual chords and tell you what scales to play over them, I am going to teach you a method that empowers you to discover and understand these chords for yourself.

At a high level, our method consists of incorporating each new sound into our tonal vision and studying it just as we have studied the seven basic chords of the major scale. In this way each new sound becomes integrated into our personal repertoire. Then whenever this sound appears in a song we will recognize it immediately, no matter what key the song might be in. And of course the new sound will also always be available for us to use in our own music.

In IFR Exercise 3: Pure Harmony you learned a wide variety of powerful exercises that you can use to enter and explore the seven basic harmonic environments of the major scale. Essentially, you could think of Exercise 4 as an endless landscape of new harmonic environments to explore. You don't need any new tools or understanding to conquer this new terrain. Since you already know how to explore any harmonic environment and make it your own, these same "exploring skills" are all you need to discover the vast world of Mixed Harmony.

As you learned in the last chapter, Mixed Harmony always involves some kind of deformation to the basic harmonic environment. These alterations create all kinds of exotic sounding scales with new melodic possibilities. So while our visual model of harmony is very easy to understand and practice, the actual sounds we create can be as abstract or as complex as we want them to be. Mastering these new sounds and learning to express something personal with them takes time. So the very first thing you should do with any new harmonic environment from Mixed Harmony is to study it patiently and lovingly, using all of the techniques you learned in Exercise 3.

For now, don't worry about trying to understand how you will eventually use these new Mixed Harmony environments. In the chapter "Playing jazz standards" you will see many examples of how these concepts appear in songs. But the real power of our method consists in studying each harmonic environment as a world of its own. This is what gives you the ability to recognize this sound in any piece of music, no matter what key it's in. So take your time with each new sound presented in this chapter. Enjoy it fully and discover the new melodic possibilities it offers.

We are now ready to begin creating all of the beautiful new sounds of Mixed Harmony. I'll try to help you plan your journey by presenting the new harmonic environments in an organized way. But really you can study them in any order that you like. I'll just try to present them in the order that more or less corresponds to how frequently they appear in our music.

Mixed Harmony - Preparation in one move

The first concept we should explore is the one I touched on briefly in the last chapter, which is to use a dominant chord to create a feeling of attraction toward a particular chord of the major scale. These dominant chords that we create ourselves are called "secondary dominants" because they plagiarize the original dominant chord, which is the 5D chord. When we use a dominant chord in this way to make the ear feel drawn to a particular chord, we say we are "preparing" that chord.

The first of these new chords that we will look at is 3D, which prepares the 6- chord. 3D means "three dominant" and it has the notes 3, #5, 7 and 2. (If you have trouble seeing why these are the four notes that make up 3D, or why 3D is the chord that prepares 6-, you can find the full explanation in the last chapter. I won't repeat the explanation for every new chord in this chapter, but in each case we are simply cutting and pasting musical shapes to new locations.)

Here is the tonal map of the new 3D harmonic environment, and the 6- chord that it prepares:

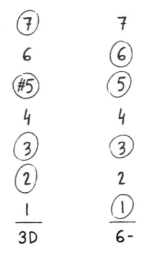

Looking at such a simple result, it's hard to get a feel for the importance of this information. But the 3D chord is so fundamental to Western music that even if you understood nothing more than the major scale plus the 3D chord, you could already play more than half of the songs ever written. In fact 3D is even more important than some of the original chords of the major scale itself.

The reason for this is has to do with what we saw in the chapter "Sun and Moon". The 1 chord and the 6- chord are the two most important tonal centers in our music. Almost every song in the world is grounded in one of these two tonal centers. So obviously the dominant chords that prepare the 1 chord and the 6- chord are also very important. You already have a lot of experience with 5D preparing the 1 chord. So for the next couple of months your top priority should be to investigate deeply the new harmonic environment of 3D and its relationship to 6-.

To hear 3D for yourself, play the following chord progression on a piano:

As you play this example you can really feel the sensation of movement when you get to the 3D chord. As soon as the note #5 makes its appearance, your entire body will feel pulled forward into the 6- chord. This is the magic of 3D.

You should also study 3D and 6- the same way you studied 5D and the 1 chord in the chapter on Tension and Release. For example you could tell musical stories for hours just over the following simple alternation:

And here is a progression that I especially like. It appears often in Latin American music, and it is the inspiration for "Song for My Father" by Horace Silver:

In Silver's tune there is one more slight alteration. He uses the chord 4D in place of 4. I will show you that chord a little later on. But first take the time to become familiar with the chords above, which are very beautiful just as they are. Notice the sweet and simple logic of this line. We start in the 6- chord and just start moving down the scale. When we finally arrive to note 3, we are at just the right place to make the jump back up to 6-, because 3D is the chord that prepares 6-. Such a perfect coincidence is a dead giveaway that this progression will be found in every country in the world. It's too catchy to go undiscovered. Play this progression on a piano and I'm sure you'll recognize its sound.

Let's move on to the next chord on our list. After the 6- chord, the next most important tonal center in our music is the 4 chord. To prepare this chord we need a new sound called 1D:

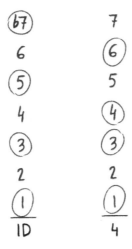

If you play these two chords on a piano, you'll notice that they sound exactly like the chords 5D and 1 which you already know. This brings us to an important point about studying Mixed Harmony. If you were to simply alternate between these two chords on a piano, your ear would not actually be hearing 1D and 4. If the only chords you play are a dominant chord and the resolution to its corresponding major chord, your ear will automatically assume that these chords are 5D and 1. This might sound very abstract but it's the same thing you've already seen with the notes of the major scale. You can't just walk up to a piano, play one single note and say, "That's what note 3 sounds like." Note 3 only sounds like note 3 in the context of the rest of the key. So the only way to hear note 3 is to play the entire scale first and then go back and play note 3 again. *Now* you are feeling what note 3 sounds like.

The same thing happens with chords. In order to really feel the sensation of 1D, our ear must first be grounded in the key of the music. One way to do that is to simply start out in the 1 chord. Here is an example that lets you really feel 1D and 4:

If you play these chords very slowly, you'll notice that you feel a sudden rush of movement as soon as you get to the 1D chord. When you start out in the 1 chord, there is nothing to suggest that we are going anywhere. The song could just stay in the 1 chord all day if you wanted it to. But as soon as that note b7 makes its appearance in the 1D chord, we feel a huge surge of energy that pushes us forward to the 4 chord. This is the sensation of 1D.

Probably the example of 1D you know best is in the song "Happy Birthday". You may not exactly be dying to include this song in your concert repertoire (unless you happen to sideline as a clown for little kids' parties). But it's worth studying because it gives you a crystal clear example of some of the most important sounds in Western harmony. And the mere fact that you have heard it a million times means that these sounds are already permanently etched into your mind. In other words, this silly song has saved you the trouble of having to spend your time learning these basic sounds. Thanks to the song, you already know these sounds. You just have to understand *which* sounds they are. So here are the chords to the song:

Play this chord progression on a piano in 3/4 time and see if you can sing the melody. (If you have trouble getting started I'll give you a hint...the melody starts on note 5.)

172

Notice that the first line of this song illustrates a concept we saw earlier about how the 1 chord and the 5D chord can be used to create the metaphor of a question and an answer. Also notice how the 1D chord works in the second line to drive us forward to the 4 chord. This is as clear as it gets. You couldn't ask for a better example of how these chords work.

Another important secondary dominant in our music is 2D. The 2D chord technically prepares the 5D chord. But since 5D creates such a strong sense of attraction forward to the 1 chord, most songs keep right on going to the 1 chord. We almost always find 2D and 5D working together to send us all the way to the 1 chord:

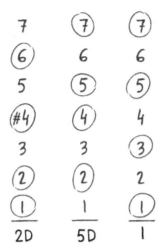

Study the progression above with Melody Paths and pay special attention to the path that starts on #4, then comes down to 4, and finally to note 3. This melody is, for me, the essence of this chord progression. Another way to understand the sound of 2D is to compare it directly to 2- in the same context. In the following example, compare the first line to the second and you'll notice the very particular sound of #4 that appears in 2D.

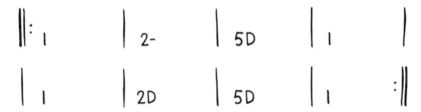

Another very common use of 2D is for it to "correct" itself back to 2- before advancing to 5D. You can find examples of this in Jobim's "Girl from Ipanema" and in "Mood Indigo" by Duke Ellington (as well as countless other popular songs).

$$\|: \quad 1 \qquad | \quad 2D \qquad | \quad 2\text{-} \quad 5D \quad | \quad 1 \qquad :\|$$

Probably the next most important secondary dominant is 6D. We already talked about the construction of this chord in the last chapter:

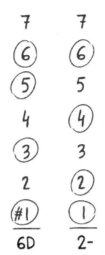

You also saw one very common use of 6D in the last chapter. That example showed how 6D might appear in a song centered around the 1 chord:

```
(7)   7    7   (7)
 6   (6)  (6)   6
(5)  (5)   5   (5)
 4    4   (4)  (4)
(3)  (3)   3    3
 2    2   (2)  (2)
(1)  (#1) (1)   1
─── ─── ─── ───
 1   6D   2-   5D
```

But another place where 6D often appears is in minor songs centered around the 6- chord. When 6- changes into 6D, all of a sudden we feel pulled forward to the 2- chord:

$$\|\!: \ 6\text{-} \ | \ 6D \ | \ 2\text{-} \ | \ 3D \ :\!\|$$

This is exactly the same thing that we saw in the major tonal center when we converted the 1 chord into 1D and then jumped ahead to the 4 chord:

$$\|\!: \ 1 \ | \ 1D \ | \ 4 \ | \ 5D \ :\!\|$$

Study the two lines above separately, but notice how each line works in the same way.

The last important secondary dominant is 7D, which prepares the 3- chord:

⑦	⑦
⑥	6
5	⑤
#④	4
3	③
#②	②
I	I
7D	3-

7D appears most commonly in minor tonality songs based on the 6- tonal center. Here is an example of how 7D might begin a line that ultimately ends in the 6- chord:

⑦	⑦	7
⑥	6	⑥
5	#⑤	⑤
#④	4	4
3	③	③
#②	②	2
I	I	①
7D	3D	6-

This is the same idea we saw earlier in the major tonal center with the chords 2D, 5D and 1. In your practicing, you should compare these two chord progressions by studying them both on the same day. Notice what is similar about the two lines, and what is different.

You now have the complete set of secondary dominants that are used to create the feeling of harmonic movement toward any chord of the major scale. The only chord we haven't learned to prepare is the 7-b5 chord. We could theoretically prepare it in the same way we prepare any other chord, by placing a dominant chord exactly one fifth above note 7. But the 7-b5 chord is so unstable that it is never used as a destination in this way. So here is a recap of the most important preparations that you should study until you have them mastered:

1 chord :	5D $\longrightarrow$ 1	
2 chord :	6D $\longrightarrow$ 2-	
3 chord :	7D $\longrightarrow$ 3-	
4 chord :	1D $\longrightarrow$ 4	
5 chord :	2D $\longrightarrow$ 5D	
6 chord :	3D $\longrightarrow$ 6-	
7 chord :	(omitted)	

Take your time learning these concepts. It wouldn't be unreasonable to spend up to a whole year just learning to integrate these new sounds into your personal understanding of music. I presented them to you quickly but there is truly a universe of material here. With just this handful of new chords you can already understand and play almost all of the popular music from every country in the world.

Mixed Harmony - Preparation in two moves

Probably the defining characteristic of the harmony found in most jazz music is a short little chord progression that uses two different steps to prepare the final destination. This is commonly called the "two five one progression".

This chord progression is nothing more than an extension of the concept we just saw. But now we prepare each chord with *two* preparatory chords:

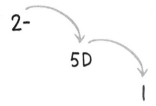

Notice that the first chord is 2-, not 2D. When we use 2D, the ear expects a final resolution in the very next chord. Remember that any secondary dominant reminds the ear of a 5D chord and fools the ear into expecting an immediate resolution. Sometimes composers play with these expectations. There is certainly nothing wrong with using 2D to prepare 5D and then going on to 1 as we saw earlier:

But what we are looking at now is different. Now we are using the 2- chord, and the ear does not expect a resolution in the very next chord. Instead the ear recognizes that the real source of attraction is the 1 chord, and that we will pass through two different states to get there:

If you want to play jazz music you need to understand this chord progression to the very last little detail. This is part of the reason I used this progression to illustrate our exercise Melody Paths in Exercise 3. I wanted to give you the drawings to get you started on discovering the inner workings of this important series of chords.

In addition to being important in itself, the above chord progression also serves as our *model* for preparing any major chord. So just as we plagiarized 5D earlier to prepare chords in one move, now we are going to plagiarize 2- and 5D to prepare chords in two moves. For example, here is the two-move progression that prepares the 4 chord:

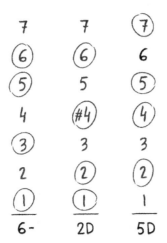

And here's the two-move progression that prepares 5D:

In fact, these two progressions together were very commonly used as a bridge in older jazz standards. One example is the bridge to "On the Sunny Side of the Street", the music of which was composed by Jimmy McHugh:

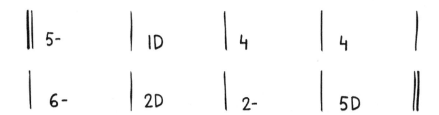

Notice that there is one additional interesting detail here. Just when the ear is expecting the 5D chord in the third measure of the second line, instead the 2- chord appears and makes us begin to feel attraction all the way to the 1 chord. This sets up the return to the 1 chord which is how the song begins. Almost every bridge ever written works in this same way. They always end with a chord progression that makes us want to go back to the top of the tune again.

Now let's look at how we prepare minor chords in two moves. First we will look at the preparation of 6-, since it serves as the model for preparing all other minor chords as well. Here is the chord progression that leads to the 6- chord:

$$
\begin{array}{ccc}
⑦ & ⑦ & 7 \\
⑥ & 6 & ⑥ \\
5 & ⑤ₛ & ⑤ \\
④ & 4 & 4 \\
3 & ③ & ③ \\
② & ② & 2 \\
\underline{1} & \underline{1} & \underline{①} \\
7{-}^{b5} & 3D & 6{-}
\end{array}
$$

Just as the 2-, 5D, 1 progression is the model for preparing all other major chords, this new progression is the model for preparing all minor chords. Here is how it works in the progression to the 2- chord:

3-♭5	6D	2-
(♭7)	♭7	7
6	(6)	(6)
(5)	(5)	5
4	4	(4)
(3)	(3)	3
(2)	2	(2)
1	(#1)	(1)

An example is the Brazilian song "Manhã de Carnaval" by Luiz Bonfa (better known in the U.S. as "Black Orpheus"). The second half of the tune begins with these lines:

‖ 6- | 7-♭5 3D | 6- | 6- |

| 3-♭5 | 6D | 2- | 2- ‖

The other minor chord that we need to learn to prepare is 3-. The progression to the 3- brings up an interesting point. We saw earlier that 7D is the chord that prepares 3-, because note 7 is exactly one fifth above note 3. But what chord do we need to place in front of the 7D chord? In other words, what is the note exactly one fifth above note 7? If you guessed note 4 you are wrong, because the interval between 7 and 4 is a *flatted fifth*. We need to place our first chord exactly a *perfect fifth* above note 7. So for the first time we need to build a chord on a root note that is outside the major scale. The note we need is #4. Here is the full progression:

#4-♭5	7D	3-
7	(7)	(7)
(6)	(6)	6
5	5	(5)
(#4)	(#4)	4
(3)	3	(3)
2	(#2)	(2)
(1)	1	1

This progression occurs in the songs "These Foolish Things" and "I Hear a Rhapsody". The bridge to both songs begins in 3- and the chords above are used to make the transition. But I think the best example of the #4-b5 chord is the very first chord of "Stella by Starlight". The unusual sound that begins this beautiful standard is precisely the sound of #4-b5.

You have now seen the complete set of chord progressions that take us to every practical destination in the major scale. I say every "practical" destination because we did not create a progression that leads us to 7-b5. The reason, as I stated earlier, is that this highly unstable chord is simply never used as the final destination of a chord progression. So I do not include it in this initial set of chord progressions that you should master. Here is our working list:

1 chord:	2- $\longrightarrow$ 5D $\longrightarrow$ 1
2 chord:	3-b5 $\longrightarrow$ 6D $\longrightarrow$ 2-
3 chord:	#4-b5 $\longrightarrow$ 7D $\longrightarrow$ 3-
4 chord:	5- $\longrightarrow$ 1D $\longrightarrow$ 4
5 chord:	6- $\longrightarrow$ 2D $\longrightarrow$ 5D
6 chord:	7-b5 $\longrightarrow$ 3D $\longrightarrow$ 6-
7 chord:	(omitted)

It's important to understand that the preparations in one move that we saw earlier are actually contained within these larger progressions. So in fact everything you have seen up until now in Exercise 4 is summarized right here on this simple chart which you can use to guide your practicing. Every one of these chord progressions should become just as familiar to you as the seven basic chords of the major scale. It will take time and practice. But the journey is a beautiful one that is well worth the effort.

Once you have become an expert in all of the progressions on this chart, there is one final detail you should consider before moving on to the next section. You have seen that the way we prepare the 1 chord and the way we prepare the 6- chord serve as models for preparing all other chords. If our destination is major, we copy the chord progression that takes us to the 1 chord. If our destination is minor, we copy the chord progression that takes us to 6-. But a common variation that occurs very often in jazz music is to interchange these sounds to create a surprise for the ear. For example, we can use the *minor* chord progression to prepare a *major* chord. The way we do this is simply to alter the scales of 2- and 5D (which prepare the 1 chord) so that they sound like 7-b5 and 3D (which prepare 6-). Then the ear is surprised when we arrive at a major chord instead of the expected minor chord. Below is the result of using the minor chord progression to prepare the 1 chord:

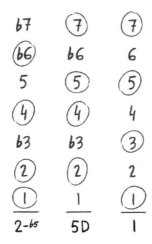

I'll leave it as an exercise for you to figure out exactly why these are the notes that produce this effect. But if you improvise for a while over the progression above, your ear should recognize that the first two harmonic environments are exactly the same as the harmonic environments of 7-b5 and 3D. The only difference is in the *names* we are using for the notes, because now we are calling our final destination "1" instead of "6". Can you find the 7-b5 harmonic environment hidden in the column above for 2-b5? Can you find the 3D harmonic environment hidden in the column above for 5D? If not, don't worry. Just play the progression and enjoy it. Someday you will be so good at visualizing these harmonic environments that you'll even spot them when they are displaced or otherwise disguised.

We can also use the same principle to prepare the 4 chord. If we first want to trick the ear into thinking that we are arriving at a minor chord, we can use the following progression:

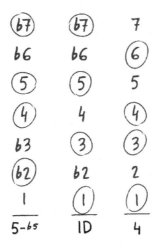

As before, the first two harmonic environments use the exact same scales we saw for 7-b5 and 3D. But now we find these scales displaced to yet another location so that the ear expects a minor chord built on note 4.

In both cases, the concept I am trying to show is really very simple. While we are in the preparation stages, we use notes that fool the ear into thinking we are moving toward a minor chord. It is only with the final appearance of the destination chord that we feel the sudden change from minor to major.

Probably the clearest example of the first progression is the song "Night and Day" by Cole Porter. The first two lines are literally just this minor progression to the 1 chord. When the ear hears the chords 2-b5 and 5D, it automatically assumes that these chords are actually 7-b5 and 3D. In other words, the ear is fooled into thinking that we are moving toward the minor tonal center 6-. Then the appearance of the major chord surprises the ear and feels like a sudden ray of sunshine. When you study this chord progression you'll see what I mean.

The bridge to Dizzy Gillespie's "A Night in Tunisia" also shows us an example of this technique:

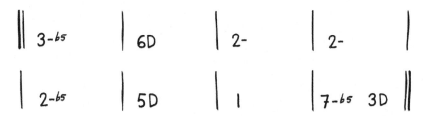

Don't be in a rush to understand all of these concepts on an intellectual level. Just begin working with the sounds that I have presented in this chapter. The logic of harmony is very simple but it's difficult to explain in words. The only way to understand it is by playing with the sounds and noticing for yourself how all of the different musical shapes can be combined to create different effects.

Mixed Harmony - Some additional colors

You can actually define and study any new harmonic environment on your own, just by thinking through the alterations that this chord causes to the original key of the song. I will leave this up to you, since there are too many possibilities to cover in a single book. But there are just a few more sounds that are so common that I would like to include them here. These additional sounds are 4D, 4- and b7D. You should study each of these harmonic environments separately, and then study them in a tonal context. A good way to do this is simply to contrast each new chord to the 1 chord. You can use Melody Paths to hear how the voices flow between the two chords, and you can use Seven Worlds Expanded and Accompanied Singing to improvise over a chord progression made up of these two chords together. Here is the drawing of the 4D harmonic environment, along with the 1 chord for reference.

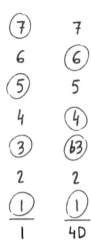

And here is the drawing of the 4- harmonic environment next to the 1 chord:

The 4- chord is used very often in jazz standards as a transitional chord between the 4 chord and the 3- chord. It's especially common in a progression that I call the "long trip home" from the 4 chord down to the 1 chord. Here is a common way to make this harmonic journey:

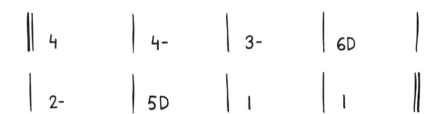

You will find variations on this basic idea in many jazz standards and bossa novas. Here are just a few examples:

After You've Gone
All of Me
All the Things You Are

Anthropology
But Not for Me
Corcovado (Quiet Nights of Quiet Stars)
I've Got You Under My Skin
Meditation
My Romance
New York, New York
Summer Samba
There Will Never Be Another You
Triste
Wave

As you can see from this partial list, one of the most powerful benefits of our tonal point of view is that we begin seeing the same basic elements in hundreds of different songs. These connections are very difficult to spot by just looking at the written chord progressions, because songs are written in all different keys.

The last important sound I want to share with you in this section is b7D. This is a dominant chord built on the note b7. It has a beautiful tense sound that is very similar to 4D. It appears often as an alternative way to create tension before the 1 chord. Some clear examples of this sound appear in "After You've Gone", "Stella by Starlight" and "There Will Never Be Another You". I will show it next to the 1 chord so that you can study the connections with Melody Paths:

Mixed Harmony - Short passages from other keys

Many songs involve short passages from other keys. This is especially common in jazz music. In most improvisation courses the standard approach to these passages is simply to mentally change keys. The preparations in one move and two moves that you saw at the beginning of this chapter are really my own concepts, and they do not appear in other courses on harmony and improvisation. Instead, the student of jazz music is instructed to simply analyze a piece of sheet music to identify all of the chord progressions of type 2, 5, 1 that occur in the piece. Every single one of these progressions is treated as if it were an actual key change. That is to say, the student it taught to forget about the original key and consider the next few measures to be in a totally different key. In our tonal language, we could call this "moving our 1" because we literally declare a new note to be note 1. The advantage of doing this is that it's very easy to play something that sounds musically correct. All you have to do is practice getting good at making lots of rapid key changes, and everything else is very easy because essentially you spend your entire life just playing the progression 2-, 5D, 1. None of the other progressions that we study in IFR are necessary if you are willing to constantly move your 1.

But for playing standards and other popular music, I don't teach harmony this way because it does not reflect the way the human ear actually feels the music. These short passages that use notes from other keys are not, in fact, a true key change. The human ear continues to feel the original key all along. And so while it's true that mentally changing keys will lead you to the new "correct notes", it's not the best approach if your goal is to express the sounds that you imagine. This doesn't mean that you can't become a great musician using the traditional approach of constantly changing keys. Many wonderful creative musicians were taught to improvise initially with scales and theory. But my personal opinion is that this is a superficial approach to understanding songs, and it only makes things even more confusing for the beginning improviser.

For this reason, when you encounter short passages from other keys in the songs you play, I encourage you to study these chords patiently and work to integrate them into your tonal awareness, just the way you have seen in this chapter. Try to understand each note relative to the *original* key, and learn to work with these notes without having to mentally change keys. Avoiding unnecessary key changes is an important part of keeping your inner composer engaged and in control.

Mixed Harmony - Genuine key changes and modal music

Genuine key changes, on the other hand, are a completely different story. Genuine key changes are not really a part of Mixed Harmony because they do not represent a deformation to the original harmonic environment. They represent a switch to a completely *new* harmonic environment altogether. Whenever there is a genuine key change in a piece of music, your ear loses all memory of the original key and has no desire to go back to it. In these cases it makes perfect sense to "move your 1". But notice that the reason we move our 1 in this case is the same reason we *don't* move it in the other case. In both cases we just want our tonal map to correspond to what our ear is actually feeling. Whenever there is a genuine key change, you ear will forget about the original key and orient itself relative to the new one. So it would be unhelpful to keep thinking in terms of the original key, since it is simply no longer relevant.

Something similar to a genuine key change happens constantly in the more modal style of jazz composition that became popular in the sixties, the best example of which is the group Miles Davis had at the time with Wayne Shorter, Herbie Hancock, Ron Carter and Tony Williams. In many of their compositions, the individual chords do not make up tonal chord progressions like we are studying in Exercise 4. Instead each new chord is a completely new harmonic environment, independent unto itself. In these compositions every single chord in a tune can feel like a genuine key change. For this reason, when we play this kind of music we too must drift constantly from one key to another if we hope to make any sense of what our ear is feeling. In the IFR method, this is what we work on in IFR Exercise 5: Free Harmony.

But right now our focus is on developing a very solid foundation in the essential sounds of Mixed Harmony. This foundation will give us a complete mastery of tonal harmony as it appears in popular music from all over the world. For jazz players this means everything from the blues and early standards up to the be-bop era. Concentrate on this material for now, in order to learn the important lessons of Mixed Harmony. For your ear, this is a necessary preparation for the totally free improvisation that we will practice later.

Summary

In Exercise 4 you learned to use a simple, compact mental model that allows you incorporate any new sound into your tonal awareness and study it just as you studied the seven basic harmonic environments of the major scale. This is a lifelong project, since there are virtually unlimited sounds that could theoretically be studied in this way. But I included in this chapter the most important sounds from Mixed Harmony so that you can get to work right away discovering them for yourself and making music with them.

I encourage you to take the time to explore each of these Mixed Harmony chord progressions very deeply. Later you'll encounter these same chord progressions in almost all of the songs you want to play. But the problem with trying to learn about harmony through songs is that most songs contain several harmonic concepts which are all worth exploring deeply. Because these chords go by so quickly, in the course of improvising over an entire song you might only get a few seconds to experience a given harmonic environment. This doesn't give you enough time to really explore the inner workings of the harmony so that you can understand what's going on

This deep exploration is exactly what we do in IFR Jam Tracks Level 4: Mixed Harmony Essentials and IFR Jam Tracks Level 5: Mixed Harmony Advanced. And when you're ready to study the more advanced topics covered in this chapter, you can add IFR Jam Tracks Level 6: Sun and Moon to your practicing. You'll find all of these resources at ImproviseForReal.com.

Time

Do you remember when you were a child, when you could lie in the grass for hours just staring at the clouds? Can you remember having all the time in the world to just reflect on your own thoughts and experiences?

Most people never notice their freedom slipping away. We just gradually come to feel that we can't allow ourselves certain luxuries. Most adults learn to live with a more or less constant sensation of being in a hurry. We don't even know why we're in such a hurry. We just know that we are.

The ironic thing is that despite all our agitation we still manage to waste huge amounts of time. We can easily be seduced into watching an hour of television or other entertainment. But most of us would never permit ourselves a full hour to just sit quietly and look at the clouds.

The secret to IFR is not any particular way of understanding harmony. Music is so simple that you would figure it out on your own if you just stuck with it for a while. In fact, just playing the notes of the major scale and really listening to them would eventually lead you to understand everything there is to know about harmony. The real secret to IFR is simply to create a daily practice in which this reflection is possible.

Some of our students proudly tell us in the first class that they are willing to work very hard. I always ask them the same question: "But are you willing to *stop* working very hard?" Most of us were taught to think of musical growth as a steady accumulation of knowledge and skills that we better try to accelerate if we want to go very far. Stories about child prodigies only confirm our suspicions that we are already running behind. Little by little, our innocent love of music is overshadowed by a growing preoccupation with improving our skills. For some, this struggle for improvement actually *becomes* their entire relationship with music. "Playing" gives way to "practicing". We are unable to fully enjoy what we're doing in the moment because we are so anxious to get where we want to go.

But the present moment is not just a relaxing break from our forward progress. The present moment *is* our forward progress. The really big discoveries are not waiting for you somewhere "out there" in the next chapter or in next week's lesson. They are right before your eyes, patiently waiting to be noticed. To see them for yourself, all you have to do is *slow down* and give your full attention what you're doing. Unfortunately, this is not easy to do in a society that constantly tells us to move faster or risk falling behind.

In summary my advice to you is this: fall behind. Lose yourself in contemplation of the simplest of sounds. Forget about "all that material" that you would like to master someday. Throw away your "to do" list. Mastery only comes from growing in your own personal understanding, and that can only happen when your mind is empty and calm. If you want to reach your highest potential as a creative musical artist, the first step is to reclaim the freedom you enjoyed as a child to lie in the grass and look at the clouds. The truth is that you've had this freedom all along.

Playing jazz standards

You don't have to master every new sound from Mixed Harmony in order to begin playing and improvising over a repertoire of songs with other musicians. You could choose songs of any style, since the concepts of harmony that you have been learning about are the same for all modern popular music. The concepts are equally applicable to gospel, soul, bluegrass, country, rock, salsa, tango, flamenco or any one of a hundred other musical styles. And you could improvise just as freely in any of these styles, even if improvisation doesn't form an important part of that style's tradition.

But there is one kind of music that is so rich and perfect for improvising that its name has become almost synonymous with improvisation. That style is jazz music. Jazz is like an improviser's paradise. It's as if an entire musical culture were created just for us. In other styles of music you're lucky if your bandmates give you permission to make the slightest variations to your part. But in jazz music it's just assumed that you have complete creative freedom to improvise everything you play. The other musicians give you plenty of space to create whatever you want, and they play off of your ideas with creative responses of their own. Suddenly it's not just about self-expression anymore. Now you can engage in a true dialogue with other musicians and have entire musical conversations.

The most powerful aspect of this communication between musicians is something that isn't even covered in this book, which is rhythm. In any good jazz group there is always an intense conversation taking place that has to do with each musician's use of *time*.

And even the songs that jazz players use as vehicles for their improvisations are so sophisticated and so lovely that they are the perfect inspiration for an improviser. With such an ideal environment made up of interesting harmony, rhythmic conversation and the creative energy of other musicians, playing jazz music can be one of the greatest pleasures on earth. This is why so many musicians continue to play and improvise over jazz music.

To study any song (regardless of style) using our tonal method, you first need to create a tonal sketch of the song. This is what lets us see how the song really works. Keep in mind that these tonal sketches are not intended to replace traditional sheet music. Instead think of them merely as teaching examples that help you see for yourself how these songs work. My goal is not to replace the standard sheet music system with a different one. My goal is to break your dependence on written music altogether.

You can create your own tonal sketch of a song starting from either a piece of sheet music or a recording:

> **Starting from written sheet music.** To make a tonal sketch from a written lead sheet or other sheet music, you first need to identify the key in which the song is written. Then you need to write out both the melody and the chords in tonal numbers relative to this key. Identify the chord shape of each chord that appears in the song: major, dominant, minor or minor with a flatted 5th. Don't worry if some of the chords are unfamiliar to you. You'll probably find lots of chord shapes constructed in unfamiliar locations. For example you might find a dominant chord built on the note b3. Even if you have no experience with this chord, the first step is just to write it in our tonal language. So you would just write "b3D" and keep going. Then do the same for each note of the melody, writing out every

188

single note using its tonal number. When the tonal sketch is finished you will be able to see exactly where any unfamiliar sounds are located. Probably you will already be familiar with the majority of the chords but there are usually at least a couple that will be new to you. For these chords that we haven't studied yet, we need to think through any changes that the chord creates in the basic harmonic environment. Basically you will be defining a new Mixed Harmony environment just like the ones we are studying in Exercise 4. Draw the column of notes the same way we did in Exercise 4, and indicate any sharps or flats necessary to create the new chord. Finally, put circles around the chord notes so you will be able to see at a glance what is really happening in the harmony at that moment. Study this new harmonic environment just as you have been studying the harmonic environments that I already showed you. In this way, you will continue to grow as a musician with each new song you play. Over time you will find that more and more of the chords are familiar to you, because you already studied them in other songs.

Starting from a recording. As your confidence with Mixed Harmony grows, it will become increasingly easy for you to make tonal sketches directly from musical recordings. You are preparing yourself for this whenever you work on the activities Follow the Melody and Follow the Harmony from Exercises 2 and 3. Your success in transcribing an entire song depends on whether or not you have personal experience with every chord in the song. Nobody can expect you to recognize a chord that you haven't studied. So don't feel bad when you come up against chords that you simply don't recognize. Whenever you're stumped, just leave that space blank on your tonal sketch and go find a written transcription of the song to find out what chord is being played at that moment. Then obviously you will want to study this unusual chord the same way we did in Exercise 4. Over time your repertoire of chords will grow and you will find more and more songs that you can transcribe entirely just by ear.

To get started we'll look at a few examples of jazz standards and write them out in our tonal language. A great place to start is the classic "Autumn Leaves". With just the very first concept from Mixed Harmony, the 3D chord, you can already play this entire song in any key. It always amazes me that even some very excellent jazz musicians will have trouble playing "Autumn Leaves" in an unfamiliar key. I think the problem is that they are getting caught up in the names of the chords and they don't realize that the entire harmony of the song is just the major scale plus the 3D chord. Here is my tonal sketch of the song. Notice that 3D is the only chord that does not come directly from the major scale.

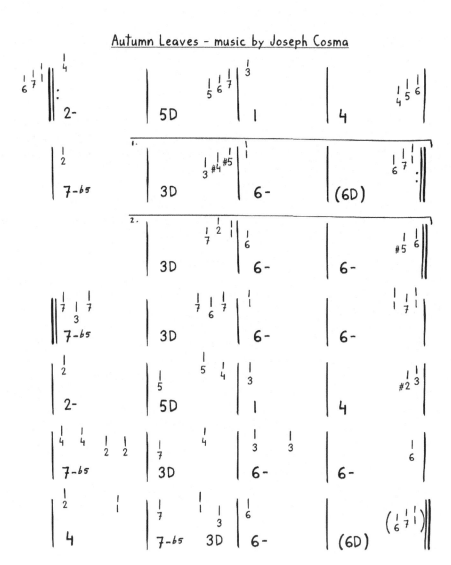

Autumn Leaves - music by Joseph Cosma

This tune is a very pretty example of a song that interlaces the two most important chord progressions we know, the path to the 1 chord and the path to the 6- chord. In my own tonal sketch there are some additional chords in parentheses but you don't need to worry about these right now. Just begin working with the song and let it be part of the way that you come to understand the 3D chord.

Here are some ideas of how you could study this or any other song to really understand it:

1. Sing the melody in numbers every day.

2. Play the melody every day in a different key.

3. Study each chord individually the way you learned to do in Seven Worlds Expanded from Exercise 3.

4. Play the chords on the piano in all different keys using Home Chords as you learned to do in Exercise 3. (This is an important exercise even for piano players. Even though it seems like a very primitive way to play chords, it gives you an important vision of

exactly *where* each note lies in the tonal octave.)

5. Practice improvising over the entire chord progression using Seven Worlds Expanded, Melody Paths and Accompanied Singing as you learned in Exercise 3. Don't forget to sing freely sometimes, without even trying to visualize where you are in the octave. This is what we talked about in the section, "Free Your Imagination" from Exercise 2.

6. Make time to listen to recordings of the song and enjoy the music without trying to analyze it in any way. Let the song soak into you on an unconscious level. Don't try to recognize the notes the way we do in Follow the Melody. Instead, remember what I told you earlier: *memorize the sound*. A true improviser creates music in the world of sounds. When you hear an especially beautiful melody, just stay there in the world of sounds and appreciate every detail that you can.

As an example of how you can practice Melody Paths, I'll give you my own drawing of the chords to the song. This is the drawing I would use to discover and practice all of the melody paths across the harmony.

7	(7)	(7)	7	(7)	(7)	7
(6)	6	6	(6)	(6)	6	(6)
5	(5)	(5)	5	5	(#5)	(5)
(4)	(4)	4	(4)	(4)	4	4
3	3	(3)	(3)	3	(3)	(3)
(2)	(2)	2	2	(2)	(2)	2
(1)	1	(1)	(1)	1	1	(1)
2-	5D	1	4	7-b5	3D	6-

Don't be overwhelmed by the amount of time and effort that we dedicate to learning each song. Remember that everything you learn from studying one song will also enable you to play many other songs. So we're not only studying "Autumn Leaves". We are also letting the song itself teach us some tremendously important concepts of basic harmony. We want to study them deeply because we will continue to see these concepts over and over again in other songs.

In the case of "Autumn Leaves", the only new concept for you is the 3D chord. So this song gives you the perfect opportunity to get comfortable with the 3D chord. Later, when you find this same chord in other songs, you won't have to study it in detail because you will already know it inside and out.

The next example is the Brazilian bossa nova "Manhã de Carnaval" by Luiz Bonfa (often listed as "Black Orpheus" in jazz fake books). This song contains everything we have seen in "Autumn Leaves" plus one more concept from Mixed Harmony, the path to the 2- chord. Here is my tonal transcription:

Manhã de Carnaval (Black Orpheus) – Luiz Bonfa

Notice that in this song, the only chords that do not come directly from the major scale are 3D (which prepares 6-) and the chords 3-b5 and 6D (which prepare 2-). In my transcription you'll also notice a diminished chord in measure 8. You'll find a complete treatment of diminished chords in IFR Jam Tracks Level 7: Diminished Chords. But for now you can just think of this as the 6D chord which performs the same harmonic function as the diminished chord indicated.

Another great song that doesn't include too many new chords is the standard "All of Me". This is a wonderful exercise in the first concept from Exercise 4, which is the use of secondary dominants to prepare new chords in just one movement.

All of Me – Gerald Marks and Seymour Warren

And here is a great song that lets you practice the paths to all three of the most important tonal centers in our music: the 1 chord, the 6- chord and the 4 chord. The song is "There Will Never Be Another You".

There Will Never Be Another You – Harry Warren and Mack Gordon

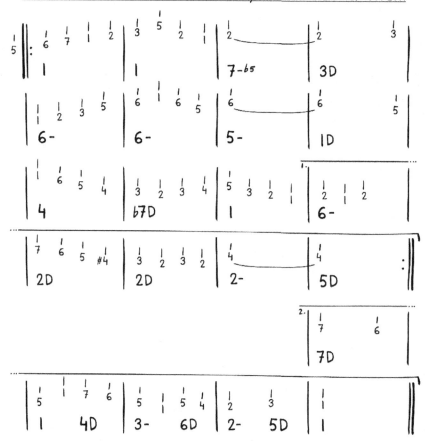

Take a minute to notice how this song works. It has a very beautiful harmony that is very simple to understand. The song starts in the 1 chord, then takes us on the path to 6- and then the path to the 4 chord. Once we arrive at the 4 chord, we begin a variation on what I call the "long trip home" from the 4 chord back down to the 1 chord. (This is the progression that I explained toward the end of Exercise 4.) This is a wonderful song to study because it is a beautiful tour through the three most important tonal centers in Western music. You couldn't ask for a better teaching example.

As you study "There Will Never Be Another You", pay special attention to the sound of 5- right after 6-. This is a very easy movement to recognize and, because it's such a pretty transition, it appears in many songs. Probably my favorite example of this movement is in the beautiful ballad by Miles Davis and Bill Evans, "Blue in Green". I don't want to include the melody because Miles' interpretation is so free that I don't feel comfortable saying what the true melody is. (And I don't entirely agree with the melody printed in most jazz fake books.) But here is the complete chord progression, and I'll leave the interpretation of the melody up to you:

Blue in Green - Miles Davis and Bill Evans

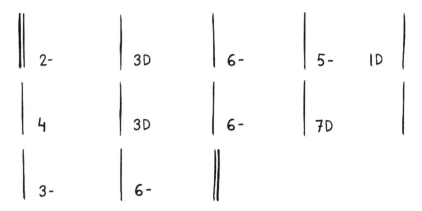

I want you to notice how easy it is to understand the harmonic movement in this tune. Look at the actual movement from each chord to the next and imagine yourself moving around your tonal map, just playing the root note of each chord. Notice that every single movement is either a simple movement up or down in the scale (for example, the move upward from 2- to 3D that begins the song) or it's one of the jumps that we have been studying (for example in the jump from 3D to 6-). So this is an excellent tune for practicing Follow the Harmony. As you begin, you might not be able to recognize all of the chords by ear because you probably haven't gained enough experience working with each of these chords separately. But use my tonal sketch to orient yourself. If you listen closely to the song and follow along in my tonal sketch, I think you can get your first taste of what it feels like to recognize chords by ear.

I could easily fill the rest of this book with more examples, but you can also make these tonal sketches for yourself. For any song that you would like to play, just identify the key of the song and then translate each note and each chord into our tonal language. But remember that our goal is not merely to translate songs into our own language and then memorize the new chord symbols. What we are really trying to do is *understand* the songs, to get to the point where we no longer need even our tonal sketch because we can *hear* the harmony in the song. The best songs for you to study in this way are songs that you love and that have a special meaning for you. These are the songs that have the most to teach you. Analyze these songs and study each new harmonic environment within them very patiently so that you can come to recognize them instantly just by the way they sound. This way you can free yourself from memorizing chord progressions and instead learn to depend on your ear as the only orientation you need.

You'll also find a complete exploration of many popular jazz standards in the IFR Standards Workout series. Each standard is broken down into its component chord progressions from Exericse 4: Mixed Harmony so that you can see exactly how these concepts appear in the songs you love. And for each standard we provide many creative insights, practice tips and backing tracks in all 12 keys to practice your soloing. You'll find the complete IFR Standards Workout series at ImproviseForReal.com.

Playing the blues

A curious feature of the IFR method is that it took us this long to get to what is normally the very first thing that any improvisation student learns: the blues. This is because the 12 bar blues, while simple in form, involves changes to the harmonic environment that we did not know how to deal with until we began working with Mixed Harmony.

Before looking at that harmony, I want to clarify what I mean by "playing the blues". The word "blues" refers to a way of making music that existed in the United States around the end of the 19th century. It is an African American creation. We should be careful not to try to reduce this enormous body of poetry and music to a few chord changes. As a teacher, I am completely unqualified to give you even the humblest notion of what the blues is really about. If you want to discover something about this beautiful tradition and what it meant to the people who created it, a good place to start would be the book "Blues People" by Amiri Baraka. It is one of the best books I have ever read about blues, jazz and African American culture.

But the word "blues" also has a different meaning for contemporary jazz musicians. When we say for example that we are going to play a "blues in F", what we are really talking about is a particular song form. This form, also called a "12 bar blues" is only one of countless song forms that existed in traditional blues music. But it is the only blues song form that jazz musicians continue to play today, and for this reason we often simply call it a "blues". It is this song form that I want to show you, so that you too can play a "blues in F" or in any other key when you are invited to.

The curious thing about the way we play a blues is that all of the chords are dominant chords. In other words, the basic harmonic environment of the song is *not* the major scale but in fact the 1D chord. This affects not only the 1D chord but also the 4D chord, as you will see in a minute. First let's just look at a typical example of blues changes:

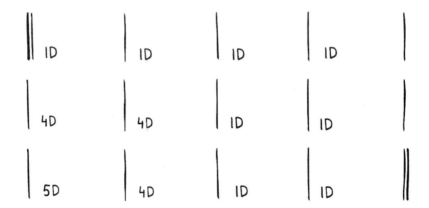

It's important to understand how these chords support the lyrics to the song. Traditionally, although the song has three lines, there are actually only two different lines of lyrics. The first line is the statement of a problem or some type of provocative phrase that leaves us guessing at its resolution. Then in the second line of the song, this very same phrase is *repeated* a second time, intensifying its impact. And finally the resolution is given in the third line of the song.

It's this connection to the lyrics that will help you understand the purpose and harmonic function of each chord. Look at the drawing above and reflect on how the harmony supports the story being told by the lyrics. In the first line, the harmony stays in the 1D chord allowing the singer to make the opening statement with no distracting changes in the background. But notice what happens in the second line while the singer repeats this opening statement. Now the harmonic background switches to the 4D chord, raising the level of suspense and helping us to perceive the urgency of the message that is being repeated. This line ends by returning to the 1D chord, creating a sensation of inevitability or even tragedy. It's the perfect harmonic complement to lend authority to the singer's words.

Finally, the harmony of the third line is what ties the whole story together. Remember that the third line of the song is the moment when the singer reveals the second half of the lyrics, the part that explains or resolves the statement presented earlier. Notice that in the harmony, the third line opens with the 5D chord creating a moment of maximum tension, just as the meaning of the story is about to be revealed. This harmonic background then relaxes slightly to the 4D chord, suggesting resignation or additional complexity in the singer's discourse. It's as though the message requires just a few more words of elaboration in order to be fully comprehended. And finally the harmony returns to the perfectly resolved 1D chord just as the singer utters the final word of the song.

I mention all of this because I think that if you can connect with the meaning of these three lines, you will feel much more inspired to make music with them. The beauty and significance of the blues is not contained in the chords themselves, nor in any clever reharmonizations that you might come up with. In order to grasp the power of this song form you need to hear it for yourself, and that means listening to lots of traditional blues artists singing songs of this form. I encourage you to take this part of your musical development seriously. Before you can truly express what *you* want to say about the blues, you need to feel the power of this tradition for yourself. So take the time to enrich your musical thinking with the poetry, the expressiveness and the sound of great blues artists. That's the only way to understand anything about the blues.

What we can do here though is to take a closer look at the sounds that are used to create these different moments in the harmony of a 12-bar blues. There are three harmonic environments that occur in the song. They are as follows:

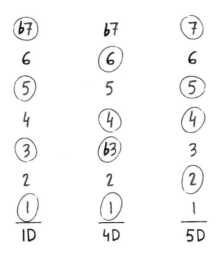

Notice that the 4D harmonic environment presented here is different from the 4D harmonic environment that I showed you in Exercise 4. The difference is in note 7. In the true 4D harmonic environment that you saw in Exercise 4, note 7 is not altered. This is an important detail and it's what gives 4D such a beautiful and distinctive sound.

But what we have in the blues is something different. The basic harmonic environment of the blues is not the major scale but in fact the 1D chord. This means that the note b7 is present already in the original harmonic environment of the song. When the 4D chord comes along and deforms this environment, the flatted 7th is still there. It's only when the 5D chord appears that this note gets corrected, since 5D requires note 7 to be natural.

It doesn't really matter if you follow my explanation or not, since it's pretty subjective anyway. Remember that our analysis of these harmonic environments is not intended to tell you which notes you are allowed to play. You can always play any note you want, expressing whatever sound you hear in your mind. So all we're really trying to do with any kind of harmonic analysis is just to create a map that corresponds to what we hear and feel when we listen to the song. The only purpose of this tonal map is to help you orient yourself in the song. So if you prefer to use a different note on your tonal map than I use on mine, that's perfectly fine. You should always try to organize harmony in whatever way sounds most natural to you.

Apart from listening to lots of blues songs, the other important thing you should do to understand blues harmony is to study these three chords and the relationships between them. I recommend using Melody Paths to investigate the connection between 1D and 4D, and also the connection between 5D and 1D. This will teach you everything there is to know about how the voices flow from each chord to the next.

Now we'll look at the song form called a "minor blues". Curiously, to play a minor blues we do not need any of the new concepts from Mixed Harmony. All three chords of the basic minor blues are contained right within the major scale itself. Following is an example of a typical minor blues. For this form as well, you should study all of the connections with Melody Paths to notice for yourself how the harmony flows through the chord changes.

6-	6-	6-	6-
2-	2-	6-	6-
3-	3-	6-	6-

Once you are comfortable playing the basic blues changes in both major and minor, you might want to think about how you can use the concepts you learned in Exercise 4 to create an additional sense of harmonic movement in these pieces. For example, here is one way that a 12 bar major blues might actually be played by jazz musicians today:

198

‖ 1D	4D	1D	5- 1D
4D	4D	1D	3-♭⁵ 6D
2-	5D	1D	2- 5D ‖

And here is an example of how a minor blues might be played:

‖ 6-	6-	6-	6D
2-	2-	6-	6-
7-♭⁵	3D	6-	6- ‖

We could go on to imagine much more sophisticated chord substitutions that would maintain only a very abstract relationship with the original song form. But I would caution you against using an overly complicated map. Inside your own imagination, you already possess an unlimited capacity for abstraction. So it's not necessary to have a complicated map in order to play sophisticated music. By keeping your mental model very simple, you can improvise much more freely and make much more sophisticated music without getting lost. Also, it's important to keep your mental model simple so that you don't become a slave to ever-changing chords. What we really want to do is just connect with the basic harmonic movement that gives the 12 bar blues its power. It is this *connection* to the overall song form that enables us to tell powerful stories with our improvisations.

If playing the blues is something you are passionate about, another resource you should know about is the IFR Blues Mastery Course. This is a complete course in blues harmony and improvisation, including all of the most popular blues song forms and chord progressions. You'll learn both the major blues and the minor blues in a variety of rhythms and styles. And you'll learn to understand the special chords and scales used in the blues so you can play confidently with other blues musicians. You'll find more details about this course at ImproviseForReal.com.

Playing scales is not improvising

By now you are probably beginning to realize how powerful the Mixed Harmony environments are as a conceptual tool. Since you can now visualize the entire harmonic flow of any piece of music, you could easily fly all over your instrument, playing the appropriate scales up and down in a way that might sound very impressive. For many beginners this new freedom of movement can be absolutely euphoric. If you have always marveled at jazz musicians who can weave in and out of chord progressions at lightning speed, it can be exhilarating to discover this ability for yourself.

But this is not the real purpose of the Mixed Harmony environments. These new concepts are not raw material to use in your improvisations. They are nothing more than *maps* of the musical terrain. Their purpose is to enable you to easily locate the sounds you *imagine*. Don't make the mistake of playing the map itself. It may seem thrilling in the beginning to fly up and down the altered scales of Mixed Harmony, demonstrating your mastery of harmony to the audience. But playing scales is not improvising, no matter how well you do it.

Remember that you are arriving very late to the party. Human beings have been playing and composing music with this material for *centuries*. No matter how much you practice, you are never going to be able to play these scales any faster or better than the millions of other musicians who came before you.

But you do have something to offer that is unique, special and priceless, and that is your imagination. This is your treasure. The mental clarity that we develop in Exercise 4 is for one purpose only, and that is to improve our ability to express the music we imagine. Don't show off your mastery of harmony as if it had some value in and of itself. Instead keep your mental clarity to yourself, a private secret that enables you to express beautiful melodies without a moment's hesitation. Real virtuosos don't waste their talent on foolish acrobatics. They use their skill for the only purpose that matters, to make each note infinitely beautiful.

Advanced jazz compositions

The material we have studied up to this point assumes a fixed tonal center with no key changes. You could say that what we have really been studying is basic tonal harmony. Relative to a particular note that we call the tonal center, you have learned to recognize the sound of all twelve notes of the tonal chromatic scale and you have learned how to use these notes to create many different kinds of harmonic movement. Most popular songs including jazz standards are based purely on these concepts of tonal harmony. So you already have all of the concepts you need in order to develop yourself as an improviser of this kind of music.

I want to share some thoughts about how you might apply these same concepts of tonal harmony to more sophisticated jazz compositions. My own experience is based on working with the music of composers like Thelonious Monk, Charles Mingus, Miles Davis, Wayne Shorter, John Coltrane and Ornette Coleman. But I think the same approach can also be helpful for studying the work of more contemporary artists like Keith Jarrett, Brad Mehldau, Marc Copland, Egberto Gismonti, Paul Bley, etc.

First of all I want to reassure you that there is nothing "difficult" about improvising over more sophisticated jazz compositions. On the contrary, the richness and the beauty of these compositions can be so inspiring that the music seems to play itself. It's much easier to make beautiful music if you are guided by an underlying compositional structure that is already fascinating and beautiful. So improvising great music over these compositions is not the problem. I think any difficulty that people have with sophisticated harmonies is really just a question of not knowing exactly how to go about studying the music in the first place.

If you want to improvise using a modern jazz composition as your material, then you need to understand every moment in that composition just as deeply as you understand the simpler songs that you are accustomed to. There is nothing difficult about this work. You just need to see clearly the size of the job you're talking about. A typical jazz standard might only include one key change, typically in the bridge. As you already know from experience, even just one key change in a tune is something you need to practice over and over again so that you can clearly see what's going on. So if a more sophisticated composition consists of fourteen measures and each measure is rooted in a different key, then you're looking at a minimum of fourteen times the amount of work involved just to form a basic idea of how the harmony flows through the piece.

And the problem actually goes deeper than that. Before we can begin to study the chord changes to a tune, we first need to decide for ourselves what the harmony of the piece really is. This is not a simple matter. Jazz composers use harmony in such abstract and ambiguous ways that it's not realistic to try to reduce their compositions to "lead sheets" like the ones we're used to seeing in fake books. And this is where most young musicians get stuck when it comes to working with more advanced material.

So just as we did with the seven notes of the major scale, our first task with complex jazz compositions is to get to know the sounds that make up the musical material we are going to be improvising with. In other words, there is no "secret" to improvising over more sophisticated music. We just need to study this music as patiently and as lovingly as we have studied everything else up to now. This is very enjoyable work and shouldn't be difficult for anyone. I'll try to give you an outline of what this work might look like for any particular piece.

Study the melody. Try to listen to several recordings of the piece, especially performances by the actual composer. Learn to sing the melody note for note and practice playing the entire melody on your instrument in all twelve keys. You might not be able to visualize the entire melody on a single tonal map because the key of the music might change several times during the course of the piece. But just embrace this challenge and figure out your own way to think about these key changes. Find some way to understand how the entire melody of the piece is connected, and learn to play the entire melody starting on any note of your instrument.

Study the entire composition. Try to get a transcription of the entire piece as performed by the composer. If that's not possible you might be able to get a copy of an arrangement for solo piano. This is much more valuable than a lead sheet because it will often contain countless details that cannot be summarized into a simple melody with chord symbols. You don't necessarily have to be able to play the entire piece on the piano at the proper tempo, since this might be too difficult. But you can still use the piano to discover and contemplate every sound in the composition, and to visualize all of the harmonic relationships between the sounds. Don't worry about trying to identify the harmony at this point. Forget about looking for scales and chords that might guide your future improvising. Just enjoy getting to know the composition for what it is.

Decide the harmony. This part is more complicated but it's nothing to fear. Remember that harmony is subjective, especially with more abstract music. So what we're looking for is not necessarily the "right answer" but rather some way to talk about what *you* feel when you listen to the harmony. The final authority on these questions should always be your own ear. So ironically, the principal technique I use for studying the most serious jazz compositions is the very first thing I ever showed you about music. In the chapter "Understanding begins with listening", I showed you a simple technique that you can use to connect with the underlying tonality that you feel whenever you listen to a song. (You might want to reread that chapter now to refresh your memory.) This is exactly what I would do to clarify the tonality of every moment in a sophisticated jazz composition. This is far more reliable than any kind of scale calculations based on written chord symbols. It also leads me to a result that is more useful to me personally because it corresponds to what I actually hear and feel when I listen to the composition. So for each new chord in the piece I would just pause the recording (or pause my own interpretation if I'm playing a written transcription), and I would identify the notes that I hear in my mind as the underlying harmonic environment of that moment. I would also identify the tonal center and then I would decide on some way to summarize this and write it down. You might express the harmony as a chord symbol similar to the ones that appear in fake books. Or you might write out an entire scale. You could even use the tonal language you learned in Mixed Harmony wherever it's appropriate. For example you might hear a particular chord as the "3D chord in the key of F", and you could just write that down. You can use any system you want, since you're the only one who needs to understand your own thinking.

Practice improvising. Once you have learned to play the entire composition (both chords and melody) on a piano, and once you have decided for yourself what is going on harmonically in the piece, you are ready to begin adding your own contribution. Practice improvising over every chord change as carefully as you studied your very first chord progressions in Pure Harmony. Especially wherever there are key changes, you will want to go over these passages many times to explore the melodic possibilities. Each change in the harmonic environment produces a particular sensation that the composer felt was important. So take the time to become intimately familiar with the way that each of these changes feels to you. And practice creating these key changes with your instrument so that you can confidently produce these same sensations for your listeners. The final step is to internalize all of this so that you can improvise melodies by ear, expressing your music exactly as you hear it in your musical imagination.

The main thing I want to impress upon you is an attitude of love and respect for the work of other composers. What I describe may seem like a lot of effort just to add a new piece to your repertoire. And it's certainly not the only way to do it. It can also be an excellent exercise in improvisation to just play through a tune using the written chord symbols on a lead sheet. But it would be just that, an exercise in improvisation. It would not give you the opportunity to enrich your own musical imagination with the deep thinking of a great composer.

So what I want to suggest is that seeing these jazz compositions as "difficult" to improvise over is really missing the point. These compositions are not quizzes. They are beautiful works of art that contain some of the most amazing musical lessons. So instead of seeing these compositions as a test of your improvisaiton skills, try to see them as great works of art that can form an essential part of your musical learning. If you give yourself time to study and enjoy each composition very deeply, and really get to know it inside and out, then the improvising will take care of itself.

Free improvisation - Feel, Imagine, Create

"Free improvisation" means different things to different people. For some it means making music with power tools and kitchen gadgets. For others it means using traditional instruments in non-traditional ways, like banging on your saxophone with a hammer or shouting into your trombone.

For me it means simply the spontaneous creation of music. There is no reason why it can't be just as beautiful as any other kind of music. Free improvisation doesn't necessarily mean avoiding everything that sounds melodic or sensible. It just means that the musicians let the direction of the music take shape in the moment.

One difference between free improvisation and traditional jazz improvisation is that free improvisers do all of their communicating with sound. Whereas a jazz player might begin a tune by calling out, "Let's play Body and Soul in Bb", a free improviser might begin a tune just by playing a few notes on the piano. What the pianist is really saying is, "Let's play something that starts like this!" The other musicians will listen for a moment and then play whatever should come next, according to their own creative imagination.

In a sense, free improvisers are like great painters who must all paint simultaneously on the same canvas. They have just a few minutes to create a masterpiece, and the only communication between them takes place in the actual paint on the canvas. Each painter decides what to paint based on what everybody else is painting.

Jazz players enjoy the same thrill of spontaneous creation but they prefer to organize themselves a bit before getting started. Jazz players agree on what they are going to paint, maybe a country scene of a farm house and a field, and they assign a specific responsibility to each painter. One would paint the background, another the farm house, another the trees, etc.

I say "jazz players" and "free improvisers" to illustrate a point about how these two ways of making music are different. But we can all play music in many different ways and there is no reason to limit ourselves to one concept or another. In a single concert I might play a couple of my own compositions note for note just like classical musicians do. I might play a whole bunch of tunes that have a loose structure with lots of room for improvisation, like jazz players do. And I might play a couple of pieces with no plan whatsoever, just like free improvisers. There is nothing right or wrong about any of this. It's all just music.

In Exercise 5 we are going to begin a new musical practice that is essentially free improvisation. But this practice is not restricted to any particular style of music. You certainly *could* practice Exercise 5 by participating in free improvisation jams with other people. But you can also practice Exercise 5 with jazz standards, rock songs or even simple children's songs. The change in Exercise 5 is an internal shift. It has to do with the mental process you use to find the notes you imagine.

In Exercise 2 - Mastery Level you learned to orient yourself in any piece of music using just one note from your instrument. The idea is that any note you play is always going to be one of the twelve notes of the chromatic scale relative to whatever key you are feeling. So simply by getting to know the sensation of all twelve notes on your tonal map, you should never need to play more than a single note in order to be perfectly oriented in any piece of music.

As I mentioned at the time, one way to practice this technique is to improvise along with your entire music collection. If you have tried this, you probably noticed that your experience varies greatly depending on the kind of music you are improvising over. With simple music that stays in the same key the whole time, you only have to orient yourself once at the beginning of the song and then you can spend the rest of the song developing your own musical ideas. With more complex music, you will notice that the key changes often. This requires you to orient yourself again every time the key changes. So obviously you have less time to develop your ideas before the next key change.

In other words, improvising over simple music lets you practice your ability to *imagine* and *create* music, whereas improvising over complex music gives you lots of practice at trying to *feel* the key of the moment.

At either extreme we miss out on part of the process. Very simple music doesn't let us practice our ability to feel where we are in the key, because they key never changes. And very complex music doesn't let us practice imagining and creating music because there isn't enough time to play even a single note before the key changes again. Most modern jazz, classical music and free improvisation is somewhere in the middle of these two extremes. The musical environment is generally in constant evolution but at a more reasonable pace. We need to pay attention to what we are feeling at all times because the key can change at any moment. But we still have plenty of time and space to develop and contribute our own ideas. This is the ideal setting to practice Exercise 5.

To understand this new approach to improvising, let's go back to that particular moment in Exercise 2 - Mastery Level when you learned to use a single note on your instrument to orient yourself in the music. What we need to do is look at the little stretch of time in between that initial "test note" and the very first note that you actually play with intention. This moment is the essence of free improvisation, and in Exercise 5 we will learn to incorporate this moment into every note we play.

The first thing you did was to *feel* where your test note was located within the tonal octave that you were feeling. In practice, this just means listening to and recognizing the sound of whatever note you are playing:

By listening to the sound of your test note, you instantly know exactly where you are in the tonal octave that you are feeling. It doesn't even matter if this is truly the "key" of the music. It makes no difference whether the other musicians are feeling the same key you are feeling.

All you need is some point of reference so that you can locate the next musical idea that want to play.

The next step is just that, to *imagine* the sound that you want to add to the music. This is a purely musical idea that occurs to you in the form of a sound:

imagine

And just as you did for your test note, you now need to locate this new musical idea within the tonal octave that you are feeling. As soon as you recognize which of the twelve notes of the tonal chromatic scale you are imagining, you can go ahead and *create* this sound on your instrument:

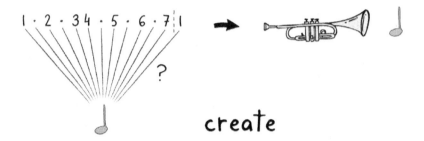

create

In Exercise 2 - Mastery Level, we only do this one time at the very beginning of our improvisation. As soon as we are oriented in the music we can just enjoy improvising because we know that the key is probably not going to change. But in Exercise 5 we are assuming that the musical environment is changing constantly. So we need to "check in" with every note we play to see whether we are still feeling the same key we were feeling a moment ago. In other words, there is no "test note" any more. Literally, every single note we play serves as the new test note. No matter how many times the key of the music changes, we will always know exactly where we are in the *new* key if we just pay attention to the sound of the last note we played.

Just like everything else in IFR, in practice this process is a lot more natural than it sounds when you first read about it. It takes a lot of words to describe these three moments, but in practice you won't actually have the sensation of performing three distinct actions. As soon as you get used to the new reality that the key can change on you at any time, you just begin to play with a heightened sensitivity to this fact and you learn to adapt to the changes as they come along.

To give you an idea of what it feels like to improvise in this way, let's walk through an example. Imagine that you are improvising in a complex musical environment that involves frequent key changes. Your internal thought process might go something like this:

"...I just played note 3, so that's mentally where I am on my tonal map...."

206

"...The next musical phrase that occurs to me is made up of the notes b6 and then 5... I'll play them now..."

"...Okay, I just played b6 and then note 5. But all of a sudden it doesn't *feel* like note 5 anymore. Now this new note feels more like note 7..."

"...Oh well. No problem. I guess now I'm on note 7. Let's see what sound I imagine next..."

"...Okay, now I hear my next musical idea in my mind, and it's note 6. So I'll play that now. I just need to move down from note 7 to note 6."

Obviously we don't actually think these thoughts verbally while we are playing, but the experience is kind of like this. The point is that whenever the feeling of a particular note surprises you, it's no cause for alarm. You just adapt to whatever you are feeling in the moment and you keep going. It's that simple.

The important thing is to realize that no matter how disoriented you might feel, you are *never* off your tonal map. You might be on one of the seven notes of the major scale or you might be on one of the little black dots. But you are always *somewhere* in that drawing. And if you want to know exactly where you are, all you have to do listen to the note you're playing and pay attention to what you feel.

Sometimes our students say that a nice benefit of the IFR method is that the only information you need to remember while you're playing is the note you're currently on. If you just keep track of where you are in the tonal octave, you'll always know where to find any other sound you can imagine. But even this statement doesn't quite capture the whole story. The truth is that you don't need to remember *anything* while you're playing. You don't need to "remember" where you are in the key because you can *hear* it. Just by listening to whatever note you play, you can instantly orient yourself in the key that you are feeling, and you can use this orientation to find any other sound that you can imagine.

So the next step in your journey as an improviser is to learn to let go of your dependence on a constant harmonic environment. If you want to play more sophisticated music, you have to accept the reality that the key you are feeling will be constantly moving. To adapt yourself to this situation you need to develop the habit of listening to *every* note you play as if you had lost your place in the tonal octave. In a sense, we are developing the habit of purposely "forgetting" where we are. Since we can no longer depend on the harmonic environment remaining constant, we need to "check in" with every single note and constantly feel where we are.

In Exercise 5 you will begin to practice making music in this way. But everything you have studied up to this point is still entirely relevant to your future musical growth. All five exercises in the IFR method are designed to be practiced in parallel. And your ability to practice Exercise 5 depends on skills that can only be acquired in the first four exercises. So if you find this new way of making music difficult or frustrating, don't torture yourself practicing Exercise 5. Instead go back and do more work on the earlier exercises. It is in the first four exercises that you will develop the knowledge, perception, sensitivity, control and mental quickness necessary to enjoy practicing Exercise 5.

Exercise 5: Free Harmony

<u>Objective</u>: To continuously improve in your ability to...

Play entirely from your own imagination, using your ear as your only reference.

Water trickling down a mountainside never gets confused about which way is down. No matter how many obstacles lie in its path, water never goes up by accident. Guided by the constant pull of gravity it flows passively downward toward the earth's gravitational center. In the same way, in any piece of music the human ear feels a constant pull toward a particular note called the *tonal center*. It is the attraction to this tonal center that makes all other notes sound the way they do. The notes that harmonize nicely with the tonal center are called "consonant notes" and the ones that create conflict are called "dissonant notes".

Music theory can actually predict which notes will sound consonant or dissonant in any given musical situation. Just knowing a few scales and some rules about when to use them is sufficient to improvise lines that sound pretty good to the ear. For this reason most improvisation methods are based entirely on teaching this theory.

In other words, as soon as possible, the students' attention is directed away from the sounds themselves toward a mathematical system of rules and formulas. Most students never notice this sleight of hand on the part of their teachers, but think for a minute about what has happened:

- The human ear feels some sounds as pleasing and others as painful.

- We can define rules predicting which notes will sound pleasing.

- We begin following these rules instead of listening to the sounds.

Do you see what has gotten lost in this process? We're using music theory to guide our improvising, but what has gotten lost is the very thing that we are theorizing *about*. Our formulas are an attempt to codify how the human ear will perceive sounds in different harmonic situations. But since you presumably have a couple of human ears attached to your head, you could actually skip all the theorizing and go straight to the authority. If you want to know if a note is beautiful, all you have to do is listen to it.

Just like water flowing down a mountainside, the ear always knows what it is feeling. And its feelings are far too subtle for simplistic labels like "right notes" and "wrong notes". The human ear is very sensitive and it has a complex personality. Every note we hear contains cultural references that are impossible to explain in words. Even in the simplest music, our clumsy theories don't even come close to telling the whole story. This is why the next step in your growth as a musician is to learn to play, think and create music entirely in the world of *sounds*.

In Exercises 1 through 4 we discovered many new concepts that were useful at the time. These concepts are only metaphors, but they gave us a way to begin making sense of the music that we hear or imagine. Here are examples of some of the metaphors we have been using up to now:

- "chord notes" and "other notes"

- "the 1 chord"

- "tension" and "relaxation"

- "note 3"

- "the 6D harmonic environment"

- "major" and "minor" tonality

- "dominant chord shape", "minor chord shape", etc.

In Exercise 5 these concepts will continue to serve us but in a different way. It's time for them to take their rightful place as nothing more than metaphors. We are no longer concerned with studying them as unique concrete things. At any given time a note might feel like note 2 and then a moment later the same note might feel like note 3. We might play a phrase that starts out sounding minor but then it switches to major and finally ends in a dominant sound. The concepts are still useful but only as passing sensations that we happen to notice. The sounds themselves don't come into this world with predefined labels.

You could think of your early musical training in IFR as something similar to the way we use fairy tales to teach children about metaphorical concepts like "good guys" and "bad guys". As adults, we know that these concepts are gross oversimplifications, and that any one of us can behave like a good guy one moment and a bad guy the next. We don't go around literally trying to label each person as a good guy or a bad guy. But these metaphors were an important tool for learning about abstract concepts like justice, fairness and the difference between right and wrong.

The musical exercises that you have been doing up to now are a little bit like musical fairy tales. In fairy tales you find very simple one-dimensional characters like kings and dragons and cats with too much curiosity. In the same way, in our musical fairy tales you find very pure musical concepts like the 6- chord. In real life it's not always possible to reduce every single person to being either a king or a dragon. And in music it's not always possible to put simple labels on every sound.

For this reason, in Exercise 5 we can no longer say whether we are improvising in the 1 chord or the 6- chord or some other chord. And we no longer care. All that matters is that we have some way to understand where we are, and some way to locate the next note we are imagining. It may turn out that *either* the 1 chord concept or the 6- chord concept might be equally useful to help us express the musical idea we are feeling. But neither concept is "correct". They are just two metaphors available to us, because we have worked on each one individually and we have learned the lessons that each one has to teach.

Exercise 5 is about practicing the art of seeing things as they really are. It represents the next step in your journey inward, to the world of the sounds themselves. The first activities in this chapter will help you build a bridge connecting the work you have done up to now with the new practice of Exercise 5. Then we'll talk about some specific ways that you can practice this new way of making music. We will begin our work with an updated look at the very first exercise in the IFR method which is Exercise 1: Landscape.

Landscape Revisited

To officially begin your practice of Exercise 5, your first assignment is to go back and read Exercise 1 again. Notice whether the words have a different meaning for you now, after everything you have learned about harmony. Then try the Exercise 1 Daily Meditation and see how that feels. Choose any interval you like, and really take your time with the exercise. Don't assume that you should be able to perform the exercise more quickly now due to all your experience playing musical intervals on your instrument. The real test of whether you have grown as a musician is whether you can now do the meditation more *slowly*.

Think about how you could expand Exercise 1 to include any musical phrase, riff, melody or chord shape that you know. For example you might allow yourself to move around your instrument using *either* the interval of a major third *or* the full arpeggio of a minor seventh chord. Imagine yourself moving up a major third, then another, then another, and then coming down through an entire minor seventh chord as you learned in Rock Jumping.

The reason why these arbitrary movements are so important to practice is that we musicians very quickly develop an impressive ability to steer around our areas of doubt. There are always a million ways to resolve any musical situation, so it's easy to improvise your entire life without ever seeing certain things clearly. If a particular movement is difficult for you to visualize, then this musical idea simply won't occur to you when you are improvising. The only way to eliminate these gaps in our understanding is to invent some silly game that *forces* us to contemplate movements that might not otherwise occur to us. It doesn't need to form a big part of your musical life, but take a few minutes each day to play around with some variation of Landscape. If you find it too easy, it's only because you're not really challenging yourself. Incorporate more difficult shapes that really stretch your mind.

You can also mix free improvisation with Exercise 1 very naturally. For example you might be doing the Exercise 1 Daily Meditation with the interval of a minor sixth, and then suddenly you feel an inspiration to play a particular melody. Go ahead and play it! This is a great skill to practice because it's precisely what happens to us all the time in free improvisation. You find yourself somewhere in your musical range when you have a sudden musical inspiration, and you must think through how to play it. Play these melodies whenever they occur to you. Then, whenever the melody has finished, you can use the last note of the melody as the new starting point for the Exercise 1 Daily Meditation in minor sixths again.

Be playful and invent your own ways to strengthen your confidence moving around your musical landscape. Don't think of Exercise 1 as a specific practice technique but rather a personal *meditation* that can be entered any number of ways. Any time your attention is focused on the purely physical details of moving around your musical landscape, you are doing Exercise 1.

Melody Revisited

In Exercise 2 you learned how to use a visual map of the major scale as a point of translation between the sounds you imagine and your instrument. In order to develop a strong personal awareness of the sounds in the major scale, we were careful to avoid using any other notes. You always knew exactly where you were in the scale, and you knew which note was being used as the tonal center. For example, in the Seven Worlds exercises you would first choose one of the seven harmonic environments to study, and then you would use this particular note as both the floor and ceiling of your musical improvisation. This simple exercise, repeated over time, enabled you to develop your musical consciousness in three very important ways:

- You practiced the *intervals* that make up each of the seven modes of the major scale.

- You learned to recognize the *sound* of each note in all seven harmonic environments.

- You came to know and recognize the overall *feel* of each harmonic environment.

In Exercise 5, there are two important ways in which our approach to Melody changes:

1. The tonal map that we use to orient ourselves is now purely subjective. Since any melody can be located on any tonal map, we can now use any tonal map we want. All that matters is that we have some way to make sense of what we are feeling.

2. We always consider our musical palette to be the entire twelve note chromatic scale. No matter which chord we feel we're in, we are always free to use any note we want.

As an example, let's say you are improvising in a sophisticated musical context that has lots of free and ambiguous sounds. Let's say you just played the note D and now you are imagining a new sound in your mind that you want to play. (The new sound you are imagining is the note F, but in our example you don't know that yet. For you it's just a sound, and your task is to figure out where this sound is located so that you can play it.)

If the musical environment is very ambiguous, then it's hard to predict what key you might be feeling in the moment. Here are just a few examples of the many possibilities:

You might feel that you just played the root of the 2- chord. (In other words, the note D that you just played feels like note 2.) As you imagine the new sound in your mind, it will feel like note 4. Moving up to note 4, you will correctly play the note F that you were imagining:

Or perhaps you were feeling something totally different. Maybe the last note you played (D) sounded to you like the fifth of the 4 chord. (In other words, the note D that you just played feels like note 1.) As you imagine the new sound in your mind, it will feel like note b3. Moving up to note b3, you will correctly play the note F that you were imagining.

Or maybe you feel that you just played the sharp fourth of the 5D chord. (In other words, the note D that you just played feels like note #1.) As you imagine the new sound in your mind, it will feel like note 3. Moving up to note 3, you will correctly play the note F that you were imagining.

We could go on imagining endless possibilities. But the point is that it doesn't matter whether you are "correct" in your assumption about where you are in the key. The fact is that *any* way of understanding where you are will give you all the information you need to play the next note you are imagining. In other words, when you are applying the tonal map to your own imagination, there is no way to be wrong. Just clarify what you feel, and you'll always be able to play what you imagine.

Depending on your level of comfort with the seven basic harmonic environments, these concepts may or may not continue to play a big role in your musical thinking. Some people have a natural tendency to imagine themselves in one of the seven environments of the major scale all the time. Other people gradually move away from the concept of the seven harmonic environments and simply start referring to any tonal center as "1". Either way of imagining the notes is perfectly fine, as long as your mental model corresponds to what you really feel in your body.

To achieve this new level of freedom, you will need to become an absolute expert in what I call the "tonal chromatic scale". By this I mean the twelve notes of the chromatic scale, relative to a particular tonal center. There can no longer be any uncertainty in your mind about how each one of these notes sounds. In free improvisation you can't count on being oriented in a scale in order to identify the notes you hear in your mind. You will have to

212

recognize them *instantly* and purely by their sound.

The good news is that you already know all of these sounds intimately. You might need to do some work to clarify which sounds are which, but you have been making music with these sounds all along. For example, think back to when you were practicing Seven Worlds from Exercise 2. Whenever you chose to use note 2 as your tonal center, your improvisation was based on the following set of notes:

2 · 3 4 · 5 · 6 · 7 1 · 2

You probably didn't think about it at the time, but as you were improvising with this material you were also getting to know the sound of two notes outside the major scale. These two notes are b3 and b7. This is because, relative to the tonal center you were feeling, the notes you were playing could also be described by the numbers shown below:

1 · 2 b3 · 4 · 5 · 6 b7 · 1

This is the same kind of analysis we performed in the chapter "Measuring distances" to determine that the 2- chord is a minor chord, but now we are extending our analysis to the entire scale. What we are really doing is analyzing this particular mode of the major scale to discover the new scale that exists at this location. But this is not just some academic exercise. It literally allows us to take the magic of the 2- chord with us no matter where we go. All those beautiful sounds and melodies that you discovered improvising in the 2- chord are actually available to you all the time, no matter what's going on around you harmonically. All you need to understand is *where* to find those sounds relative to whatever tonal center you are feeling in the moment. This is the significance of the second scale shown above.

The other purpose of studying the connection between the two scales drawn above is so that you can learn the lessons that each mode of the major scale has to teach you. Looking at the second scale drawn above, you can see that this particular mode of the major scale has already made you an expert in the sound of the two outside notes b3 and b7. My own personal opinion is that one of the most beautiful lessons of mode 2 is the sound of the major sixth in a minor chord. (Notice in the second scale drawn above that note 3 is flatted but note 6 is natural.) This is a unique combination that only occurs in mode 2. For me, this is the essential beauty of the second harmonic environment. But you can decide for yourself what you think is important and special about each mode of the major scale. I just want you to begin to look at these sounds in a more abstract context, the one shown in the second drawing above.

I want to emphasize that I am *not* suggesting you memorize the new scale and look for opportunities to spit it out in your solos. That's not the point. The new drawing is simply a new way to see the notes of mode 2. They are the same notes but now we are seeing them from a different point of view. The benefit of studying each mode in this way is that you will eventually come to have a command of the entire octave. Every one of the twelve notes in the tonal chromatic scale will be filled with meaning for you, because it will remind you of all of the different harmonic environments in which that sound appears.

One way to practice these new note names is to simply go back to the same accompaniments you used when you were first studying the 2- chord. Maybe you used a recording that you created yourself, or maybe you used IFR Jam Tracks Level 1: Seven Worlds. Either way, now you can practice improvising over this same accompaniment using the new note names shown in the second drawing above as your tonal map. One of the fastest and most effective ways to learn to use this new tonal map is with the exercise Sing the Map, but now you would sing the new numbers (1, 2, b3, etc.).

Once you have learned to see mode 2 of the major scale from these two different points of view, you should go on to study all of the other harmonic environments in the same way. Mode 3 of the major scale has an especially interesting sound because it starts right off the bat with a half step:

$$3 \quad 4 \quad \cdot \quad 5 \quad \cdot \quad 6 \quad \cdot \quad 7 \quad 1 \quad \cdot \quad 2 \quad \cdot \quad 3$$

$$1 \quad b2 \quad \cdot \quad b3 \quad \cdot \quad 4 \quad \cdot \quad 5 \quad b6 \quad \cdot \quad b7 \quad \cdot \quad 1$$

Again, you can practice this new view of the notes using the same accompaniments you used when you first began to study the 3- chord. The only difference is that now you will use the new numbers (1, b2, b3, etc.) to think about the notes you are playing. You should do the same for all of the remaining modes as well. We'll go through them quickly now.

Mode 4 of the major scale is almost exactly like mode 1. (Mode 1 is just the major scale in its original order.) The only difference between mode 4 and mode 1 is the sharp fourth which gives this scale an even lighter feeling than mode 1:

$$4 \quad \cdot \quad 5 \quad \cdot \quad 6 \quad \cdot \quad 7 \quad 1 \quad \cdot \quad 2 \quad \cdot \quad 3 \quad 4$$

$$1 \quad \cdot \quad 2 \quad \cdot \quad 3 \quad \cdot \quad \#4 \quad 5 \quad \cdot \quad 6 \quad \cdot \quad 7 \quad 1$$

Mode 5 is also very similar to mode 1, with the only altered note being the flatted seventh. This scale has a sound that is just slightly darker than the major scale itself in mode 1. This is the sound that characterizes much of blues, funk and rock music.

$$5 \quad \cdot \quad 6 \quad \cdot \quad 7 \quad 1 \quad \cdot \quad 2 \quad \cdot \quad 3 \quad 4 \quad \cdot \quad 5$$

$$1 \quad \cdot \quad 2 \quad \cdot \quad 3 \quad 4 \quad \cdot \quad 5 \quad \cdot \quad 6 \quad b7 \quad \cdot \quad 1$$

If the above scale looks familiar to you, it's because you saw it already in Exercise 4. At that time we called it the 1D harmonic environment.

Mode 6 is very similar to mode 2. The only difference is that mode 6 has a flatted sixth whereas mode 2 has a natural sixth:

```
6  ·  7  1  ·  2  ·  3  4  ·  5  · |6
1  ·  2  b3 ·  4  ·  5  b6 ·  b7 · |1
```

And finally, we arrive to mode 7 which has the strangest sound of all due to its flatted fifth:

```
7  1  ·  2  ·  3  4  ·  5  ·  6  · |7
1  b2 ·  b3 ·  4  b5 ·  b6 ·  b7 · |1
```

That's all of them. As I said before, there isn't any new musical content here. You have already been improvising freely with all seven modes of the major scale since Exercise 2. Your ears and your hands are already very accustomed to working with this material. What we are practicing now is simply a different point of view from which we see the notes.

Practice this new consciousness using the exercise Sing the Map as you have been doing all along, but this time use the new numbers. The new numbers don't replace the old numbers, but you should learn to see the notes from *both* points of view at once. Since you are already an expert in the tonal point of view (the first scale shown in all of the above drawings), now you just need to dedicate some time to developing the modal point of view (the second scale shown in the above drawings).

I want to say again that our work is not about memorizing the seven modes of the major scale, nor about looking for places to insert them in our improvised music. The reason we are taking this new look is to discover that we *already* know the sound of all twelve notes of the tonal chromatic scale. The many hours you have spent improvising in the seven basic harmonic environments of the major scale have already taught you the sound of every single note in the tonal chromatic scale:

```
1 b2  2  b3  3  4  b5  5  b6  6  b7  7 |1
```

And *this* is truly the palette of melodic colors available to you whenever you are improvising. Our work in Melody Revisited is about learning to orient ourselves in this tonal chromatic scale no matter what is going on around us.

Pure Harmony Revisited

In the chapter "The seven harmonic environments" we defined chords as being the root, 3rd, 5th and 7th of any particular scale. We called these four notes the "chord notes" and we set aside the remaining three notes of the scale as "other notes". It turns out that this was a bit of an oversimplification. But it was useful at the time because it enabled us to begin working with the seven harmonic environments and get to know how they sound and feel.

The time has come to begin including these "other notes" in our understanding of the chord. The concept of a chord doesn't need to be limited to just four notes. It can be extended beyond the 7th to include the 9th, 11th and 13th. In reality these are just notes 2, 4 and 6 of the next octave. So the true theoretical definition of the entire 1 chord is better represented by the following picture:

So just as you're learning to think in terms of the twelve-note tonal chromatic scale in your updated look at Melody, we can now adopt a different point of view toward the "other notes" in each of the seven harmonic environments. This new point of view is to understand them not as "other notes" but as *extensions* of the chord itself. Instead of imagining two different categories of notes as we learned to do in Pure Harmony, now we see all notes as part of a continuum, the one showed in the drawing above.

Just as I mentioned in our updated look at Melody, it's important to realize that this new practice has nothing to do with looking for places to insert 9ths and 13ths in your music. We just want to *become aware* of these sounds and learn to feel them as extensions of the chord itself. Don't worry about how you'll use these sounds in your music. Just enjoy them and let them penetrate deep into your musical consciousness. Trust that these sounds will enrich your musical imagination, and that this will all come out naturally in the music you imagine.

You should investigate the upper chord extensions for all of the harmonic environments that you have seen in both Pure Harmony and Mixed Harmony. But concentrate especially on the seven basic harmonic environments of the major scale, since this is where all of the other sounds come from. Take a new look at Exercise 3 and think about how you could modify the activities in that chapter to include the entire extended chord in your awareness. You can actually retain the concept of "chord notes" and "other notes" but you need to be more sophisticated in your use of this metaphor. Look again at the drawing above and notice that over the span of two octaves you still see the same familiar pattern of alternating circles. What is new is the idea that note 1 can be a chord note in one octave and an other note in the next octave! Obviously this is a contradiction but don't be alarmed. All we're really trying to do is grow in our own ability to feel each note as *either* a chord note or an other note. Even this statement is a little too simplistic. But I think you'll discover exactly what I mean when you try it yourself.

A good place to start is the exercise Seven Worlds Expanded from Exercise 3. After choosing your starting note and the harmonic environment you want to explore, play all seven notes of this harmonic environment over a *two octave* range on your instrument. Improvise for a few minutes using all seven notes of the scale. Then improvise for a few minutes using just the extended chord over this two octave range: the root, 3rd, 5th, 7th, 9th, 11th and 13th. I think if you do this, you will be able to feel the 9th, 11th and 13th not as "other notes" but as extensions of the chord itself.

This concept can be unsettling because it raises theoretical questions that seem paradoxical. "How can the same note be both a chord note *and* an other note? How do I know when to think of the 2nd as really the 9th?" The answer is that both of these concepts (the 2nd and the 9th) are only metaphors. When we study the "other notes," imagining them to be notes 2, 4 and 6, we are practicing one particular way of using these notes. And when we study them as the 9th, 11th and 13th, we are practicing a different way of using them. Neither way is "correct". We just want to develop our own ability to see the notes from both points of view, and so we practice that consciousness in the specific way I described, using Seven Worlds Expanded from Exercise 3. But this awareness then becomes a part of you, and you don't need to think about it consciously anymore. Once you have learned to appreciate the notes in this new way, your expanded sensitivity will automatically enrich your music.

In summary, our updated practice with Pure Harmony includes both of the following steps:

1. We are going to focus on the upper chord extensions and discover their particular sounds. And we will expand our musical imagination to be able to appreciate these notes as chord notes.

2. We will remember to let go of all of these concepts when we are actually creating our music. Whenever we are improvising we will always listen to each note as it really is and we will play from our imagination, without trying to put labels on the notes we play.

Mixed Harmony Revisited

In Exercise 4, I showed you a long list of altered harmonic environments that create different sounds and feelings. But whenever we are improvising freely, our attraction to any particular tonal center is purely a subjective one. As a consequence, many of the Mixed Harmony environments from Exercise 4 can be interchanged, simplified or even forgotten.

As an example, consider the following chord progression that leads us to the Dm chord:

$$\| \text{ E-7}^{b5} \quad | \text{ A7} \quad | \text{ Dm} \quad | \text{ Dm} \quad \|$$

If we were to encounter this progression in the key of F we would immediately recognize it as the progression to the 6- chord:

$$\| \text{ 7-}^{b5} \quad | \text{ 3D} \quad | \text{ 6-} \quad | \text{ 6-} \quad \|$$

If on the other hand we were playing a song in the key of C, we would understand the above progression as the path to the 2- chord:

$$\| \text{ 3-}^{b5} \quad | \text{ 6D} \quad | \text{ 2-} \quad | \text{ 2-} \quad \|$$

And if we were playing a song in the key of D major, we might even think of the above progression in the following way:

$$\| \; 2\text{-}^{b5} \quad | \; 5D \quad | \; 1\text{-} \quad | \; 1\text{-} \quad \|$$

Whenever you are playing actual songs like the jazz standards we looked at just after Exercise 4, these differences are very important. Contrary to the way most music schools teach improvisation, the fact is that the three chord progressions above are *not* the same, even if they all lead you to play the exact same notes. What is different is your tonal orientation, which is the most important thing in the world to a true improviser. Real improvisers aren't looking for rules and shortcuts to get to the "correct notes". What we are after is a command of the octave, the ability to visualize where we are and to locate any sound we might imagine. This is why we treat every chord progression in Mixed Harmony as something unique and special that must be studied independently.

This is still true in Exercise 5. We still consider every one of the above progressions to be unique and special. What is new in Exercise 5 is that our perception of these progressions is now entirely *subjective*. Since we are no longer anchored to a specific key, we might feel any one of the above progressions (as well as countless others) at any given moment. Our only orientation is our own ear. And so a natural complement to your new approach to Melody is a simplification in your use of Mixed Harmony.

As I mentioned earlier, different people have a tendency to feel harmony in different ways. Some people naturally orient themselves in the harmonic environments that you studied in Exercises 3 and 4, while others tend to feel *any* tonal center as "note 1". In the case of the progression to Dm shown above, the person who tends to orient himself in the major scale would probably feel the above progression as 7-b5, 3D, 6- while the person oriented in the tonal chromatic scale would probably feel it as 2-b5, 5D, 1-.

But the fact is that in a free improvisation setting both of these interpretations are correct. In fact *any* interpretation is correct. The chords above might even feel to you like the progression to an unusual tonal center like 4-. But if that's what you feel then it's perfectly fine to interpret the sounds in that way. As you saw earlier in our updated look at Melody, the only thing you need in order to play the next sound you imagine is some way to orient yourself in whatever key *you* feel.

So our new practice in Exercise 5 is to apply your knowledge of Mixed Harmony in a more flexible way. Whenever you are improvising freely, be on the lookout for the sensations that you discovered in the altered harmonic environments of Exercise 4. Even though you are no longer tied to a specific key, these sensations will still come up for you. And when they do, you can immediately orient yourself in whatever Mixed Harmony concept you are feeling at that moment.

Exercise 5: New exercises in Feel, Imagine and Create

The rest of the activities in Exercise 5 are organized roughly into the three skill areas of Feel, Imagine and Create. Obviously there is a lot of overlap between the different areas, and many of the following activities could be listed in more than one area. But I have tried to associate each activity with the skill area that it most directly benefits, so that you can easily pick an activity to work on any particular skill area you feel like practicing.

feel

Feel refers to your ability to recognize the sounds that you hear or imagine. It is what enables you to orient yourself in whatever key you are feeling by listening to the sound of the last note you played. It is also what enables you to locate on your tonal map the next note you are imagining.

Invisible Staircase. This is a fascinating exercise that you can perform alone or with other people. It consists of playing a few random notes on a piano and then using your ear to "fill in" the missing notes. Start by playing a simple repeating pattern on the piano using three notes. You can choose any notes you want, so don't shy away from strange combinations and unusual sounds. Play a little pattern with these notes and listen to it a few times. Then match the highest of these notes with your voice. Starting at this pitch, just start coming down a musical scale singing whatever notes seem to naturally occur to you. Singing this scale is like walking down an "invisible staircase" that connects the three random notes you were playing. Almost always the notes you imagine will form a perfect major scale, and many times this will be the *only* major scale that includes all of the notes you were playing on the piano. In other words, your subconscious musical mind is able to instantly imagine the one key that happens to contain the three notes you were playing. If there is no major scale that contains all three of the notes you were playing, then your subconscious mind will imagine the key in which the three notes make the most "sense". This is a natural ability that all people possess. (If you don't believe me, try this exercise on complete beginners or even little children. You'll be amazed at how often they fill in the missing notes with a perfect major scale, even if they have no idea what a major scale is!) We all do this naturally because the music we have been exposed to during our lifetime has created a kind of subliminal programming that causes our ear to naturally try to feel the major scale *all the time*. As soon as you hear the first few notes of any piece of music, your subconscious mind automatically imagines the entire major scale (or "key") that contains those notes. This is an important exercise because it shows you that the key of the music is subjective. "Tonality" actually occurs inside your own mind. Even when presented with three completely random notes, your subconscious mind automatically fills in the remaining notes based on an imaginary key. This key feels just as real to you as if you were literally hearing all seven notes on the piano. Practice this exercise and learn to find this "invisible staircase" inside you. Once you connect with it, you will be able to improvise your own beautiful music over even the most strange or sophisticated musical environments.

Moving Chord Shapes. A warm-up exercise I often practice with advanced students is to accompany them with one particular chord shape on the piano (for example "minor") while the student improvises. Then periodically I move this chord shape to a new location. The student must then orient himself or herself in the new key. It is very important that you don't go fumbling around for the new notes. Remember that the question is not, "What is the new key?" The question is always, *"Where* in the new key am I?" The student's job is to just stay put on whatever note he or she happens to be playing when the key changes. The student needs to *feel* where this note is located on the new tonal map, and then continue improvising in the new key. You can practice this yourself with

IFR Jam Tracks Level 8: Modal Mastery. First you'll learn to master key changes using a single chord shape exactly as I do with my private students. Once you get good at orienting yourself within a single moving chord shape, you can move on to more advanced tracks that freely mix all different chord shapes (major, minor, dominant and minor b5) in all different locations. At this level you will be playing even the most sophisticated jazz harmonies entirely by ear.

Moving Progressions. An extension of the last idea is to do the same with entire chord progressions. The most important are 2-, 5D, 1 (the path to major) and 7-b5, 3D, 6- (the path to minor). This practice is especially useful to jazz players because jazz standards are filled with quick little 2-5-1 progressions from other keys. What many people don't realize is that the key change *itself* has a particular sound that you can learn to recognize by ear. So for example, if you're improvsing over a song and suddenly there is a key change going up a major third, the sound of this ascending major third key change is absolutely unique and it's something you can recognize by ear. All you need is the opportunity to practice jamming over this exact key change the same way you learned chords and chord progressions. All of this is part of what we do in IFR Jam Tracks Level 8: Modal Mastery.

Follow the Melody, Revisited. In Exercise 2 you learned to listen to a recording and follow along with the melody to identify every note as one of the seven notes of the major scale. In the updated version, we have the same two changes that we saw earlier in this chapter for Melody Revisited. The two changes are that (1) the key is no longer constant and (2) the melody note can be any one of the twelve notes in the tonal chromatic scale. To practice this new ability, it's best to work with music that is harmonically sophisticated but rhythmically slow. Any slow piece by a 20th century classical composer will be excellent. As you listen to the music, try to identify every single note as one of the twelve notes of the tonal chromatic scale. When you feel the key change, forget about the old key and immediately orient yourself in the new one. Don't worry about keeping track of how many times you feel the key change. Just try to keep up with the melody and pay attention to what each note makes you feel. If you fall behind, just pause the music and clarify what you are feeling. By singing a few notes up or down in the scale you imagine, you should be able to recognize where you are. The mastery level of this practice is to pick up your instrument and play what the soloist plays, note for note. Try to shadow the melody, doubling it perfectly just a split second behind.

imagine

Imagine refers to your ability to imagine sounds that tell a meaningful story. Whenever you work on Imagine, try to forget about all of the technical work involved in actually playing your ideas on your instrument. This is your time to work on cultivating the ideas themselves.

Playing Other People's Music. At last we arrive at the only place in the entire IFR method where I will mention studying the music of other people. We study other people's music the same way we study the seven notes of the major scale. Our only objective is to discover new sounds and possibilities. We never study other people's music with the intention of consciously copying them or trying to force their ideas into our music. Playing a classical piece or a transcription of a beautiful jazz solo note for note is a way of giving your respect to the musician who played it. It says that you are interested in hearing and contemplating what that person had to say. It shows that you are curious, thoughtful and open minded. The reason I tell you not to copy other musicians' phrases is not because I don't want you to learn from them. On the contrary, it's because I *do* want you to learn from them! It's the same as if you were listening to your wise old grandfather telling you a story. If your attention is on looking for clever sounding phrases that you can steal from your grandfather so that you can sound just as smart as he sounds, then you're missing out on the real treasure that he is trying to give you. But if you just *listen,* if you listen with patience and an open mind and just reflect on the things he tells you, *this* is the way to eventually become as wise as your grandfather someday. So study classical compositions and arrangements and solo transcriptions and anything else that you find beautiful. Practice these pieces over and over again until you can play them by heart. Enjoy every note and celebrate the gorgeous music that has been created by others. This is one of the great treasures of modern life, and it's yours to enjoy as much as you want. But play their music with sincerity and respect. Don't cheapen the art form by focusing on clever sounding phrases that you can rip off. Make sure you get the real gift they have to offer you, which is to enrich your musical imagination with their beautiful ideas. Play their music without thinking about how you will use it. Trust that the musical nourishment you receive will all come out in your own music someday.

Sing Freely, Revisited. In this activity from Exercise 2, I encouraged you to sing music freely sometimes without making any attempt to orient yourself in a key or put names on the notes you sing. The updated version of this practice is to do the same over the most sophisticated music you can find. Try it with contemporary jazz music and 20th century classical composers like Hindemith, Shostakovich, and Bartok. It will feel strange in the beginning but don't let your initial clumsiness discourage you. Your ear is an absolute musical genius that can imagine beautiful melodies even in the most difficult or unusual harmonic environments. But your ear can't perform for you unless you give it plenty of opportunities to practice. You need to be just as patient with your imagination as you are with your physical technique. You might need to practice singing freely over sophisticated music every day for *years* before you really start to feel confident. But take comfort in knowing that every minute you dedicate to this kind of exercise forces your mind to grow in ways that you don't even notice. So try not to get too hung up on the desired result. Just take time to enjoy singing freely over very complex musical environments, and you'll be giving your imagination the experiences it needs in order to grow.

Memorize the Sound. This last exercise is to sing your favorite melodies or solos note for note. Don't try to sing the numbers or even think about where you are on the tonal map. Just play a recording of your favorite solo and try to sing along with the soloist. You probably won't be able to sing the entire solo the first time through. It takes lots of practice to sing an entire solo note for note. But you'll be amazed how much more detail you notice in the solo when you begin to sing along with it. If there are phrases that you especially like, stop the recording and sing them in slow motion. Clarify the sound of every single note so that you can sing the melody clearly at any tempo. Don't worry about trying to figure out what the notes are. Just *memorize the sound* and trust your own ability to translate these sounds to numbers whenever they occur to you during your improvisations.

create

Create refers to your ability to express on your instrument the sound that you are imagining. This means understanding where the sound is located on your tonal map (which is part of *Feel*) and then being able to execute the required musical interval on your instrument.

Technical Studies. One of the most important things you can do to make it easier to express your music is to develop a high level of physical mastery over your instrument. This includes the Exercise 1 Daily Meditation but it goes far beyond that to include every aspect of your physical relationship with your instrument. Many people do not realize the extent to which creativity and physical technique are interrelated. But having a high level of control over your instrument is absolutely essential to the creative process. If playing your instrument is difficult for you, your brain dedicates an enormous amount of energy to managing this physical process. You may not be aware of it, but your music suffers in every way from this energy drain. Your rhythm is not as sharp, your sound is not as beautiful and your ideas are not nearly as lively. But it would be wrong to conclude that you have a problem with rhythm or creativity, even if those are the symptoms you are experiencing. The problem is often with your physical technique. Simply put, playing your instrument is requiring too much brain power. The only way to overcome this problem is to study the physical aspects of playing your instrument with an excellent teacher. So make it a priority to study deeply the most basic movements involved in playing your instrument. You will be amazed at how much your creativity improves after just a few months of serious technical study.

Solo Free Improvisation. An excellent daily practice for the free improviser is simply to pick up your instrument once every day and, without any warm-up whatsoever, create a totally spontaneous free improvisation from the *very first note* you play. Tell a story, and create a short musical poem that stands by itself as a perfect statement of some very precise thing. It may help to first get in touch with your own emotions before you begin. Pause for a moment before you begin playing and decide what you are feeling in your heart and body in that very moment. I'll let you in on a tremendous secret of musical performance. It's a lot easier to express something that you are actually feeling. So take a minute to check in with yourself and notice all the thoughts and feelings running through your mind. Play all that. You really can do it if you just *believe in yourself*. You may not always love what you were able to create. But just like every other aspect of our art, be patient with yourself and give yourself the opportunity to practice. If your dream is to be able to improvise beautiful pieces for an audience someday, then start practicing now.

Add-a-Part Recordings. Many students of jazz music are familiar with add-a-part recordings designed specifically for practicing improvisation. There are hundreds of these products on the market, and some are of very excellent quality. The recordings consist of a professional jazz group playing well-known tunes, where the only part missing is your instrument. For example a piano student can buy the version in which the piano part is missing, but all other instruments are present. These recordings typically come with sheet music for the songs so that you can read along and improvise with the group. You can turn these products into a fantastic exercise in Free Harmony by simply throwing away the sheet music. This is as close as you can get to the experience of improvising freely in a jazz context using nothing but your ear to orient you. Even if you don't feel that you are

100% successful in the beginning, I encourage you to make this a regular part of your practice routine.

Fearlessly Participate. Another important practice is to fearlessly participate in any musical conversation without worrying about how successful you will be. This means picking up your instrument anytime music is playing in your home and playing right along with it. It also means doing this in real live social situations like jams with other people. This requires you to be comfortable with the possibility that you might not always play a brilliant solo. If you can handle that, then you are on your way. Once the ego is out of the way, there is no limit to how fast you can learn because life presents so many opportunities to practice. Think about how much faster a person learns a new language if he is living in a country where he is immersed in the language and must use it for everything he does. Try to create a musical life for yourself in which you are immersed in the language of free improvisation. If you fearlessly participate in all of the musical conversations that life offers, your confidence will grow so fast that soon you won't even remember that you were insecure at first.

Group Free Improvisation. Obviously, the best preparation for free improvisation is free improvisation itself. Take the initiative to invite friends over to your house to experiment with free improvisation. Even just one other person is enough to give you a rewarding experience. Some of the most beautiful improvised music I have ever heard was created by just a duo. For people interested in sincere improvisation (in which the musicians really listen to each other and try to create something together), I think small formats like duo and trio work best. But no matter what happens you will always learn something and grow from the experience. Even on the days when you get together with someone and you can't make music at all, these can be some of the most valuable lessons of all. At the time it can be frustrating because you're not sure why it didn't work. But after you have played with a hundred musicians you'll start to see the patterns and you'll begin to understand what you need in order to make music. The only way to discover this is through experience. So don't wait to begin your career as a free improviser. Start today and give yourself permission to learn as you go. Remember that discovering what *doesn't* work is just as important as discovering what does.

Summary

In Exercise 5 we learned ways to practice applying our musical skills to a harmonic environment that is ambiguous or in constant movement. In this setting we cannot rely on a constant tonal center so we need to incorporate our feelings into every note we play. The same concepts of tonal harmony that we learned in earlier exercises are still just as relevant, but we must now apply these concepts in a subjective way based on what we feel in the moment. Here is a summary of the new exercises that will help you develop this ability:

1. Landscape Revisited

2. Melody Revisited

3. Pure Harmony Revisited

4. Mixed Harmony Revisited

5. Feel exercises

  - Invisible Staircase

  - Moving Chord Shapes

  - Moving Progressions

  - Follow the Melody, Revisited

6. Imagine exercises

  - Playing Other People's Music

  - Sing Freely, Revisited

  - Memorize the Sound

7. Create exercises

  - Technical Studies

  - Solo Free Improvisation

  - Add-a-Part Recordings

  - Fearlessly Participate

  - Group Free Improvisation

As with all of the other exercises in this book, you'll find a wealth of tools to accelerate your mastery at ImproviseForReal.com. For your Exercise 5 practice, a great resource is IFR Jam Tracks Level 8: Modal Mastery. This course will lead you step by step through the entire process of becoming a confident free improviser. At each step the harmonic materials become just a little more abstract, so that you can move at your own pace and gain confidence as you go.

The journey begins

The way that can be told of is not an unvarying way;

The names that can be named are not unvarying names.

It was from the Nameless that Heaven and Earth sprang;

The named is but the mother that rears the ten thousand creatures, each after its kind.

- Lao Tzu, China, 550 B.C.

In the Japanese martial arts, when a student reaches the level of black belt he earns what is called Shodan, which means "beginning degree". The journey doesn't end there. On the contrary, this is the moment when the journey *begins*. Earning the level of Shodan means that you have been exposed to the full set of ideas, and now you can begin to study.

During the time that you have spent learning about and practicing the IFR method, you have earned your own "beginning degree" of sorts. You have gained a deep personal understanding of harmony, you have developed a mastery over the sounds of our musical system and you have learned how to express any musical idea that you can imagine in any key on your instrument.

But just as in the martial arts, your journey as an improviser has only just begun. You now have a powerful set of skills that enable you practice your art. But your contribution as an artist depends on what you actually do with these skills. In your moment of self-expression, what will you say? What do you *need* to say?

When you listen to the greatest improvisers, you feel something in your soul that can't be put into words. You feel overcome by an immense and powerful voice that seems to tell the whole story of our shared human experience. Their music transcends harmony, and their message seems infinitely larger than the individual notes that they might be playing.

This is the eternal mystery of music. We can talk about music all day long but we can never capture its essence in words. Music, just like all of nature, belongs to the Nameless. Our attempts to explain it in words or reduce it to techniques just create more of those ten thousand creatures that Lao Tzu wrote about so long ago.

And this is the last idea that I would like to leave you with on the subject of music. I hope that your journey forward leads you to a deeper knowledge of yourself and a deeper connection with the people around you. And I hope that you never forget that the real magic of music is not in the notes. It's in those powerful moments of human expression that remind us of the significance and the majesty of this life we have been given.

About the author

My name is David Reed. I want to thank you for reading my book. The truth is that I never set out to become a writer, nor a teacher of music for that matter. I never wanted to create a "different" way of thinking about harmony. Like most young musicians, I just wanted to play.

But for most of my life I felt like I was on the outside of music, looking in at something that I couldn't fully understand. I would sit in the park under a tree for hours playing simple chords and melodies on my guitar. I was fascinated by beautiful sounds and I wanted to hear them over and over again. But everything I knew how to play was isolated. I had no global vision of what I was doing, no way to relate the sounds of one melody to the sounds of another. For this reason, improvisation didn't come naturally for me either. The first several years that I studied music I couldn't improvise anything. People would encourage me to just "go with the flow" and play "whatever comes out". But nothing ever came out!

Despite my limitations, I loved music more than anything else in the world. My father was a jazz trumpet player and I grew up listening to records by Miles Davis, Chet Baker and Billie Holiday. I started playing the guitar when I was nine. A few years later I was playing in rock bands, singing in our school choir and now also playing the trumpet. When I was sixteen, I got a steady gig playing in a local jazz quintet. That was one of the best learning experiences of my life. We played for four straight hours every Friday and Saturday night for almost two years while I was still in high school.

I don't have a music degree. In college I studied a lot of different things that interested me, from quantum mechanics to experimental fiction. But the idea of going to a music school didn't appeal to me at all. I already had a very personal relationship with music, and I didn't like the idea of a bunch of college professors telling me how jazz is supposed to be played. But at the same time, I was fascinated by jazz harmony and I wanted to understand it. I read every book about music theory that I could get hold of. I transcribed entire albums by Charlie Parker, Chet Baker and Sonny Rollins. One summer I spent every day in the college music library listening to the complete discography of Miles Davis, back to back from his first record to his last. I even used to put Ornette Coleman albums on my CD player and set them to repeat all night long because I thought it would somehow nourish my mind while I slept.

My fascination with music would eventually lead me to study and play in New York, Los Angeles, Argentina, Brazil, Uruguay, Senegal, Guinea Bissau and Spain. It was in Barcelona, Spain that the IFR method was actually created. For seven years I taught classes in musical improvisation for all instruments. I had the opportunity to work with hundreds of students of all different ability levels and backgrounds. In addition to giving me the chance to explore alternative models of visualizing harmony, the experience also forced me to reexamine my own beliefs and attitudes about improvisation. All of the really big discoveries that led to the creation of this method are the result of this period of experimentation in Barcelona.

Some other important events took place in my life during my time in Barcelona. I changed the tuning of my guitar to allow for a totally visual approach to harmony, which required me to relearn how to play the guitar. I began practicing Aikido, which has given me a new perspective on every aspect of my life, particularly my music and my teaching. And the most important event was that I fell in love with a beautiful young violin player named Mireia who is now my wife. Mireia created all of the illustrations that appear in this book. She also created many of the IFR courses and learning materials, including our entire ear training program.

It took me many years to find all of the pieces to my own personal puzzle. Today, musical improvisation is the greatest source of pleasure in my life. I am very thankful for this gift and I am happy to share it with as many people as I can. I don't claim to play any better than the next person. And I don't really care about that. But I do hope that this book can help you in some small way to find your own pleasure in music.

Made in the USA
Las Vegas, NV
07 November 2022

58988687R00129